THE
EVERYTHING
WEEKNIGHT GLUTEN-FREE
COOKBOOK

Dear Reader,

Growing up, I ne~~~~~~~~~~~~~~~~~rgy.
It wasn't until col~~~~~~~~~~~~~~~ Now,
I know over thirt~~~~~~~~~~~~~~ of gluten intolerance. T~~~~~~~~~~~~u hear
about on a daily ~~~~~~~~~~~rgy,
there are now m~~~~~~~~~~~ants
that cater to peo~~~~~~~~~~f these
are still really ex~~~~~~~~~~ have
to live without th~~~~~~~~~~

But it doesn't ~~~~~~~~~~g the
foods you used ~~~~~~~~~~emade
your favorites ~~~~~~~~~~ without
any complicat~~~~~~~~~~pes,
from decaden~~~~~~~~~~at will
have even yo~~~~~~~~~~

This book ~~~~~~~~~~nto
ones your kid~~~~~~~~~~t.
What's stoppi~~~~~~~~~~

Claire

Welcome to the EVERYTHING® Series!

These handy, accessible books give you all you need to tackle a difficult project, gain a new hobby, comprehend a fascinating topic, prepare for an exam, or even brush up on something you learned back in school but have since forgotten.

You can choose to read an Everything® book from cover to cover or just pick out the information you want from our three useful boxes: e-questions, e-facts, and e-alerts. We give you everything you need to know on the subject, but throw in a lot of fun stuff along the way, too.

We now have more than 400 Everything® books in print, spanning such wide-ranging categories as weddings, pregnancy, cooking, music instruction, foreign language, crafts, pets, New Age, and so much more. When you're done reading them all, you can finally say you know Everything®!

QUESTION

Answers to
common questions

FACT

Important snippets
of information

ALERT

Urgent
warnings

PUBLISHER Karen Cooper

MANAGING EDITOR, EVERYTHING® SERIES Lisa Laing

COPY CHIEF Casey Ebert

ASSISTANT PRODUCTION EDITOR Alex Guarco

ACQUISITIONS EDITOR Lisa Laing

SENIOR DEVELOPMENT EDITOR Brett Palana-Shanahan

EVERYTHING® SERIES COVER DESIGNER Erin Alexander

Visit the entire Everything® series at *www.everything.com*

THE
EVERYTHING®
WEEKNIGHT GLUTEN-FREE COOKBOOK

Claire Gallam

Avon, Massachusetts

An Everything® Series Book.
Everything® and everything.com® are registered trademarks of F+W Media, Inc.

Published by Adams Media, a division of F+W Media, Inc.
57 Littlefield Street, Avon, MA 02322 U.S.A.
www.adamsmedia.com

Contains material adapted and abridged from *The Everything® Gluten-Free Baking Cookbook* by Carrie S. Forbes, copyright © 2013 by F+W Media, Inc., ISBN 10: 1-4405-6486-8, ISBN 13: 978-1-4405-6486-4; *The Everything® Gluten-Free Cookbook,* by Rick Marx and Nancy T. Maar, copyright © 2006 by F+W Media, Inc., ISBN 10: 1-59337-394-5, ISBN 13: 978-1-59337-394-8; *The Everything® Gluten-Free Slow Cooker Cookbook* by Carrie S. Forbes, copyright © 2012 by F+W Media, Inc., ISBN 10: 1-4405-3366-0, ISBN 13: 978-1-4405-3366-2; *The Everything® Guide to Living Gluten-Free* by Jeanine Friesen, copyright © 2013 by F+W Media, Inc., ISBN 10: 1-4405-5784-7, ISBN 13: 978-1-4405-5184-0; and *The Everything® Wheat-Free Diet Cookbook* by Lauren Kelly, copyright © 2013 by F+W Media, Inc., ISBN 10: 1-4405-5680-6, ISBN 13: 978-1-4405-5680-7.

ISBN 10: 1-4405-8315-3
ISBN 13: 978-1-4405-8315-5
eISBN 10: 1-4405-8316-1
eISBN 13: 978-1-4405-8316-2

Printed in the United States of America.

10 9 8 7 6 5 4 3 2 1

Library of Congress Cataloging-in-Publication Data
Gallam, Claire.
  The everything weeknight gluten-free cookbook /
Claire Gallam.
    pages cm
  Includes index.
  ISBN 978-1-4405-8315-5 (pb) -- ISBN 1-4405-8315-3
(pb) -- ISBN 978-1-4405-8316-2 (ebook) -- ISBN 1-4405-
8316-1 (ebook)
1. Gluten-free diet--Recipes. I. Title.
  RM237.86.G35 2014
  641.5'638--dc23
                                2014026561

Always follow safety and commonsense cooking protocol while using kitchen utensils, operating ovens and stoves, and handling uncooked food. If children are assisting in the preparation of any recipe, they should always be supervised by an adult.

Many of the designations used by manufacturers and sellers to distinguish their products are claimed as trademarks. Where those designations appear in this book and F+W Media, Inc. was aware of a trademark claim, the designations have been printed with initial capital letters.

Nutritional analysis by Nicole Cormier, RD.
Photographs by Claire Gallam.

This book is available at quantity discounts for bulk purchases. For information, please call 1-800-289-0963.

Contents

Acknowledgments

First and foremost, I need to thank my husband Elliot. Without your support, patience, admiration, understanding, and encouragement, I'd never be able to continue to do what I love. I also want to thank you for always pushing me to take on new projects and challenge myself in the kitchen. Without you, I could not have written this book or created the amazing recipes inside of it. Thank you for always taste testing, hand modeling, dish washing, food buying, and everything else you did to help make this book a possibility. I also want to thank one of my best friends, Melanie, for opening my eyes to the world of gluten-free eating and cooking. Thank you for testing these recipes and giving me your feedback. Most of the recipes in here were made with you in mind. I also need to thank my mom, for showing me how incredibly romantic, beautiful, and fun cooking can be. And my dad, for always standing by me and being my number one fan. I have to also thank my brothers, the original Realistic Nutritionist taste testers—the ones who ate everything I made, even when it was neon green. And to my friends, my cousins, and my fans, whose continued support helps me to turn my dreams into a reality.

Introduction

A FEW YEARS AGO, a gluten allergy or celiac disease diagnosis meant one thing: You'd no longer be able to eat the foods you once loved. You had to say goodbye to pizza nights with your roommates, happy-hour beers with your coworkers, and birthday cakes with your family. The foods you grew up eating, the ones you looked forward to as a kid, were now completely off-limits. The only gluten-free options in supermarkets and restaurants were either overpriced or unappetizing. Living gluten-free meant drastically changing your life, and food became more of a necessity rather than something you enjoyed.

However, due to an increase in diagnoses of celiac disease and gluten intolerance and new scientific research, a gluten-free diet is not as deprived and bland as it once was. Large food brands, popular chefs, top restaurants, and food writers are coming up with good-tasting and easy gluten-free mixes, dishes, and recipes. People suffering from a gluten allergy are now welcomed with aisles of food to choose from in most supermarkets, and at many restaurants you'll find an entire menu of gluten-free choices.

However, the cost of these products is still much higher than their counterparts. For example, a package of high-quality, gluten-free frozen pizzas can cost up to three times the amount of regular frozen pizzas. Gluten-free baking mixes are also at least $1–$1.50 more per box than standard cake, cookie, or brownie mixes. At some restaurants, a gluten-free sub for pasta or bread can set you back more than $5 more as well. There may be more options, but the high cost of these options can be a huge financial strain for families and people on a tight budget.

So instead of spending double on takeout pizza or a sub at the local deli on those busy weeknights, why not save your pennies and make something even better at home? Here, you'll find hundreds of easy-to-make, lower-cost, gluten-free dishes that taste amazing and can be made after a long day at work or school. There are recipes that appeal to every important person in your life, from your meat-loving husband to your picky kids to your vegan friends, and everyone in between.

The recipes aren't overly difficult or complicated. In fact, all of these recipes were developed for beginning and intermediate cooks. Besides being easy, recipes in this collection are substantially more economical than store-bought or takeout items. Most of the ingredients can be purchased at your local supermarket. Dishes are comprised of mostly fresh fruits, vegetables, meat, poultry, dairy, and healthy fats. A few recipes call for gluten-free flours or blends. See Chapter 1 for information on choosing gluten-free flours for cooking and baking from scratch. Also, the nutritional information is listed for each recipe, which will make it even easier to stay in shape and pursue a healthy, gluten-free lifestyle.

Life is busy enough, and dinner should be the last thing you stress about. And with the recipes in this book, cooking a healthy, home-cooked meal doesn't mean you'll be spending hours in the kitchen. Make a plan on the weekend and follow these simple, easy-to-pull-together recipes for the busy nights during the week. A healthy dinner on the table doesn't have to take longer than 45 minutes. Some recipes are for hands-off, slow cooker meals that you can start in the morning and forget about until you get home—to the lovely aroma of dinner that's ready to eat!

Enjoy!

CHAPTER 1

Living Gluten-Free

Due to the increase in awareness of celiac disease and gluten intolerance, there is more information than ever available for those who are recently diagnosed. However, even with the abundance of information out there, you may still struggle with understanding what your new gluten-free diet entails and how you can make it work in your busy life. Here you'll find information about gluten and gluten intolerance, along with tips for making the transition to the gluten-free lifestyle as seamless as possible. You'll see how easy it can be to create tasty and nutritious weeknight dinners, without spending all your time in the kitchen.

Gluten Defined

Gluten is the term used for several types of proteins found in wheat, barley, and rye. The proteins gliadin and glutelin are found in these grains and together form a substance called gluten. Gluten is a "storage protein," which means that it holds the key ingredients for these grains to continue proliferating.

Gluten is primarily found in foods like bread, pasta, cakes, muffins, crackers, and pizza dough. Wheat, barley, and rye are used in many baked goods because the gluten in these grains provides excellent elasticity, structure, and texture. Gluten is what causes pizza to have a chewy, stretchy texture. It gives French bread its soft, white center and chewy crust. Gluten makes cinnamon rolls stretchy, soft, and light. It helps give structure to bread dough when rising, so that the bread becomes tall and stays tall after baking and cooling.

Avoiding gluten can be difficult for several reasons. The biggest reason is that ingredients containing gluten are not required by law to be listed on food labels. However, by law, the top eight food allergens must be listed on every food label in the United States, and wheat (which is a primary source of gluten) is one of them. So although you may not see "gluten" in the ingredients list, you can look for food allergen information, for example, "contains wheat."

When you are removing gluten from your diet, you will also need to avoid these foods (most are derivatives of wheat), which also contain gluten:

- Barley
- Bulgur
- Couscous
- Durum flour
- Farina
- Graham flour
- Kamut
- Rye
- Semolina
- Spelt
- Triticale (a cross between rye and wheat)

As a matter of fact, it's often a good idea (especially when you first receive a diagnosis of celiac disease) to only eat foods that are either naturally gluten-free or actually are labeled "gluten-free" until you have a better understanding of how to read food and nutrition labels.

Allergy, Intolerance, or Celiac Disease?

So what's the difference between a gluten allergy, a gluten intolerance, and celiac disease? Simply put, the main difference between a food allergy and a food intolerance is that a food allergy affects the immune system, while a food intolerance does not. Those who suffer from wheat allergies can experience anything from sneezing, itching, headaches, and nausea to swollen limbs and overall aches and pains. Wheat intolerance is much more common, and those who have it usually have a delayed onset of symptoms, as long as two to three days after consuming the food. These people suffer with various degrees of symptoms, ranging from stomach discomfort to chronic headaches and diarrhea.

FACT

There are no "typical" signs and symptoms of celiac disease, according to the Mayo Clinic. Celiac patients often report having a wide range of symptoms that can be anything from well-known signs such as diarrhea, constipation, or malabsorption of nutrients to migraine headaches, "brain fog," loss of memory, joint pain, irritability, depression, neuropathy, infertility, and osteoporosis.

However, celiac disease is an intestinal disorder caused by an intolerance to gluten. Gluten irritates the intestinal lining, interfering with the absorption of nutrients and water. Unlike certain food allergies, celiac disease is not something you grow out of, and those with the disease must maintain constant vigilance to keep their diet gluten-free. Untreated, the disease can lead to severe complications and potential long-term illness. The disease is permanent, and damage to the small intestine will occur every time gluten is consumed, regardless of whether symptoms are present. Reactions among people who suffer from this disease vary, but they are inevitable. The only treatment is strict adherence to a 100 percent gluten-free diet.

Changing to a Gluten-Free Lifestyle

The most important rule for following a gluten-free and wheat-free diet is to read ingredient labels carefully. There are many foods out there that contain some type of wheat ingredient that might surprise you. For example, did you know that soy sauce could contain wheat? Even dairy products like ice cream may have some wheat in them. If you are unsure of which ingredients might contain wheat, call the manufacturer.

If you've been diagnosed with celiac disease, the first thing you will want to do is gather all the information you can. Ask your doctor to recommend a nutritionist or registered dietitian who can give you a better understanding of what going gluten-free really means. A nutritionist may also request that your doctor order tests to help you discover if you have any additional food sensitivities or nutritional deficiencies. These tests may include a bone scan or tests of vitamin D, calcium, iron, zinc, B_{12}, folate, or thyroid levels. Once your doctor and nutritionist have a better picture of what's going on in your body, they can help you to determine the best plan of action and what gluten-free foods will be the most nutritious choices for your body.

FACT

It was once thought that only children suffered from celiac disease and only had certain symptoms such as diarrhea, stunted growth, and sometimes an enlarged stomach. In the 1950s and early 1960s, doctors didn't know exactly what caused celiac disease, but they knew bananas and rice didn't seem to negatively affect the health of their patients. Children who were diagnosed with celiac disease during that time were sometimes called "Banana Babies" because bananas were so frequently prescribed by their doctors.

Maintaining a healthy, gluten-free lifestyle involves eating a well-balanced, gluten-free diet that is high in protein and normal in fats. Common nutrient shortages among people with celiac disease include deficiencies in calcium; the vitamin B complex; and vitamins A, C, D, K, and E. If you have celiac disease, it's important to eat a carefully balanced diet to ensure that you're getting all the vitamins your body needs.

Research Is Key!

Do some online research to find local grocery stores that have gluten-free foods, along with local restaurants with gluten-free items on their menus. Thankfully, now almost every supermarket chain in the United States offers some gluten-free options in their aisles. For a more complete selection, visit health-food stores like Whole Foods, who offer a more complete selection of gluten-free items due to their focus on healthy, whole ingredients.

Community Resources

If you're feeling alone, try to find local gluten-free resources for your daily life, such as community support groups, books to help educate yourself and your family, gluten-free recipes and menus, and even gluten-free shopping guides. Chances are, your community may even have a gluten-free bakery that offers baked goods like pizza, sandwich bread, cakes, and cookies.

Another great source of information is your community or county extension agency. There will generally be an agent who specializes in the food resources and support groups in the community. This is also a great organization to contact if you would like to find out about regional farms that sell fresh organic produce and meats, which are usually gluten-free. These farms may also make and sell hygiene products like goat's milk soap and lotions. Often if these products are organic, they typically will not contain gluten, although you will have to ask to be sure.

Ask Questions

Every time you visit a restaurant, make sure to assess the knowledge of the wait staff and kitchen staff. Even though the description of the dish may seem harmless, it is the way foods are prepared that poses a problem. For example, once chicken becomes Chicken Parmesan, it is no longer wheat-free.

To be safe, ask your server for a gluten-free menu and inquire about the steps taken in the kitchen area to prevent cross-contamination. If a waiter or chef doesn't understand what gluten-free means, it may be a sign that gluten-free options are not available. Never be afraid to ask specific questions—your health is important! Most restaurants take allergy and intolerance issues very seriously, and will take your questions and concerns seriously as well.

Gluten-Free Diet Basics

The best part about following a basic gluten-free diet is that you'll be eating more fresh, natural, and unprocessed foods. Which means you will not only be following a gluten-free diet, but a nutritionally balanced and healthy one.

It's often recommended when starting a gluten-free diet to start with naturally gluten-free foods. These foods include:

- Beans
- Eggs
- Fish
- Fruits
- Milk, cheese, and plain yogurt
- Nuts and seeds
- Rice
- Unseasoned fresh chicken
- Unseasoned fresh meats
- Vegetables

Most of these foods (except for the beans and rice) are located around the perimeter of your grocery store, where most of the fresh foods are. Most naturally gluten-free foods will not come in a bag or box. Other than canned fruits or vegetables, rice, beans, and nuts, you can find most gluten-free foods in their natural state in the produce, meat, and dairy sections.

Give Gluten the Boot!

The thought of having to change your entire diet due to celiac disease or gluten sensitivity can feel completely overwhelming. No more bread? No pasta, pizza, doughnuts, or cookies?

While this may have been true even five years ago (at least as far as purchasing these items in a local grocery store or restaurant), the gluten-free food industry has come a long way. There are many companies that produce high-quality and readily available gluten-free products like sandwich breads, pastas, flours, cookies, and snacks. Most large grocery stores now have a gluten-free section, where you can find substitutions for many of your gluten-rich favorite foods.

But before you jump into buying a whole bunch of gluten-free processed foods, take a look at your kitchen. You may already have a fair amount of food that is already gluten-free. You will also need to identify foods that contain gluten, which you will need to avoid.

Here are some naturally gluten-free foods that you can keep:

- Baking ingredients such as baking powder, baking soda, salt, individual herbs and spices (not seasoning blends, which may contain gluten), oils, and sugar
- Canned, frozen, and jarred foods such as plain vegetables, beans, dried beans, fruits, peanut butter (and other nut butters), plain jams, jellies, and honey
- Canned tuna and chicken
- Eggs
- Fresh and frozen fruits and vegetables of all types
- Fresh and frozen unseasoned meats, chicken, and fish
- Milk and nondairy milk substitutions
- Natural cheeses ("cheese foods" often contain wheat)
- Plain rice (not seasoned rice mixes, which usually contain gluten)
- Unseasoned nuts

What to Get Rid Of—Products That Contain Gluten

Other foods in your pantry should be moved to a designated "gluten section" or removed entirely. This includes any food that lists "flour" as an ingredient on the label. This will include most "cream of" soups, noodle soups, baking mixes, pancake mixes, all-purpose and self-rising flours, even some nonstick baking sprays, and, of course, breads, bagels, frozen pancakes, waffles, cookies, and crackers.

BREAD PRODUCTS
- Bagels
- Bread
- Croutons
- Muffins
- Pancake and waffle mixes
- Pastries
- Pies
- Pita bread
- Rolls

BREAKFAST CEREALS
- Cream of Wheat
- Farina
- Most dry cereals and sweetened kid's cereals
- Some brands of oatmeal

CANDY

- Jordan almonds
- Licorice
- Some caramels
- Some nut candies

CONDIMENTS

- Barley malt
- Ketchup
- Malt vinegar
- Marinades
- Mustard
- Some salad dressings
- Soy sauce
- Worcestershire sauce

DESSERTS

- Cakes and frostings
- Chocolates
- Graham crackers
- Some flavored ice creams
- Sherbet

DRINKS

- Ale
- Beer
- Fruit drink mixes
- Instant chocolate drink mixes
- Lager
- Malted milk
- Root beer
- Some soft drinks
- Some sports and nutritional powdered drinks

FOOD ADDITIVES AND INGREDIENTS

- Artificial colors and flavors
- Caramel coloring and flavoring
- Ground spices and seasonings
- Modified food starch
- Shortening
- Vanilla and other extracts
- Vegetable gum
- Vegetable protein
- Vegetable starch

GRAINS

- Cereal grains
- Couscous
- Matzo meal
- Orzo
- Seasoned rice mixes
- Spelt
- Tabbouleh
- Triticale (a combination of wheat and rye)

JARRED AND CANNED FOODS

- Alfredo sauce
- Bouillon cubes
- Canned fruits
- Gravies
- Some canned meats
- Some canned vegetables
- Some chicken and beef broth brands
- Some soups

MEATS AND SEAFOOD

- Chicken nuggets
- Fish sticks
- Fried or breaded meats
- Imitation crab, shrimp, and bacon
- Meatballs
- Processed deli meats
- Some brands of sausages
- Some hotdogs

PASTA

- All kinds except those labeled wheat- or gluten-free
- Soba noodles

SNACKS

- Some chips
- Cookies (including cookie crumbs and cookie dough)
- Crackers
- Dry-roasted nuts
- Granola bars
- Popcorn

Even some nonfood items may have wheat in them. If your allergy is severe enough, even simply touching wheat can cause an allergic reaction. Call the manufacturer to find out if there is wheat in products like these that you may use:

- Cosmetics
- Glue
- Lotions and creams
- Medications
- Ointments
- Pet foods
- Playdoughs, clays, and putties
- Shampoo
- Sunscreens
- Vitamins

Although this is a very detailed list, it doesn't contain every item that might have gluten. Be sure to consult the ingredient list or your doctor if you're unsure about an item in your pantry.

Buying Gluten-Free

Buying gluten-free specialty items can be very expensive. Gluten-free foods often cost as much as 400 percent more than their traditional wheat counterparts. For example, a loaf of regular bread may cost about $1.50, while a generally much smaller loaf of gluten-free bread can easily cost over $6.00.

Because specialty gluten-free foods can be so expensive, it's cost-effective to eat as many naturally gluten-free foods as you can. Buying fruits and vegetables in season can help with food costs, along with purchasing canned or frozen versions during the winter months.

QUESTION

Does wine contain gluten?
Most wines made from grapes, apples, cherries, berries, and other fruits are gluten-free; however, flavored wines may not be gluten-free. Although not yet a common fining agent in the winemaking process, gluten's use has been gaining popularity. Scientists began studying its suitability several years ago, when concerns about mad cow disease were raised over gelatin, the industry's preferred fining agent. Pea protein, milk protein, egg whites, and fish glue have all been used for wine fining. Bentonite clay can also be used and is both gluten-free and vegan.

Generally speaking, it is more difficult to find gluten-free foods in the center aisles of a grocery store. Most of the items located there are pro-cessed and will require careful label reading. Some items, like rice, sugar, and canned beans, are gluten-free. Many other items, like seasoned rice packets, crackers, canned soup, and snack bars, are likely to contain gluten. Reading the fine print on labels can be a long process at first. Once you find a few items and brands that you know are gluten-free, double-checking the label will go much faster.

In addition to the grocery store, you can also stock up on many fresh items at your local farmers' market. These markets may be more accommo-dating to the gluten-free lifestyle than you might expect. All of the fresh fruits and vegetables will be gluten-free, and many may even be organic. The pro-ducers who sell at these markets take great pride in bringing their customers products that are superior to what they will find in a grocery store. Vendors selling processed foods like meats, jellies, and sauces will know the ingredient list for their goods, and they will also have a complete understanding of the manufacturing process. They will know if their food has come into contact with gluten and will be able to warn you away from dangerous items.

Talk to the sellers. Ask them about their products and the processes they use. Not only will this enhance your farmers' market shopping experience; it will allow you to make educated decisions about whether or not the food is safe for you to eat.

Gluten-Free Flours

There are hundreds of types of gluten-free flours to choose from in many grocery stores. Many of these flours, like rice, bean, and potato, are meant to be used together. Because gluten-free flours don't contain the unique elastic properties of wheat flour, they don't have the same ability to produce baked goods that are light yet sturdy. Gluten-free baked goods often have a much better texture and taste when you combine a variety of flours that have different properties. However, some gluten-free all-purpose blends work directly on their own.

Here are the most common gluten-free flours available:

- Arrowroot starch
- Blanched almond meal/flour
- Brown rice flour
- Chia flour
- Chickpea flour
- Coconut flour
- Cornmeal
- Cornstarch
- Hemp flour
- Millet flour
- Oat flour
- Potato flour
- Quinoa flour
- Sorghum flour
- Tapioca flour

When baking gluten-free recipes, you need a binder, which helps replace the action of gluten in baked goods. The most commonly used binder in gluten-free baking is xanthan gum. This is a powder made from a strain of bacteria that is grown on corn. When xanthan gum is introduced to a liquid, the mixture becomes thick and sticky. This quality helps give structure to gluten-free baked goods. If you're allergic to corn products, you can use guar gum in place of the xanthan gum. Whole psyllium husks are used for many vegan baked items in place of gums.

Many breads need yeast to help the dough rise. The best yeast to use in slow cooker baking is a fast-acting yeast that doesn't need to be mixed with water to become activated. This type of yeast is usually called "rapid rise," "instant," or "bread machine yeast." This yeast will be mixed with the dry gluten-free ingredients when making the bread.

Gluten-Free for Kids

Making the change to a gluten-free diet is a huge undertaking for anyone, but it is especially difficult with children. Children may not understand why certain foods make them sick; they don't have the same level of understanding that an adult does. They may not see the connection between that delicious soft pretzel at the mall and the stomachache that they get hours later. Thankfully, understanding parents can be there to help their children transition and have a relatively normal life, while still maintaining a gluten-free diet.

Children may need to maintain a gluten-free diet for a variety of reasons, including celiac disease, gluten intolerance, or to help alleviate symptoms of autism or attention deficit hyperactivity disorder (ADHD). Regardless of the reason, it's important to understand that this is a change that will affect the whole family, not just the affected child. Some families decide that if one person has to eat gluten-free, they will all eat gluten-free. This removes any temptations and possible conflicts that may arise by having foods that contain gluten in the house.

Other families decide to have a "shared kitchen," where both gluten and gluten-free products coexist. Often in these cases, the family dinner is the one meal that is 100 percent gluten-free. This allows everyone to sit down and enjoy a meal together without anyone being treated differently. This arrangement is also much easier on the person preparing the meal, since the possibility of cross-contamination during meal preparation will be reduced or eliminated.

In a shared kitchen, meals that are less formal or not attended by the entire family may contain a mixture of gluten-free and regular foods. During these meals, cross-contamination needs to be considered when preparing the food.

ALERT

If you have a shared kitchen, try to make both the gluten-free and the gluten-filled meals and snacks similar. If a child eating a regular diet is having cookies, have cookies for the gluten-free child as well. That way, everyone gets a treat and no one feels deprived while eating a gluten-free diet.

The importance of sticking to a gluten-free diet needs to be clearly explained to your child with celiac disease or gluten intolerance. He needs to know that any amount of gluten can make him sick. If he sneaks a cookie from a friend or eats his sister's crackers, he will get ill again, and it will take a while for him to get better.

If your child is old enough, have her help you read labels. Make a game of seeing if she can find products that are gluten-free. With new labeling laws coming into effect, more manufacturers are beginning to print "gluten-free" directly on the package. Since so many products are now available in gluten-free versions, involving your child in the shopping process can help her feel more in control of her new diet. Help your child understand that what she eats won't necessarily change, but it's where that food comes from that will change. For a child already accustomed to convenience or restaurant foods, foods that will now be off-limits, the transition may be made easier by explaining that a favorite takeout pizza can be replaced with a homemade gluten-free pizza.

Cooking Weeknight Meals from Scratch

Since many gluten-free items at the store, including many weeknight dinner short-cuts, cost so much money, the easiest way to save is to make most of your meals and snacks from scratch. Despite how busy and challenging your current lifestyle may be, learning how to make some of your own gluten-free foods from scratch can actually save you time in the long run, even on those busy weeknights.

Not only are homemade foods healthier than their store-bought counter-parts; they are generally cheaper as well. Gluten-free ingredients will most likely be more expensive than regular baking ingredients for a long time to come, but it's still cheaper to make most foods from scratch.

Homemade dinners also contain less sodium, preservatives, and partially hydrogenated oils. When you make your bread, cake, muffins, and pizza crust at home, you completely control what ingredients go into your food. You can add additional fiber or less sugar. You can decide to make a food egg-free or dairy-free.

Another good reason to make gluten-free foods from scratch is that many people who have gluten sensitivities also have additional food sensitivities or allergies. Most of the recipes in this book are gluten-free and soy-free already. For additional options, see Appendix B for egg replacements and vegan substitutes.

For those who are busy working full-time jobs, shuffling kids to practices and plays, and finding time to balance exercise and mental health, preparing a healthy, gluten-free weeknight meal can seem nearly impossible. That's why so many of the recipes in this book take less than 45 minutes to prepare or can be made and frozen days in advance.

Your schedule is demanding, and yet you still need healthy, nutritious, and gluten-free dinners you can prepare with ingredients you probably have on hand. And that's what you'll find here. In addition, many of the recipes are for slow cooker meals, like the Red Wine–Braised Beef Short Ribs with Mushrooms in Chapter 6 and the Slow Cooker Thai Curried Chicken Soup in Chapter 4, which means you can throw them together in the morning before work or school and come home to a fully prepared meal. Look for the slow cooker icon SC on these recipes.

Some of the meals can be made a few days in advance, like the Puttanesca Sauce in Chapter 3, the Slow Cooker Pulled Pork in Chapter 7, or the Broccoli Cheddar Soup in Chapter 4. These recipes will make it easier than ever to enjoy homemade, gluten-free meals, even on your busiest days. Some of the desserts, like the Hummingbird Cake with Cream Cheese Icing in Chapter 16, can be started one night and finished the next for an impressive dessert with minimal effort. These make-ahead recipes are designated by the MA icon.

We hope you enjoy the delicious weeknight meals in this book and look forward to hearing about how these dishes brought your family back to the dinner table.

CHAPTER 2

Appetizers and Snacks

Light Gorgonzola and Ricotta Torte Appetizer

This is light and delicious. You will find that it's best made in a springform pan.
Serve warm or at room temperature.

INGREDIENTS | SERVES 6 | 40 MINUTES

1 (16-ounce) tub fresh whole-milk ricotta cheese

4 ounces Gorgonzola cheese, crumbled

1 teaspoon fresh oregano, or ¼ teaspoon dried

1 teaspoon fresh lemon juice

1 teaspoon freshly grated lemon zest

1 teaspoon salt

½ teaspoon freshly ground black pepper

3 egg whites, beaten stiff

½ cup chopped toasted hazelnuts

1. Preheat oven to 350°F.

2. Process the cheeses, oregano, lemon juice, zest, salt, and pepper in a food processor until very smooth. Place in a bowl and fold in the beaten egg whites.

3. Spray the inside of a 10" springform pan with gluten-free cooking spray. Add the cheese mixture, and bake for about 30 minutes or until slightly golden.

4. Sprinkle with hazelnuts. Cool slightly and serve in wedges.

PER SERVING Calories: 267 | Fat: 21g | Protein: 16g | Sodium: 821mg | Fiber: 1g | Carbohydrates: 5g | Sugar: 1g

The Ties That Bind

Gluten is the glue that holds breads, cakes, and piecrusts together. When you substitute gluten-free flours for gluten-containing flours, you must use eggs or other stabilizers such as guar gum or xanthan gum to hold things together. However, as well as eggs work for some recipes, forget about making gluten-free pasta—you need so much guar gum or xanthan gum that it gets slimy.

Hearty Mushrooms Stuffed with Spicy Beef

This filling dish is wonderful on a chilly night. You can even increase the portions and serve these mushrooms for lunch with a bowl of soup on the side.

INGREDIENTS | SERVES 4 | 45 MINUTES

6 ounces lean ground beef

1 large egg

2 tablespoons gluten-free chili sauce

1 teaspoon minced fresh garlic

½ cup chopped red onion

1" fresh gingerroot, peeled and minced

⅛ teaspoon ground cinnamon

½ teaspoon dried red pepper flakes

½ teaspoon freshly ground black pepper

½ teaspoon salt

8 very large fresh mushrooms

Water (enough to cover bottom of pan)

8 teaspoons freshly grated Parmesan cheese

¼ cup pine nuts

1. To make the filling, place the beef, egg, chili sauce, garlic, onion, spices, pepper, and salt in a food processor and mix thoroughly.

2. Carefully remove the stems from the mushrooms and pack them with the filling.

3. Preheat the oven to 325°F. Place the mushrooms in a baking pan and add enough water to cover the bottom of the pan.

4. Sprinkle with cheese and pine nuts. Bake for 35 minutes.

PER SERVING Calories: 210 | Fat: 12g | Protein: 19g | Sodium: 682mg | Fiber: 2g | Carbohydrates: 8g | Sugar: 3g

The Versatile Mushroom

Today, you can get really excellent commercially grown exotic mushrooms. Mushrooms can be called wild only if gathered in the wild. Try baby bellas, which are small portobello mushrooms. Shiitakes and oyster mushrooms are also great additions and have a bolder, more striking flavor. If you have no budgetary constraints, buy morels or chanterelles.

Devilish Egg-Stuffed Celery

Eggs are incredibly versatile. You can prepare them simply for kids or exquisitely for adults, as in this different take on deviled eggs. In this recipe, you devil the whole egg.

INGREDIENTS | SERVES 12 | 30 MINUTES

6 large hard-cooked eggs, peeled

2 tablespoons mayonnaise

6 drops Tabasco sauce

¼ teaspoon freshly ground white pepper

1 teaspoon celery salt

1 tablespoon gluten-free Dijon mustard

2 tablespoons chopped onion

1 clove garlic, chopped

¼ teaspoon salt

2 tablespoons heavy cream

4 stalks celery, cut into thirds

For garnish:

3 teaspoons salmon caviar

3 teaspoons gluten-free capers

3 teaspoons green peppercorns

2 tablespoons chopped fresh parsley

1 teaspoon hot or sweet Hungarian paprika

1. Place all ingredients except the celery and the garnishes in a food processor and blend until smooth.

2. Spread the mixture in the celery, cover with foil or plastic wrap, and chill. Add garnishes just before serving.

PER SERVING Calories: 67 | Fat: 5g | Protein: 4g | Sodium: 342mg | Fiber: 0g | Carbohydrates: 1g | Sugar: 0g

An International Flavor

Chili sauce and mayonnaise will add a Russian flavor to the eggs. Salmon caviar as a garnish will add a Scandinavian touch. Change the amount of heat and the herbs and you will have a different taste sensation. Experiment to find the flavor combinations you like best.

Sweet Potato Chips

Sweet potatoes are loaded with vitamin A and very delicious when fried and salted. Eat these chips plain or with your favorite dip.

INGREDIENTS | SERVES 6 | 15 MINUTES

2 large sweet potatoes, peeled
3 cups canola oil
1 teaspoon salt
½ teaspoon freshly ground black pepper

1. Slice the potatoes thinly with a mandoline.

2. Heat the oil in a deep-fat fryer to 375°F.

3. Fry for about 3–4 minutes, depending on the thickness of the chips. When the chips are very crisp, remove from the oil and drain.

4. Sprinkle chips with salt and pepper.

PER SERVING Calories: 41 | Fat: 5g | Protein: 0g | Sodium: 393mg | Fiber: 0g | Carbohydrates: 0g | Sugar: 0g

Avocado-White Bean Hummus

Simple yet impressive, this appetizer will wow your guests. It also makes a delicious and healthy alternative to mayonnaise on your favorite sandwich.

INGREDIENTS | SERVES 10 | 10 MINUTES

1 (15-ounce) can cannellini beans, drained and rinsed
1 ripe avocado, pitted and diced
1 large garlic clove, coarsely chopped
¼ cup water, plus more as needed
Juice of 1 medium lemon
2 tablespoons extra-virgin olive oil
1 teaspoon kosher salt
2 tablespoons coarsely chopped fresh cilantro
¼ teaspoon freshly ground black pepper

1. Place the cannellini beans, avocado, garlic, water, lemon juice, olive oil, salt, chopped cilantro, and pepper in a food processor fitted with a blade attachment or a high-speed blender.

2. Process until smooth, scraping down the sides of the bowl as needed. If the dip is too thick, pulse in more water, a tablespoon at a time, until the desired consistency is reached. Serve with Baked Corn Tortilla Chips (see recipe in this chapter).

PER SERVING Calories: 94 | Fat: 6g | Protein: 3g | Sodium: 362mg | Fiber: 4g | Carbohydrates: 8g | Sugar: 1g

Fresh Wheat-Free Croutons

These croutons can be made in advance and stored in the refrigerator, then crisped up at the last moment. They're the perfect addition to any salad.

INGREDIENTS | SERVES 4 | 30 MINUTES

½ cup extra-virgin olive oil

2 cloves garlic, minced or put through a garlic press

4 slices wheat-free bread, thickly cut, crusts removed

1½ teaspoons salt

1 teaspoon ground black pepper

⅛ teaspoon red pepper flakes

1. Preheat the broiler to 350°F.

2. In a small bowl, mix the oil and garlic together. Brush both sides of the bread with the garlic oil. Sprinkle with salt, black pepper, and pepper flakes.

3. Cut each slice of bread into 6 cubes, to make 24 cubes. Spray a cookie sheet with gluten-free nonstick spray. Place the cubes on the sheet and broil until well browned on both sides, 3–4 minutes each side.

4. Put the cookie sheet on the bottom rack of the oven. Turn off the oven and leave the croutons to dry for 20 minutes.

5. Store in an airtight container until ready to use.

PER SERVING Calories: 242 | Fat: 27g | Protein: 0g | Sodium: 885mg | Fiber: 0g | Carbohydrates: 1g | Sugar: 0g

Grilled Portobello Mushrooms with Balsamic Glaze

This vegan salad is filling and hearty any time of the year. If you haven't tried to grill portobellos, now is the time! You get the meaty flavor of meat without actually using any!

INGREDIENTS | SERVES 6 | 30 MINUTES

3 cups baby arugula

3 large portobello mushrooms

1 cup balsamic vinegar

1 tablespoon turbinado sugar

1 teaspoon wheat-free soy sauce

1. Place the arugula on a large platter. Prepare a grill to medium-high heat.

2. Clean mushrooms and remove stems and any debris. Grill for 10 minutes, turning once. Place mushroom caps on top of the arugula.

3. In a small saucepan, heat the vinegar, sugar, and soy sauce to a boil. Reduce heat to low and simmer for about 15–20 minutes or until the mixture thickens. Remove from heat and let cool.

4. Once balsamic glaze has cooled a bit, pour evenly over portobellos and arugula. Serve immediately or at room temperature.

PER SERVING Calories: 56 | Fat: 0g | Protein: 1g | Sodium: 64mg | Fiber: 1g | Carbohydrates: 11g | Sugar: 10g

Spicy Cheddar Hamburger Dip `SC`

A hearty dip with ground beef and garlic, this dish could also be served over cooked rice for a Mexican-inspired gluten-free meal.

INGREDIENTS | SERVES 6

1 pound ground beef
½ cup finely chopped onion
4 cloves garlic, peeled and crushed
½ jalapeño pepper, seeded and minced
¼ teaspoon salt
1 (15-ounce) can tomato sauce
½ teaspoon oregano
1 (8-ounce) package cream cheese
1 cup shredded Cheddar cheese
1 teaspoon gluten-free chili powder

1. Brown ground beef in a medium skillet over medium-high heat with the onion, garlic, and jalapeño. Drain the fat and pour browned ground beef mixture into a greased 2.5-quart slow cooker.

2. Add salt, tomato sauce, oregano, cream cheese, Cheddar cheese, and chili powder.

3. Cover and cook on high for 2–3 hours or on low for 5–6 hours.

4. Serve with gluten-free corn tacos or rice chips.

PER SERVING Calories: 362 | Fat: 27g | Protein: 23g | Sodium: 756mg | Fiber: 2g | Carbohydrates: 8g | Sugar: 5g

Pineapple Teriyaki Drumsticks `SC`

Serve this crowd-pleasing favorite as a hearty appetizer. Pair leftovers with steamed rice for a great lunch that tastes like a trip to the islands.

INGREDIENTS | SERVES 12

12 chicken drumsticks
1 (8-ounce) can pineapple rings in juice
¼ cup gluten-free teriyaki sauce or gluten-free soy sauce
1 teaspoon ground ginger
¼ cup gluten-free hoisin sauce

1. Arrange the drumsticks in a single layer on a broiling pan. Broil for 10 minutes on high, flipping the drumsticks once halfway through the cooking time.

2. Drain the juice from the pineapple into a 4–6-quart slow cooker. Add the teriyaki sauce, ginger, and hoisin sauce. Stir to combine.

3. Cut the pineapple rings in half. Add to the slow cooker.

4. Add the drumsticks to the slow cooker and stir to combine. Cover and cook on low for 4–6 hours or on high for 2–3 hours.

PER SERVING Calories: 142 | Fat: 7g | Protein: 15g | Sodium: 446mg | Fiber: 0g | Carbohydrates: 5g | Sugar: 3g

Mini Pizza in a Flash

A mini pizza is about the quickest dinner or lunch you can make. It doesn't require many ingredients, and it's easy to personalize it for different tastes. Top these pizzas with your choice of meat or vegetables or add some fancy toppings like balsamic glaze, gourmet cheeses, and gluten-free cured meats!

INGREDIENTS | SERVES 2 | 10 MINUTES

1 gluten-free bagel, split in half

2 tablespoons pizza, spaghetti, or tomato sauce

¼ cup shredded mozzarella cheese

1. Preheat the oven to 350°F.

2. Place the bagel halves on a cookie sheet. Spread the pizza sauce over each bagel half. Top with mozzarella cheese.

3. Bake 5–8 minutes, or until the cheese is melted.

PER SERVING Calories: 237 | Fat: 8g | Protein: 12g | Sodium: 477mg | Fiber: 1g | Carbohydrates: 30g | Sugar: 1g

Baked Corn Tortilla Chips

Who says tortilla chips have to be laden with fat and calories to taste good? These tasty chips are perfect with all kinds of dips and salsas.

INGREDIENTS | SERVES 6 | 20 MINUTES

24 (6-inch) round corn tortillas

1 teaspoon kosher salt

Read the Label!

Some corn tortillas are made with wheat gluten! Thoroughly reading the labels will help keep you informed because sometimes they don't advertise that they contain wheat.

1. Preheat the oven to 350°F.

2. Cut tortillas into large triangular slices. Lay slices out in a single layer on a baking sheet and sprinkle with salt.

3. Bake 8–12 minutes, or until chips start to lightly brown. Repeat with remaining tortilla slices. Let cool for 10 minutes before eating.

PER SERVING Calories: 209 | Fat: 3g | Protein: 5g | Sodium: 436mg | Fiber: 6g | Carbohydrates: 43g | Sugar: 1g

Tiny Chickpea Crepes

Chickpea (garbanzo bean) flour gives a slightly nutty flavor that goes well with many dips and fillings. They not only add nuttiness, but also fiber and protein to these fluffy and soft crepes.

INGREDIENTS | SERVES 12 | 20 MINUTES

2 cups chickpea flour

2 cloves garlic, crushed

1 teaspoon Tabasco sauce or other red hot sauce

1 teaspoon salt

1½ cups water

¼ cup olive oil, for frying

1. Mix flour, garlic, hot sauce, salt, and water in a blender, pulsing and scraping the mixture down the sides.

2. Heat the oil in a medium nonstick pan over medium-high heat. Add 1 tablespoon of the batter for 1½" crepes.

3. Cook until very crisp on the bottom, about 3–4 minutes; do not turn. Remove from pan and place on paper towels or a platter.

PER SERVING Calories: 122 | Fat: 6g | Protein: 5g | Sodium: 213mg | Fiber: 2g | Carbohydrates: 12g | Sugar: 2g

Crab and Artichoke Dip with Pine Nuts

This luscious dip isn't just for pairing with your favorite chips, vegetables, or gluten-free breads. You can slather this creamy crab dip right on top of your favorite fish for an added richness.

INGREDIENTS | SERVES 4 | 20 MINUTES

¼ cup nonfat plain Greek yogurt

4 ounces shredded crabmeat

1 (4-ounce) jar chopped artichoke hearts, drained

1 ounce low-fat cream cheese, softened

½ tablespoon lemon juice

1 teaspoon salt

1 teaspoon ground black pepper

½ teaspoon oregano

1 tablespoon pine nuts

½ teaspoon olive oil

1. Preheat oven to 350°F.

2. In a medium bowl, mix yogurt, crabmeat, artichokes, cream cheese, lemon juice, salt, pepper, and oregano. Stir to combine.

3. Transfer dip to a small baking dish or ramekin. Top with pine nuts and olive oil.

4. Bake for about 13–15 minutes, or until bubbly and lightly browned. Serve hot.

PER SERVING Calories: 127 | Fat: 8g | Protein: 10g | Sodium: 734mg | Fiber: 3g | Carbohydrates: 4g | Sugar: 1g

Piquant Artichoke and Spinach Dip

This is the perfect dip for parties and entertaining. Serve with corn or rice crackers or sliced vegetables. Or you can just eat it with a spoon!

INGREDIENTS | MAKES 2 CUPS | 15 MINUTES

1 (10-ounce) package frozen chopped spinach, thawed

2 tablespoons extra-virgin olive oil

1 (12-ounce) jar artichoke hearts, drained and chopped

4 ounces cream cheese

8 ounces sour cream

2 cloves garlic, finely chopped

½ bunch scallions, chopped

2 tablespoons fresh lemon juice

¼ teaspoon freshly grated nutmeg

1 tablespoon shredded or grated Parmesan cheese

1. Drain the thawed spinach, squeezing it with paper towels, until the extra liquid is gone.

2. Heat the olive oil in a large skillet over medium heat and add the spinach; cook until just soft, about 5 minutes.

3. Remove pan from heat and add the rest of the ingredients, stirring to mix. Serve warm or cold.

PER SERVING (2 TABLESPOONS) | Calories: 84 | Fat: 7g | Protein: 2g | Sodium: 66mg | Fiber: 2g | Carbohydrates: 4g | Sugar: 1g

Spicy Gorgonzola Dip with Red Pepper "Spoons"

This is one of those dishes that totally benefits from more fresh herbs. Try using fresh chives, basil, and oregano.

INGREDIENTS | MAKES 2 CUPS | 15 MINUTES

6 ounces Gorgonzola cheese, at room temperature

4 ounces mayonnaise

4 ounces cream cheese, at room temperature

2 ounces roasted red peppers (jarred is fine)

2 teaspoons fresh chopped herbs (such as oregano, basil, and chives)

½ teaspoon salt

½ teaspoon freshly ground black pepper

¼ teaspoon hot pepper sauce

4 medium sweet red bell peppers

1. Put all ingredients but the raw red peppers into a food processor and blend until smooth. Scrape into a serving bowl.

2. Wash, core, and seed the red bell peppers, and then cut into chunks (these will be your "spoons"). Place the red pepper spoons around the dip.

PER SERVING (2 TABLESPOONS) | Calories: 247 | Fat: 23g | Protein: 6g | Sodium: 659mg | Fiber: 1g | Carbohydrates: 6g | Sugar: 3g

Sicilian Eggplant Rolls

Make these in advance and warm them up when you're ready to eat them.
The rolls make a great appetizer or side dish for dinner.

INGREDIENTS | SERVES 8 | 40 MINUTES

1 (1-pound) medium eggplant, peeled

1 tablespoon salt

½ cup olive oil

½ cup rice flour

1 cup ricotta cheese

¼ cup Sicilian olives, pitted and chopped

¼ cup Parmesan cheese

Salting Eggplant

Salting and stacking eggplant slices under a weight will drain off the bitterness that some seem to harbor. Be sure to use a plate with steep sides or a soup bowl under the eggplant—some give off a lot of juice when salted.

1. Cut the eggplant in very thin (1/8") slices with a mandoline. Salt the slices and stack them on a plate; let sit under a weight for 15 minutes to release the liquid.

2. Pat the eggplant slices dry with paper towels.

3. Heat the oil to 300°F. Dip the slices in flour and fry until almost crisp, about 2 minutes per side.

4. Drain the slices and then place a spoonful of the cheese and some chopped olives on the end of each slice. Roll and secure with a toothpick.

5. Heat oven to 300°F. Sprinkle the rolls with Parmesan cheese and bake for 8 minutes. Serve warm.

PER SERVING Calories: 170 | Fat: 10.5g | Protein: 7g | Sodium: 1,023mg | Fiber: 2g | Carbohydrates: 12g | Sugar: 1.5g

Strawberry Guacamole

The addition of the strawberries gives this guacamole a perfect sweetness. It's great with chips, but you can also pair it with your favorite enchiladas or tacos!

INGREDIENTS | MAKES 6 CUPS | 15 MINUTES

6 medium ripe avocados, peeled and pitted

2 large heirloom tomatoes, chopped

2 cups chopped strawberries

1 small red onion, peeled and chopped

2 medium bell peppers, seeded and chopped

Juice from 2 medium lemons

1 teaspoon salt

½ teaspoon ground black pepper

2 tablespoons chopped cilantro

1. In a large bowl, mash the avocados with a potato masher or the back of a fork.

2. Mix in the tomatoes, strawberries, red onion, bell peppers, lemon juice, salt, pepper, and chopped cilantro.

PER SERVING (¼ CUP) | Calories: 91 | Fat: 7.5g | Protein: 1g | Sodium: 103mg | Fiber: 4g | Carbohydrates: 7g | Sugar: 2g

Spicy Salmon Cucumber Bites

These flavorful bites are the perfect weeknight dinner appetizer. Each morsel is crunchy, fresh, juicy, and slightly spicy and can be made in 15 minutes flat.

INGREDIENTS | SERVES 6 | 15 MINUTES

2 medium cucumbers

6 ounces smoked salmon, flaked

4 ounces creamy gluten-free horseradish sauce

¼ cup chopped chives

1. Peel cucumbers and slice each into 12 slices.

2. Top each cucumber slice with salmon and a dab of horseradish sauce.

3. Garnish with chives.

PER SERVING Calories: 48 | Fat: 1g | Protein: 9g | Sodium: 221mg | Fiber: 0.5g | Carbohydrates: 4g | Sugar: 2g

Crispy Tofu Nachos MA

*Tofu replaces ground beef in these cheesy nachos, making them
a healthier option for a fun family snack.*

INGREDIENTS | SERVES 8

1 (15-ounce) block extra-firm tofu

1 tablespoon olive oil

½ (1-ounce) package taco seasoning

1 (5.5-ounce) bag Food Should Taste
Good Jalapeño Tortilla Chips

1½ cups low-fat Cheddar cheese

1½ cups part-skim mozzarella cheese

1 jalapeño pepper, seeded and chopped

1 (14-ounce) can diced tomatoes,
drained

1 habanero pepper, seeded and
chopped

½ (4-ounce) can mild green chilies

1 medium ripe avocado, peeled, pitted,
and mashed

½ cup chopped fresh cilantro

Tasty Tofu

Tofu doesn't have much flavor on its own—
it takes on the taste of the ingredients
added to it. For the best-tasting tofu,
always marinate it for at least an hour in
your favorite spices or gluten-free
marinades.

1. Preheat oven to 425°F. Grease a baking sheet with gluten-free nonstick cooking spray. Wrap the tofu in paper towels and stack heavy plates on top to drain the water. Remove wet paper towels and repeat 2 more times.

2. Once drained, chop the tofu into 1" cubes. In a large bowl, toss tofu with olive oil and taco seasoning. Cover with plastic wrap and chill for at least 1 hour. After an hour, spread tofu in an even layer on the baking sheet and bake for 20 minutes. Use a spatula to break the tofu apart and bake for another 20–25 minutes, or until crispy. Remove from oven and set aside.

3. Reduce heat to 350°F. Grease an oval baking dish with gluten-free nonstick cooking spray. Arrange a layer of the tortilla chips along the bottom. Top with a third of the tofu, ½ cup Cheddar, ½ cup mozzarella, and half of the sliced jalapeño pepper. Add another layer: more chips, more tofu, tomatoes, ½ cup Cheddar, and ½ cup mozzarella. Finally, top with habanero pepper, chilies, remaining jalapeño, and remaining cheese.

4. Bake for about 15–20 minutes, or until cheese is melted. Garnish nachos with avocado and cilantro. Serve immediately.

PER SERVING Calories: 345 | Fat: 16g | Protein: 16g | Sodium: 625mg | Fiber: 5g | Carbohydrates: 20g | Sugar: 4g

Garlic Slow-Roasted Artichokes

Artichokes aren't just for cheesy and creamy dips. The best thing about these slightly spicy artichokes is they are slow roasted, so you just pop them in the slow cooker and let it do the cooking.

INGREDIENTS | SERVES 2

¼ cup low-fat mayonnaise

3 tablespoons sriracha sauce

1 large artichoke

1½ cloves garlic, chopped

1 cup water

2 tablespoons lemon juice

½ teaspoon salt

½ teaspoon ground black pepper

1. In a small bowl, mix mayonnaise and sriracha. Cover and refrigerate while you cook the artichoke.

2. Chop the stems off the artichoke. Then slice the tips off the leaves and discard. Push garlic into the center and between leaves of the artichoke.

3. Pour the water into a 4–6-quart slow cooker. Place the artichoke in the center. Sprinkle lemon juice, salt, and pepper over artichoke.

4. Cook on high for about 3 hours, or until fork-tender.

5. Serve artichoke with mayonnaise sauce.

PER SERVING Calories: 246 | Fat: 2g | Protein: 3g | Sodium: 963mg | Fiber: 5g | Carbohydrates: 12g | Sugar: 1g

Gluten-Free Soft Pretzel Bites

There's nothing better than a soft, baked pretzel. These soft pretzel bites have everything you love in the larger ballpark pretzels in an easier-to-eat small size. Dip these bites into your favorite gluten-free spicy mustard.

INGREDIENTS | SERVES 12

½ cup plus 2 tablespoons warm (110°F) water

1½ teaspoons active dry yeast

1 tablespoon sugar

1 cup gluten-free all-purpose flour

¾ cup almond meal

½ teaspoon baking powder

½ tablespoon xanthan gum

½ tablespoon honey

3 tablespoons unsalted butter, melted

½ teaspoon salt

2 tablespoons cornmeal

¼ cup baking soda

1 large egg white mixed with 2 tablespoons water

2 tablespoons coarse sea salt

1. In a large bowl, mix water, yeast, and sugar together. Let sit until the yeast starts to bubble and foam, about 10 minutes. Pour the mixture into the bowl of a stand mixer fitted with a dough hook.

2. Add flour, almond meal, baking powder, and xanthan gum and stir to combine. Turn on the mixer and add honey, butter, and salt. Mix on medium-high speed until the dough starts to come together and pulls apart from the bowl. Mix another 1–2 minutes, or until dough is soft and elastic.

3. Place the dough on a lightly floured surface and knead a minute or so with your hands until very smooth. It might be a little sticky, but don't add too much more flour.

4. Place the dough in a large oiled bowl and cover with greased plastic wrap. Set in a warm spot and let double in size for about 1 hour. Turn the dough onto a lightly floured surface and roll into a log. With a sharp knife, slice into 6 even slices. Cut each slice into fourths. Score the bites evenly with a sharp knife.

5. Preheat oven to 450°F. Line two baking sheets with parchment paper and sprinkle with cornmeal.

6. Bring 5 cups water to a medium boil in a large pot. Stir in baking soda. Toss the bites into the baking soda water and boil for about 30–60 seconds. Remove from the water with a slotted spoon, shaking off the excess water.

7. Place the bites on the parchment paper. Brush with egg mixture and bake for about 15 minutes, or until golden brown. While still hot, sprinkle with coarse sea salt.

PER SERVING Calories: 93 | Fat: 4g | Protein: 2g | Sodium: 2,566mg | Fiber: 1g | Carbohydrates: 12g | Sugar: 2g

CHAPTER 3

Sauces, Dressings, and Spreads

Creamy Mushroom and Cognac Sauce

This goes great over wheat-free pasta, polenta, or rice. Or add an extra 1½ cups of broth to the recipe and turn it into soup.

INGREDIENTS | SERVES 4 | 20 MINUTES

½ cup cognac

1 (4-ounce) package dried porcini or Asian black mushrooms

3 tablespoons unsalted butter

3 tablespoons chestnut flour

4 shallots, minced

10 ounces button mushrooms, bases of stems removed

¼ teaspoon nutmeg

1 cup gluten-free beef broth

1 cup heavy cream

1 tablespoon fresh thyme

½ teaspoon salt

½ teaspoon freshly ground black pepper

1. Place the cognac and dried mushrooms in a small saucepan and add water to cover. Simmer over low heat for 10 minutes. Remove from the stove and cool. Purée in the blender until very smooth.

2. Melt the butter over medium heat in a medium saucepan, and stir in the chestnut flour, stirring until well blended. Add the shallots and button mushrooms, stirring constantly for 3–4 minutes.

3. Whisk in the rest of the ingredients, including the puréed mushroom and cognac mixture. (At this point you can add 1½ cups extra broth if making soup.)

PER SERVING Calories: 497 | Fat: 35g | Protein: 8g | Sodium: 523mg | Fiber: 5g | Carbohydrates: 29g | Sugar: 2g

Roasted Garlic Sauce with Cheese

Roasting garlic is simple and makes the garlic milder, softer, and sweeter. Use this sauce with vegetables, spaghetti squash, salads, rice, or tomatoes.

INGREDIENTS | MAKES ¾ CUP

1 head garlic, unpeeled, dampened

1 tablespoon unsalted butter

1 teaspoon cornstarch

½ cup milk

¼ cup gluten-free chicken broth

2 tablespoons minced Italian flat-leaf parsley

2 tablespoons extra-virgin olive oil

1 teaspoon vinegar or lemon juice

1 teaspoon salt

½ teaspoon freshly ground black pepper

2 tablespoons Parmesan cheese

1. Preheat the oven to 300°F.

2. Wrap the dampened garlic in aluminum foil and roast in oven for 60 minutes. Cool until you can handle it. Cut off the tip ends and squeeze garlic out of the shells and into a small bowl; set aside.

3. In a medium saucepan, melt butter over low heat and stir in the cornstarch. Continue to cook for 3–4 minutes over low heat. Whisk in the milk, chicken broth, parsley, and olive oil.

4. Add vinegar or lemon juice, salt, pepper, cheese, and reserved garlic.

5. Place mixture in the blender and process until smooth. Pour into a serving bowl.

PER SERVING (¼ CUP) | Calories: 203 | Fat: 17g | Protein: 9g | Sodium: 1,044mg | Fiber: 0g | Carbohydrates: 8g | Sugar: 2g

Greek Eggplant and Olive Sauce

*Garlic and mint provide the unmistakable flavors of Greece.
This sauce is perfect for wheat-free pasta, rice, or even vegetables.*

INGREDIENTS | SERVES 4 | 20 MINUTES

2 tablespoons flax meal

½ cup rice flour mixed with 1 teaspoon salt

1 medium eggplant, peeled and cubed

⅓ cup extra-virgin olive oil

2 cloves garlic, minced

½ cup kalamata or other black Greek olives, pitted and chopped

10 mint leaves, coarsely chopped

½ cup finely snipped chives

Juice of ½ lemon

1. In a shallow bowl, mix the ground flax with the flour and salt. Dredge the eggplant cubes in flour mixture.

2. In a medium saucepan, heat the olive oil over medium-high heat. Add the eggplant and sauté until brown, about 10 minutes.

3. Once brown, lower heat and add the garlic; sauté for another 3 minutes.

4. Add the rest of the ingredients and serve.

PER SERVING Calories: 301 | Fat: 20g | Protein: 4g | Sodium: 598mg | Fiber: 6.5g | Carbohydrates: 30g | Sugar: 3g

Spicy Spinach and Lobster Sauce

*Serve this sauce over rice pasta, which can be found in
Asian markets and some specialty supermarkets.*

INGREDIENTS | SERVES 4 | 40 MINUTES

1 (1½-pound) lobster

2 tablespoons butter

2 tablespoons cornstarch

1 cup gluten-free chicken or clam broth, heated

1 cup heavy cream

3 cups fresh baby spinach, rinsed and stems trimmed

1 tablespoon dry sherry

⅛ teaspoon ground nutmeg

1 teaspoon hot red pepper flakes

½ teaspoon salt

½ teaspoon freshly ground black pepper

1. Plunge the lobster into plenty of boiling salted water. Cook for 15 minutes. Cool; crack the shell and remove the meat. Set the meat aside.

2. In a large saucepan, melt the butter over medium heat and add the cornstarch, stirring until smooth. Whisk in the broth. Add the cream and heat.

3. Stir in the spinach and cook until wilted. Add the sherry, nutmeg, red pepper flakes, and reserved lobster. Sprinkle with salt and pepper.

PER SERVING Calories: 460 | Fat: 30g | Protein: 35g | Sodium: 920mg | Fiber: 1g | Carbohydrates: 10g | Sugar: 1.5g

Citrus Dipping Sauce for Shrimp and Oysters

One of the best things about this sauce is its versatility.
You can use it with fried scallops, cold seafood, or chicken.

**INGREDIENTS | MAKES 1½ CUPS |
15 MINUTES**

½ cup marmalade
¼ cup wheat-free soy sauce
¾ cup fresh orange juice
1 teaspoon gluten-free Dijon mustard
1 teaspoon honey
Juice of ½ lime
Juice of ½ lemon
1" piece gingerroot, peeled and minced
½ teaspoon salt
¼ teaspoon freshly ground black pepper

Place all ingredients in a small saucepan and boil until well blended. Cool and store in the refrigerator.

PER SERVING (2 TABLESPOONS) | Calories: 47 | Fat: 0g | Protein: 0.5g | Sodium: 410mg | Fiber: 0g | Carbohydrates: 12g | Sugar: 10g

Sweet and Hot Yellow Tomato Coulis

This is excellent drizzled over shrimp, fish, or poultry.
Its fresh taste will keep in the refrigerator or freezer.

**INGREDIENTS | MAKES 1½ CUPS |
10 MINUTES**

4 large yellow tomatoes, cored and chopped
2 cloves garlic, peeled and halved
3 shallots, chopped
½ cup extra-virgin olive oil
1 tablespoon orange juice
1 tablespoon finely chopped parsley
1 teaspoon salt
½ teaspoon freshly ground black pepper

Put all ingredients in blender. Purée. Serve cold or warm the sauce over low heat.

PER SERVING (¼ CUP) | Calories: 191 | Fat: 18g | Protein: 1.5g | Sodium: 400mg | Fiber: 1.5g | Carbohydrates: 7g | Sugar: 3.5g

Spicy Tomato Salsa

Salsa made with fresh tomatoes and herbs is such a treat. Of course, you can vary it tremendously. Have fun with this recipe, adding extras from your garden.

INGREDIENTS | MAKES ABOUT 1½ CUPS | 15 MINUTES

10 large, fresh plum or Roma tomatoes, blanched in boiling water and peeled

¼ cup lemon juice

3 cloves garlic, minced

2 ears cooked corn, kernels cut from the cob

1 teaspoon cumin

2 medium onions, peeled and quartered

½ teaspoon salt

¼ teaspoon hot pepper sauce

½ cup chopped fresh cilantro or parsley

Mix all ingredients in a food processor, pulsing until coarsely chopped. Refrigerate until ready to serve.

PER SERVING (¼ CUP) | Calories: 47 | Fat: 0g | Protein: 1.5g | Sodium: 207mg | Fiber: 1g | Carbohydrates: 11g | Sugar: 2g

Tropical Fruit Salsa MA

The sweet blend of fruits and vegetables makes a wonderful and unique salsa. Try it with pork, lamb, or any kind of fish.

INGREDIENTS | MAKES ABOUT 1½ CUPS

1 large mango, peeled, seeded, and diced

1 cup fresh pineapple, diced

½ medium red bell pepper, seeded and diced

¼ cup minced red onion

½ teaspoon freshly grated lime zest

Juice of ½ lime

½ teaspoon salt

Mix all ingredients in a bowl and cover. Refrigerate for 2 hours. Serve at room temperature.

PER SERVING (¼ CUP) | Calories: 44 | Fat: 0g | Protein: 0.5g | Sodium: 198mg | Fiber: 1.5g | Carbohydrates: 11g | Sugar: 9g

White and Red Grape Sauce for Poultry and Game

This is wonderful with chicken, turkey, or duck.
For an exciting taste, try it with bison or venison.

INGREDIENTS | MAKES 2 CUPS | 30 MINUTES

2 tablespoons unsalted butter

2 shallots, chopped

2 tablespoons cornstarch

1 cup gluten-free chicken broth, warmed

½ cup seedless red grapes, washed and halved

½ cup seedless green grapes, washed and halved

¼ cup dry white wine

1 teaspoon rosemary leaves

10 fresh basil leaves

1 teaspoon gluten-free Worcestershire sauce

½ teaspoon salt

½ teaspoon freshly ground black pepper

1. In a medium saucepan over medium heat, melt the butter and sauté the shallots until they are soft, about 5 minutes. Stir in cornstarch and cook for 4 minutes. Whisk in the warm broth and add the grapes, wine, rosemary, and basil. (For a variation, you can add ½ cup of heavy cream or some lemon juice.) Bring to a boil and cook for 10 minutes, until grapes are softened.

2. Add the Worcestershire sauce, salt, and pepper. Serve hot.

PER SERVING (½ CUP) | Calories: 139 | Fat: 7g | Protein: 2g | Sodium: 574mg | Fiber: 0.5g | Carbohydrates: 16g | Sugar: 6g

Apple, Cranberry, and Walnut Chutney

This chutney is excellent with duckling, chicken, and, of course, turkey. It's easy to make and will keep for 2 weeks in the refrigerator. Or make a lot and freeze it.

INGREDIENTS | MAKES 2 CUPS | 25 MINUTES

2 tablespoons vegetable oil

½ cup finely chopped shallots

2 cups fresh or frozen cranberries

2 medium tart apples, peeled, cored, and chopped

½ cup brown sugar

¼ cup cider vinegar

2 ounces water

1 teaspoon grated orange zest

½ teaspoon ground coriander seed

½ teaspoon salt

½ teaspoon ground black pepper

½ cup chopped walnuts, toasted

1. Heat oil in a large heavy saucepan over medium-high heat. Sauté the shallots until softened, about 5 minutes.

2. Stir in cranberries, apples, brown sugar, vinegar, water, zest, coriander, salt, and pepper. Cook, stirring constantly, for 15 minutes, or until berries have popped and the sauce has become very thick.

3. Stir in toasted walnut pieces. Serve warm or store in the refrigerator for up to 2 weeks.

PER SERVING (¼ CUP) | Calories: 141 | Fat: 5g | Protein: 2g | Sodium: 153mg | Fiber: 2g | Carbohydrates: 25g | Sugar: 19g

Incredible Hollandaise Sauce

This sauce can be varied enormously. It's perfect on fish, lobster, or hot vegetables, especially asparagus, artichokes, and broccoli. Add another egg yolk to make a richer sauce.

INGREDIENTS | MAKES 1¼ CUPS | 15 MINUTES

2 sticks (1 cup) unsalted butter

2 large egg yolks

1 tablespoon freshly squeezed lemon juice

⅛ teaspoon cayenne pepper

½ teaspoon salt

1. Melt the butter in a small, heavy saucepan over very low heat. Put the egg yolks, lemon juice, and cayenne in the jar of a blender or food processor. Blend well.

2. With the motor running on low, add the hot butter, a little at a time, to the egg mixture.

3. Return to the pan you used to melt the butter. Whisking, thicken the sauce over low heat, adding salt. As soon as it's thick (about 5 minutes), pour into a bowl, a sauce boat, or over the food.

PER SERVING (2 TABLESPOONS) | Calories: 173 | Fat: 19g | Protein: 1g | Sodium: 122mg | Fiber: 0g | Carbohydrates: 0g | Sugar: 0g

Spicy Marinara Sauce MA

This sauce is perfect for a variety of dishes. You can adjust the spiciness by increasing or decreasing the red pepper flakes.

INGREDIENTS | SERVES 10

3 tablespoons extra-virgin olive oil

1 medium onion, peeled and finely chopped

6 garlic cloves, minced

1 teaspoon dried oregano

1 teaspoon dried parsley

¾ teaspoon dried rosemary

1 cup fresh basil leaves, torn

¾ teaspoon marjoram

½ teaspoon crushed red pepper flakes

2 (28-ounce) cans crushed tomatoes

1 medium red bell pepper, seeded and finely chopped

½ cup dry white wine

1 teaspoon salt

½ teaspoon freshly ground black pepper

1. Heat the olive oil in a large pan over medium heat. Add onion, garlic, and spices. Cover and cook for 10 minutes.

2. Lower the heat, add all other ingredients, and simmer gently for 75 minutes.

PER SERVING Calories: 85 | Fat: 4g | Protein: 2g | Sodium: 462mg | Fiber: 2g | Carbohydrates: 9g | Sugar: 5g

Puttanesca Sauce SC

Don't be afraid of the anchovies in this dish. They simply melt away and add a complex flavor to this spicy, salty, garlicky sauce.

INGREDIENTS | SERVES 6

4 anchovies in oil

1 tablespoon olive oil

4 cloves garlic, minced

1 medium onion, peeled and diced

1 cup sliced black olives

1 (28-ounce) can crushed tomatoes

1 (15-ounce) can diced tomatoes

1 tablespoon crushed red pepper

2 tablespoons drained nonpareil-sized capers

1 tablespoon sugar

What Is Sautéing?

Sautéing is a method of cooking that uses a small amount of fat to cook food in a shallow pan over medium-high heat. The goal is to brown the food while preserving its color, moisture, and flavor.

1. Pat the anchovies with a paper towel to remove any excess oil.

2. Heat the olive oil in a large, nonstick skillet and add the anchovies, garlic, and onion. Sauté until the anchovies mostly disappear into the onion and garlic and the onions are soft, about 3–5 minutes.

3. Place the onions, anchovies, and garlic into a 4–6-quart slow cooker. Add the remaining ingredients. Stir to distribute the ingredients evenly. Cook on low for 10–12 hours.

4. If the sauce looks very wet at the end of the cooking time, remove the lid and cook on high for 15–30 minutes before serving.

PER SERVING Calories: 104 | Fat: 5g | Protein: 2.5g | Sodium: 291mg | Fiber: 4g | Carbohydrates: 14g | Sugar: 8g

Basic Cream Sauce

This cream sauce is the basis for a lot of cooking. You can use milk instead of cream, but don't substitute margarine for butter. Try stirring in ⅛ teaspoon nutmeg, 1 teaspoon gluten-free Dijon mustard, or 1 tablespoon snipped fresh chives for a bit of extra flavor.

INGREDIENTS | MAKES 2 CUPS | 10 MINUTES

3 tablespoons unsalted butter

3 tablespoons corn flour

2 cups heavy cream, warmed

½ teaspoon salt

¼ teaspoon ground black pepper

1. In a small saucepan over medium-low heat, melt the butter and stir in the flour. Sauté and stir for 4–5 minutes. Add the warm cream or milk, whisking constantly until thickened to desired consistency.

2. Just before serving, add salt and pepper.

PER SERVING (2 TABLESPOONS) | Calories: 128 | Fat: 13g | Protein: 1g | Sodium: 85mg | Fiber: 0g | Carbohydrates: 2g | Sugar: 0g

Beyond the Basics

Once you learn to make a basic cream sauce, you can add mustard, sautéed mushrooms, oysters, shrimp, herbs, and all kinds of luscious things. You can pour the sauce over fish or shellfish, poultry, and/or vegetables.

Creamy Cheddar Sauce with Ham and Sherry

This is excellent over vegetables, spaghetti squash, or rice.

INGREDIENTS | MAKES 2½ CUPS | 10 MINUTES

3 tablespoons unsalted butter

3 tablespoons corn flour

2 cups whole milk, warmed

⅔ cup grated sharp Cheddar cheese

¼ cup minced smoked ham

2 teaspoons sherry

½ teaspoon salt

¼ teaspoon freshly ground black pepper

1. In a medium saucepan over medium-low heat, melt butter and stir in flour. Cook, stirring, for 4–5 minutes. Add warm milk, whisking constantly until thickened to desired consistency.

2. Remove from the heat and stir in the cheese, ham, sherry, salt, and pepper. Serve.

PER SERVING (½ CUP) | Calories: 214 | Fat: 16g | Protein: 8g | Sodium: 462mg | Fiber: 0g | Carbohydrates: 9g | Sugar: 5g

Hazelnut, Sour Cream, and Ham Sauce

This sauce is so rich, you won't need much of it. Use it to top 8 ounces of gluten-free pasta for a very good side dish with seafood, fish, or chicken.

INGREDIENTS | SERVES 4 | 10 MINUTES

¼ cup olive oil

4 shallots, minced

1 cup hazelnuts, toasted, peeled, and coarsely chopped

1 cup finely diced Virginia ham

1½ cups sour cream (not nonfat or low-fat)

¼ teaspoon freshly ground black pepper

½ teaspoon celery salt

1. Heat the oil in a medium skillet over medium heat. Sauté the shallots about 5 minutes, until soft. Add the toasted hazelnuts, ham, and sour cream.

2. Turn heat down to low, and as soon as sour cream is hot, sprinkle with pepper and celery salt. Serve hot.

PER SERVING Calories: 417 | Fat: 37g | Protein: 13g | Sodium: 813mg | Fiber: 3g | Carbohydrates: 11g | Sugar: 4g

Creamy Mustard-Mayo Sauce

This is a great everyday sauce you can use with your favorite fish, chicken, or pasta recipes. The mustard adds just the right kick of spice and flavor to the creamy, decadent mayo. It also makes a great dip for Gluten-Free Soft Pretzel Bites (see recipe in Chapter 2).

INGREDIENTS | MAKES ¾ CUP | 5 MINUTES

6 tablespoons gluten-free Dijon mustard

⅓ cup mayonnaise

1 tablespoon minced Italian herbs

½ teaspoon salt

½ teaspoon ground black pepper

Whisk all ingredients together in a small bowl. Use immediately or refrigerate for up to 1 week.

PER SERVING (2 TABLESPOONS) | Calories: 99 | Fat: 10g | Protein: 1g | Sodium: 444mg | Fiber: 1g | Carbohydrates: 1g | Sugar: 0g

Lower-Fat Version

To cut calories in this sauce, try substituting lower-fat mayonnaise in place of regular mayonnaise. You could also replace some or all of the mayonnaise with low-fat Greek yogurt for a tangier, healthier alternative.

Alfredo Sauce with Parsley

The eggs in Alfredo sauce are lightly cooked when mixed with hot pasta.
You can also try it with spaghetti squash instead of pasta.

INGREDIENTS | MAKES 1½ CUPS | 15 MINUTES

1 tablespoon unsalted butter
2 tablespoons minced shallots
1 cup heavy cream
1 cup fresh or frozen baby peas
½ cup grated Parmesan cheese
2 large eggs
1 tablespoon cracked peppercorns
½ teaspoon salt
½ cup chopped fresh parsley

Cracked Peppercorns

When a recipe calls for cracked or coarsely ground black pepper, there's an easy way to prepare it. Place a tablespoon or so of peppercorns on a chopping board. Press a heavy frying pan down on the peppercorns and rock it around gently. You will then have cracked pepper. Many pepper grinders also have a setting for a coarse grind. You generally have to loosen the screw at the top of the grinder to make the pepper coarse.

1. In a medium saucepan over medium heat, melt the butter and sauté the shallots for 3–4 minutes. Add cream and peas. Bring to a boil, and thicken, cooking for about 6 minutes, stirring constantly.

2. Remove from heat and stir in cheese.

3. In a separate, large serving bowl, beat eggs. Whisk in a tablespoon of the cream sauce; stirring constantly, add the remainder of the sauce, a little at a time. (Be careful—if you put the hot sauce into the eggs too quickly, they will scramble.)

4. Add pepper, salt, and parsley.

PER SERVING (½ CUP) | Calories: 480 | Fat: 42g | Protein: 15g | Sodium: 784mg | Fiber: 3g | Carbohydrates: 13g | Sugar: 3g

Avocado and Cilantro Ranch Dressing

Even the pickiest eaters can't seem to get enough of ranch dressing. This variety is even creamier with a bolder flavor thanks to the cilantro. Make a big batch of this on weekends for use throughout the week on salads and vegetables.

INGREDIENTS | SERVES 10 | 10 MINUTES

½ medium ripe avocado, peeled and pitted

2 tablespoons buttermilk

½ cup full-fat mayonnaise

½ cup low-fat plain Greek yogurt

3 teaspoons white wine vinegar

1 tablespoon chopped fresh dill

½ teaspoon onion powder

2 tablespoons chopped fresh cilantro

⅛ teaspoon garlic powder

½ teaspoon salt

½ teaspoon ground black pepper

1. Place the avocado, buttermilk, mayonnaise, yogurt, and vinegar in a blender. Blend until puréed. Transfer mixture to a medium bowl.

2. Whisk in dill, onion powder, cilantro, garlic powder, salt, and pepper.

3. Serve immediately or refrigerate up to 1 week.

PER SERVING Calories: 102 | Fat: 10g | Protein: 3g | Sodium: 191mg | Fiber: 1g | Carbohydrates: 2g | Sugar: 1g

Creamy Tzatziki MA

Tzatziki is a traditional Greek sauce that's often used on gyros or in salads. Although it can be bought, it's so easy to make at home with just a few simple ingredients. Try it on chicken kebobs and fresh cucumber salad.

INGREDIENTS | MAKES 1½ CUPS

3 tablespoons olive oil

1 tablespoon white vinegar

2 cloves garlic, minced finely

½ teaspoon salt

¼ teaspoon ground white pepper

1 cup low-fat Greek yogurt, strained

1 cup sour cream

2 medium cucumbers, peeled, seeded, and diced

1 teaspoon chopped fresh dill

1. Combine olive oil, vinegar, garlic, salt, and pepper in a medium bowl. Mix until well combined.

2. In a separate bowl, blend the yogurt with the sour cream using a whisk. Add the olive oil mixture to the yogurt mixture and mix well.

3. Stir in the cucumber and dill. Cover bowl with plastic wrap and refrigerate overnight.

PER SERVING (2 TABLESPOONS) | Calories: 88 | Fat: 8g | Protein: 3g | Sodium: 129mg | Fiber: 0g | Carbohydrates: 4g | Sugar: 3g

Bourbon, Brown Sugar, and Peach Sauce

Bourbon isn't just for mint juleps and cocktails. In this brown sugar and peach sauce, the bourbon adds the right amount of smoky depth to balance the sweetness of the fruit and sugar. Try this sauce over ice cream or crumbles.

INGREDIENTS | SERVES 4 | 15 MINUTES

6 tablespoons high-quality bourbon

4 tablespoons pure clover honey

2 tablespoons dark brown sugar

1 cinnamon stick

2 tablespoons unsalted butter

2 tablespoons lemon juice

2 teaspoons gluten-free pure vanilla extract

4 large peaches, peeled and sliced

1. Heat bourbon, honey, sugar, cinnamon stick, and butter in a heavy saucepan over medium-high heat. Cook, stirring constantly, until sugar is dissolved, about 5 minutes. Stir in the lemon juice, vanilla, and peaches.

2. Reduce heat to low and simmer until peaches are softened and almost caramelized, about 6–8 minutes.

3. Remove the cinnamon stick. Transfer mixture to a blender and purée, or serve as is.

PER SERVING Calories: 271 | Fat: 6g | Protein: 2g | Sodium: 5g | Fiber: 3g | Carbohydrates: 42g | Sugar: 39g

Sticky and Spicy Barbecue Sauce

Everyone needs at least one foolproof barbecue sauce in their cooking repertoire, and this one should be yours. It's incredibly easy to make and is sticky and sweet with the right amount of spice. And it goes well with just about anything!

INGREDIENTS | MAKES 1½ CUPS | 30 MINUTES

1 tablespoon extra-virgin olive oil

½ large onion, peeled and diced

2 small chipotle peppers, chopped

1 tablespoon crushed red pepper

1 cup low-sugar gluten-free ketchup

¼ cup molasses

½ tablespoon light corn syrup

¼ cup honey

2½ tablespoons light brown sugar

4 tablespoons red wine vinegar

1 tablespoon gluten-free Worcestershire sauce

1 teaspoon salt

½ teaspoon ground black pepper

1. Heat oil in a medium saucepan over medium heat. Stir in the onion and chipotle pepper. Cook until softened, about 6–7 minutes.

2. Reduce heat to low and whisk in the crushed red pepper, ketchup, molasses, corn syrup, honey, brown sugar, vinegar, and Worcestershire sauce. Add salt and pepper.

3. Cover and simmer for about 15–20 minutes, or until thickened.

PER SERVING (2 TABLESPOONS) | Calories: 80 | Fat: 1g | Protein: 1g | Sodium: 439mg | Fiber: 0g | Carbohydrates: 17g | Sugar: 15g

Strawberry Rhubarb Jam

Jam is so easy and tasty to make at home. This quick, sweet, and simple strawberry rhubarb jam will instantly become a favorite in your house!

INGREDIENTS | MAKES 3½ PINTS

1½ pounds fresh strawberries, hulled and chopped

1½ pounds rhubarb, diced

1¾ cups sugar, divided

¼ cup lemon juice

Perfect Jam

The key to a perfect jam (without pectin or gelatin) is to let the berries reduce naturally on their own over very low heat. Resist the urge to overstir or meddle. Use a candy thermometer to make sure you don't over-cook the jam.

1. Place strawberries, rhubarb, 1 cup sugar, and lemon juice in a large saucepan. Carefully mash the strawberries with a fork or wooden spoon while mixing with the other ingredients.

2. Cook over medium heat until sugar has completely dissolved, about 3–5 minutes. Taste the mixture and add another ¼–¾ cup sugar. Cover and reduce heat to low. Simmer jam for about 20 minutes, or until mixture reaches 220°F.

3. Remove from heat and immediately transfer to sterile canning jars. Cover with lid and chill for at least 1 hour.

PER SERVING (2 TABLESPOONS) | Calories: 31 | Fat: 0g | Protein: 0g | Sodium: 1mg | Fiber: 0g | Carbohydrates: 8g | Sugar: 7g

Rich Caramel, Pecan, and Coffee Sauce

This rich and crunchy sauce was made for ice cream. Try it over your favorite gluten-free coffee cake for a truly decadent breakfast treat.

INGREDIENTS | MAKES 1 CUP

2 tablespoons egg substitute
¼ cup granulated sugar
3½ tablespoons water, divided
½ teaspoon cinnamon
⅛ teaspoon salt
1 cup pecan halves
⅓ cup brewed medium blend coffee
⅓ cup heavy cream
½ cup brown sugar
½ cup superfine sugar
¼ cup unsalted butter, melted
1 teaspoon pumpkin pie spice

1. Preheat oven to 225°F. Grease a large baking sheet.

2. Whisk the egg substitute, granulated sugar, and ½ tablespoon water until fluffy. Stir in the cinnamon, salt, and pecans. Spread the pecan mixture evenly over the baking sheet.

3. Bake for about 1 hour, stirring every 20 minutes. Remove from oven and set aside to cool.

4. In a small bowl, whisk the coffee and cream together. Set aside.

5. In a medium saucepan, whisk brown sugar, superfine sugar, and 3 tablespoons water together. Heat over medium-high heat until the sugar dissolves. Cook until the sugar is golden in color, about 4–5 minutes.

6. Remove from heat and whisk in ¼ cup of the coffee mixture, stirring until thickened. Keep adding the coffee mixture, whisking very well after each addition. Let cool slightly and then whisk in the butter and pumpkin pie spice.

7. Stir in the crunchy pecans and serve immediately.

PER SERVING (2 TABLESPOONS) | Calories: 311 | Fat: 20g | Protein: 2g | Sodium: 53mg | Fiber: 1g | Carbohydrates: 35g | Sugar: 33g

CHAPTER 4

Stocks, Soups, and Stews

African Peanut Soup SC

Peanut butter is an excellent source of protein. Feel free to play around with the seasonings in this unique soup. A small pinch of curry powder would be an excellent addition.

INGREDIENTS | SERVES 6

2 tablespoons olive oil

2 medium onions, peeled and chopped

2 large red bell peppers, seeded and chopped

4 cloves garlic, minced

1 (28-ounce) can crushed tomatoes, with liquid

8 cups gluten-free vegetable broth

¼ teaspoon ground black pepper

¼ teaspoon chili powder

½ cup uncooked brown rice

⅔ cup crunchy peanut butter

½ cup fresh chopped cilantro

Peanut Allergies and Intolerances

Peanut allergies are very serious and can be life-threatening. If you have a child or family member who has peanut allergies, you can use almond butter or cashew butter in this recipe instead. Both can be found at specialty food stores, or you can make your own by grinding soaked almonds or cashews in a high-powered blender.

1. Heat olive oil in a large skillet. Cook onions and bell peppers until softened, about 3–4 minutes.

2. Add garlic and cook for 1 minute more, stirring constantly. Add cooked vegetables to a greased 6-quart slow cooker.

3. Add tomatoes and their liquid, broth, ground pepper, chili powder, and brown rice to the slow cooker. Cover and cook on high for 4 hours or on low for 8 hours.

4. One hour prior to serving stir in the peanut butter. Heat for an additional 45–60 minutes until soup has been completely warmed through. Garnish with cilantro.

PER SERVING Calories: 323 | Fat: 20g | Protein: 11g | Sodium: 324mg | Fiber: 5g | Carbohydrates: 30g | Sugar: 10g

Italian Wedding Soup `SC`

This is a delicious light soup with spinach and meatballs. When making the meatballs, use a light touch or they will become tough during cooking.

INGREDIENTS | SERVES 8

1 slice gluten-free bread, crumbled

¾ cup 1% milk

½ pound ground beef

1 cup grated Parmesan cheese, divided

1 large egg

½ small onion, peeled and finely minced

⅓ cup chopped fresh parsley

2 tablespoons chopped fresh basil

1 teaspoon dried oregano

1 teaspoon garlic powder

1 teaspoon salt

⅛ teaspoon red pepper flakes

1 cup chopped celery

1 cup chopped onion

8 cups gluten-free chicken broth

1 (10-ounce) package frozen spinach, defrosted and drained

3 cups cooked small gluten-free pasta

1. Place bread in a medium bowl and pour milk over it. Let sit 10 minutes, then gently squeeze out excess liquid. Put bread in a large bowl; discard milk.

2. Add the ground beef, ½ cup Parmesan cheese, egg, minced onion, parsley, basil, oregano, garlic powder, salt, and red pepper flakes to bowl with bread. Gently toss to combine. Roll the meat mixture in your hands to create tiny meatballs.

3. Add celery, chopped onion, chicken broth, meatballs, and spinach to a greased 6-quart slow cooker and cook on high for 4 hours or on low for 8 hours.

4. Add ½ cup cooked pasta to each bowl of hot soup and garnish with 1 tablespoon Parmesan cheese.

PER SERVING Calories: 332 | Fat: 11g | Protein: 23g | Sodium: 933mg | Fiber: 3g | Carbohydrates: 33g | Sugar: 7g

Gluten-Free Pasta

When choosing gluten-free pasta for soup, look for small shapes such as ditalini or anellini. You can find these specialty pasta shapes from a gluten-free company called Le Veneziane and can order them through Amazon.com.

Thick and Hearty Lancashire Lamb Stew

Make a double recipe and freeze half for another busy day. Cook beans the old-fashioned way or use canned cannellini beans instead.

INGREDIENTS | SERVES 6

¼ cup olive oil

½ cup brown rice flour

1 teaspoon salt

½ teaspoon ground black pepper

2 pounds lamb stew meat

2 slices bacon, chopped

4 cloves garlic

2 large onions, peeled and chopped

2 carrots, peeled and chopped

2 bay leaves

2 cups gluten-free chicken broth

1 cup dry white wine

½ bunch parsley

2 tablespoons dried rosemary

Juice and zest of ½ lemon

2 teaspoons gluten-free Worcestershire sauce

3 (13-ounce) cans white beans, drained and rinsed

1. Heat the olive oil over medium-high heat in a large skillet.

2. In a shallow bowl, combine the flour, salt, and pepper. Dredge the lamb in the flour mixture.

3. Brown the meat in the hot oil, about 1 minute on each side. Remove from pan and drain.

4. In the same pan, cook the bacon until crisp. Place lamb and bacon in a 6-quart slow cooker. Add remaining ingredients to the slow cooker.

5. Cover and cook on high for 4 hours or on low for 8 hours.

PER SERVING Calories: 680 | Fat: 29g | Protein: 43g | Sodium: 1,520mg | Fiber: 14g | Carbohydrates: 55g | Sugar: 7g

Tortilla Soup SC

This soup tastes even better the next day. Have it for dinner one day and lunch the next.

INGREDIENTS | SERVES 8

1 teaspoon cumin

1 teaspoon chili powder

1 teaspoon smoked paprika

⅛ teaspoon salt

1 (25-ounce) can crushed tomatoes

1 (14-ounce) can fire-roasted diced tomatoes

3 cups gluten-free chicken broth

2 cloves garlic, minced

1 medium onion, peeled and diced

1 (4-ounce) can diced green chilies, drained

2 habanero peppers, seeded and diced

1 cup fresh corn kernels

2 cups cubed cooked boneless chicken breast

1. Place cumin, chili powder, paprika, salt, tomatoes, broth, garlic, onion, chilies, and peppers in a 4–6-quart slow cooker. Cover and cook on low for 6 hours.

2. Add the corn and cooked chicken. Cover and cook for an additional 45–60 minutes.

PER SERVING Calories: 153 | Fat: 3g | Protein: 15g | Sodium: 657mg | Fiber: 3g | Carbohydrates: 18g | Sugar: 5g

Put the Tortilla in Tortilla Soup

Slice 4 corn tortillas in half, then into ¼" strips. Heat ½ teaspoon canola oil in a shallow skillet. Add the tortilla strips and cook, turning once, until they are crisp and golden. Drain on paper towel–lined plates. Blot dry. Divide evenly among the bowls of soup before serving.

Slow Cooker Thai Curried Chicken Soup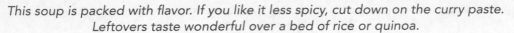

This soup is packed with flavor. If you like it less spicy, cut down on the curry paste.
Leftovers taste wonderful over a bed of rice or quinoa.

INGREDIENTS | SERVES 6

2 pounds boneless, skinless chicken, cubed

½ teaspoon salt

½ teaspoon ground black pepper

1 tablespoon peanut oil

4 cloves garlic, minced

1 tablespoon minced fresh ginger

2 teaspoons red curry paste

1 teaspoon curry powder

1 teaspoon turmeric

1 teaspoon cumin

1 (13.5-ounce) can coconut milk

4 cups gluten-free chicken broth

1 tablespoon fish sauce

Juice of 1 medium lime

1 cup sliced mushrooms

1 medium onion, peeled and chopped

1 medium red bell pepper, seeded and chopped

1 jalapeño pepper, seeded and sliced

½ cup sliced scallions

6 lime wedges

1. Sprinkle the chicken breasts with salt and pepper. Set aside.

2. Heat oil in a large skillet over medium-high heat. Sauté garlic and ginger for 1–2 minutes, until tender.

3. Stir in the chicken and cook while stirring for 5–8 minutes, until browned and no longer pink.

4. Place the chicken mixture in a 4–6-quart slow cooker. Add curry paste, curry powder, turmeric, cumin, coconut milk, broth, fish sauce, and lime juice. Stir to combine. Cook on low for 6 hours.

5. Add mushrooms, onion, red pepper, and jalapeño and let cook another 30 minutes, until they soften. Garnish with sliced scallions and lime wedges.

PER SERVING Calories: 443 | Fat: 24g | Protein: 39g | Sodium: 1,386mg | Fiber: 4g | Carbohydrates: 20g | Sugar: 3g

Shrimp Bisque with Scallops

This is an elegant first course or a delicious light supper. It's very easy to make in advance, adding the cream at the last minute when heating.

INGREDIENTS | SERVES 6 | 30 MINUTES

2 minced shallots

1 clove garlic, minced

2 tablespoons butter

2 tablespoons cornstarch

1 tablespoon tomato paste

4 cups shrimp shell broth (see sidebar) or bottled clam broth

½ pound shrimp, cleaned and deveined

½ pound bay scallops

½ teaspoon salt

½ teaspoon freshly ground black pepper

1 cup heavy cream

¼ cup chopped parsley

6 tablespoons dry sherry

Shrimp Shell Broth

Shrimp shell broth makes a flavorful addition to seafood soup. Next time you are preparing shrimp, reserve the shells. Add 1 cup water, 1 cup wine, and a bay leaf to the shells from a pound of shrimp. Bring to a boil, lower heat, and simmer, covered, for 20 minutes. Strain and use as broth in your soup.

1. In a large stockpot over medium-high heat, sauté the shallots and garlic in the butter for 2–3 minutes.

2. Blend in cornstarch and tomato paste. Add broth and bring to a boil. Then lower heat and simmer for 10 minutes.

3. Spoon in the shrimp and scallops and cook for 2–3 minutes. Season with salt and pepper.

4. Let cool for 5 minutes. Using blender, blend in batches until puréed. Return to the pot and stir in cream.

5. Ladle soup into bowls. Top each bowl with parsley and a tablespoon of sherry.

PER SERVING Calories: 298 | Fat: 20g | Protein: 27g | Sodium: 350mg | Fiber: 0g | Carbohydrates: 9g | Sugar: 2g

Tasty Taco Soup

This wonderful soup can be made into a chili if you reduce the amount of broth. Garnish with Cheddar cheese, sour cream, or extra cilantro.

INGREDIENTS | SERVES 8 | 45 MINUTES

3 tablespoons extra-virgin olive oil, divided

1½ pounds lean ground beef (you can also use ground turkey or chicken)

1 medium onion, peeled and chopped

3 cloves garlic, minced

1 medium red or yellow bell pepper, seeded and chopped

1 cup diced tomatoes

1½ cups frozen corn

1 tablespoon chili powder

¼ teaspoon red pepper flakes

¼ teaspoon oregano, dried

½ teaspoon paprika

1 tablespoon cumin

3 tablespoons chopped fresh cilantro

1 teaspoon salt

½ teaspoon freshly ground black pepper

1 (15-ounce) can red kidney beans, thoroughly rinsed and drained

1 (4.5-ounce) can green chili peppers

3 cups gluten-free chicken broth

1½–2 cups water (depending on how much liquid you want)

Juice of ½ lime

1. In a large stockpot or Dutch oven over medium heat, warm 2 tablespoons of the oil and add the ground meat. Cook for 5–8 minutes, until completely browned and no longer pink. Remove from heat and place meat into a bowl.

2. In the same pot over medium heat, heat the remaining tablespoon oil, onion, and garlic for 3–4 minutes, until they soften.

3. Add the bell peppers, tomatoes, corn, spices, and cilantro. Season with salt and pepper and mix well. Add the kidney beans and chili peppers and mix again. Add the meat back to pot along with chicken broth, water, and lime juice. Mix well and bring to a boil.

4. Cover and reduce heat to low. Simmer for 30 minutes.

PER SERVING Calories: 298 | Fat: 12g | Protein: 25g | Sodium: 915mg | Fiber: 5g | Carbohydrates: 25g | Sugar: 4g

Do You Love Sour Cream?

If you are looking for a healthier alternative, why not substitute plain Greek yogurt for sour cream? Greek yogurt is also thick and creamy but has much less fat and fewer calories. Greek yogurt is also much higher in protein.

Lentil and Sausage Soup with Quinoa and Kale

This soup is hearty enough for a complete meal. It is packed with protein and can be easily frozen in an airtight container.

INGREDIENTS | SERVES 6

1 tablespoon grapeseed oil

3 cloves garlic, minced

1 pound gluten-free turkey sausage, casings removed (can also use pork or chicken sausage)

½ cup diced carrots

½ cup diced celery

½ cup diced onion

1 tablespoon dried basil

1 tablespoon dried oregano

1 teaspoon dried rosemary

½ teaspoon dried thyme

8 cups low-sodium gluten-free chicken broth

16 ounces dried lentils, rinsed

1½ cups cooked quinoa

5 cups kale, rinsed and stems removed

4 tablespoons grated Parmesan cheese

1. Place oil and garlic in large stockpot or Dutch oven. Cook for 1–2 minutes until garlic softens.

2. Add sausage and cook over medium-low heat until browned and no longer pink inside, about 5–8 minutes. Break the sausages up into bite-sized pieces.

3. Add diced vegetables and seasonings. Stir well and slowly add the broth, lentils, and quinoa. Turn heat to high and bring to a boil. Cover soup and reduce heat to low. Simmer for 45–60 minutes until lentils become soft.

4. Add kale in the last 5–10 minutes. Top with Parmesan cheese.

PER SERVING Calories: 632 | Fat: 15g | Protein: 47g | Sodium: 650mg | Fiber: 26g | Carbohydrates: 76g | Sugar: 8g

Manhattan Red Clam Chowder

You can transform Rhode Island Clam Chowder to Manhattan with the addition of some tomatoes.

INGREDIENTS | SERVES 6 | 40 MINUTES

1 recipe Rhode Island Clam Chowder (see recipe in this chapter)

1 (28-ounce) can chopped tomatoes with their juice

¼ cup chopped parsley

Add tomatoes to the last step of the recipe for Rhode Island Clam Chowder. Garnish with chopped parsley and serve hot.

PER SERVING Calories: 305 | Fat: 13g | Protein: 14g | Sodium: 1,081mg | Fiber: 5g | Carbohydrates: 35g | Sugar: 6g

Onion Soup with Poached Eggs

This comforting soup is a wonderful light supper. Everything but the eggs can be made in advance.

INGREDIENTS | SERVES 4

4 slices bacon

2 medium Vidalia onions, peeled and thinly sliced

2 medium red onions, peeled and thinly sliced

2 medium yellow onions, peeled and thinly sliced

4 tablespoons extra-virgin olive oil

1 tablespoon chickpea flour

4 cups low-salt gluten-free beef broth

¼ cup dry red wine

1 bay leaf

1 tablespoon thyme

1 tablespoon wheat-free Worcestershire sauce

½ teaspoon salt

½ teaspoon freshly ground black pepper

4 large eggs

¼ cup chopped fresh parsley

1. In a medium skillet, fry the bacon until crisp and drain on paper towels; when cool, crumble.

2. In a large stockpot over medium heat, sauté the onions in the olive oil for 2–3 minutes. Stir in the flour and cook for 3–4 minutes, stirring to get rid of the lumps.

3. Add the broth, wine, bay leaf, thyme, and Worcestershire sauce. Cover and simmer over low heat for 1 hour.

4. Just before serving, raise the heat, and add salt and pepper. Swirl the soup and add the eggs one at a time, directly to the soup. Remove the eggs after 1 minute. Ladle soup and 1 egg each into 4 warm bowls and garnish with chopped parsley.

PER SERVING Calories: 419 | Fat: 29g | Protein: 16g | Sodium: 881mg | Fiber: 4g | Carbohydrates: 22g | Sugar: 9g

Rhode Island Clam Chowder

*This recipe is very traditional. Many cooks now substitute bacon for salt pork,
but it's better to make it the traditional way.*

INGREDIENTS | SERVES 4 | 40 MINUTES

2 dozen cherrystone clams (2" across)

3 ounces salt pork, chopped finely

1 large onion, peeled and chopped

1 carrot, peeled and chopped

2 stalks celery with tops, chopped finely

2 large Idaho potatoes, peeled and chopped

1 tablespoon cornstarch (more if you like it really thick)

2 bay leaves

1 teaspoon dried thyme

1 teaspoon celery salt

1 tablespoon wheat-free Worcestershire sauce

3 cups clam broth

½ teaspoon freshly ground black pepper

½ cup chopped fresh parsley

1. Scrub the clams and place them in a large pot. Add 2 cups water, cover, and boil until the clams open. Remove them to a large bowl and let cool; reserve the juice. When cool, remove the clams, discard the shells, and chop the clams in a food processor.

2. In a soup pot over medium heat, fry the salt pork until crisp. Drain on paper towels. Add the vegetables to the pot and sauté until soft, about 8 minutes. Blend in the cornstarch and cook for 2 more minutes, stirring.

3. Add the reserved clam juice and the bay leaves, thyme, and celery salt to the pot. Stir in the Worcestershire sauce, clam broth, the chopped clams, and the salt pork. Cover and simmer for 15 minutes. Before serving remove bay leaf. Add black pepper, garnish with chopped fresh parsley, and serve hot.

PER SERVING Calories: 421 | Fat: 18g | Protein: 19g | Sodium: 1,609mg | Fiber: 4g | Carbohydrates: 45g | Sugar: 4g

Is That Clam Alive or Dead?

Always run clams under cold water and scrub vigorously with a brush. To test for life, tap two clams together. You should hear a sharp click, not a hollow thud. If the clam sounds hollow, tap it again, and then, if still hollow-sounding, discard it.

Indian Mulligatawny Soup MA

This is a staple in India and best made a day in advance. You may have to thin it out with more water or broth if it gets too thick.

INGREDIENTS | SERVES 6

1 large sweet onion, peeled and chopped

4 cloves garlic, chopped

2 tablespoons minced fresh gingerroot

1 hot pepper, serrano or poblano, cored, seeded, and chopped

½ cup unsalted butter

1½ tablespoons Madras curry powder

¼ cup rice flour

10 cups gluten-free chicken broth

2 cups red lentils

1 (13.5-ounce) can unsweetened coconut milk

1 teaspoon salt

½ teaspoon freshly ground black pepper

6 sprigs fresh coriander leaves

6 lemon slices

1. In a large stockpot over medium heat, sauté the onions, garlic, ginger, and pepper in the butter until soft.

2. Blend in the curry powder and rice flour. Cook for 4 minutes; add the chicken broth and lentils, mixing thoroughly. Simmer, covered, for 1 hour or until the lentils are very tender.

3. Cool and then purée in the blender. Add the coconut milk, salt, and pepper and reheat. Garnish with coriander sprigs and lemon slices.

PER SERVING Calories: 695 | Fat: 36g | Protein: 27g | Sodium: 2,156mg | Fiber: 21g | Carbohydrates: 70g | Sugar: 3g

Healthy Soup

The healing qualities of chicken soup plus the healthful properties of Indian herbs and spices make this a very nourishing soup. The name means "pepper water."

Harvest Corn Chowder with Bacon

Use fresh ears of corn—the tiny kernels are unbelievably sweet and tender.
Frozen or canned corn just won't taste the same in this soup.

INGREDIENTS | SERVES 6 | 45 MINUTES

½ pound bacon

2 large sweet onions, peeled and finely chopped

2 large Idaho potatoes, peeled and chopped

1 medium red bell pepper, seeded and chopped

3 tablespoons cornstarch mixed with ¼ cup water until smooth

1 quart homemade or canned low-salt gluten-free chicken broth

3 cups fresh corn removed from cob

1 tablespoon salsa

1 cup whole milk

1 cup heavy cream

1 teaspoon salt

½ teaspoon freshly ground black pepper

¼ teaspoon ground nutmeg

1 bunch fresh parsley, washed, stems removed, chopped

1. Fry bacon and drain on paper towels; when cool, crumble and set aside, reserving grease in pan. Sauté the onions, potatoes, and pepper in the bacon grease for 10 minutes, stirring often.

2. Add the cornstarch/water mixture and, stirring constantly, ladle in the chicken broth. Bring to a boil. Cover, lower heat, and simmer for 30 minutes.

3. Stir in the rest of the ingredients. Taste and season with additional salt and pepper as needed. Do not boil after adding the cream. Serve hot, sprinkling the top with the crumbled bacon.

PER SERVING Calories: 623 | Fat: 36g | Protein: 16g | Sodium: 700mg | Fiber: 6g | Carbohydrates: 63g | Sugar: 9g

Spicy Vegetarian Chili `SC`

*Have a chili party and offer diners their choice of a hearty
beef chili and this zesty and flavorful vegetarian chili.*

INGREDIENTS | SERVES 8

2 tablespoons olive oil

1½ cups chopped yellow onion

1 cup chopped red bell pepper

2 tablespoons minced garlic

2 serrano peppers, seeded and minced

1 medium zucchini, diced

2 cups frozen corn

1½ pounds portobello mushrooms
(about 5 large), stemmed, cleaned, and
cubed

2 tablespoons chili powder

1 tablespoon ground cumin

1½ teaspoons salt

¼ teaspoon cayenne pepper

2 (15-ounce) cans diced tomatoes

2 (15-ounce) cans black beans

1 (15-ounce) can tomato sauce

2 cups gluten-free vegetable stock, or
water

¼ cup chopped fresh cilantro leaves

Pick Your Own Garnishes

A fun way to serve this chili is to prepare
and chill bowls of chopped avocados, sour
cream, shredded cheese, crushed tortilla
chips, and salsa. Allow diners to garnish
their own bowls of chili when it's time to
eat.

1. In a large, heavy pot, heat the oil over medium-high heat. Add the onions, bell peppers, garlic, and serrano peppers, and cook, stirring, until soft, about 3 minutes.

2. Add softened vegetables to a greased 4–6-quart slow cooker. Add remaining ingredients, except for cilantro.

3. Cover and cook on high for 4–6 hours or on low for 8–10 hours. Stir in cilantro before serving.

PER SERVING Calories: 244 | Fat: 5g | Protein: 11g |
Sodium: 1,422mg | Fiber: 12g | Carbohydrates: 43g | Sugar: 12g

Carrot, Parsnip, and Squash Soup

This delicious soup is made with not one but three root vegetables! Not only is this creamy soup delicious; it's one you can make a few days in advance. Here it is paired with crispy gluten-free bread, but it also works with freshly made croutons, too!

INGREDIENTS | SERVES 2 | 35 MINUTES

3½ teaspoons sesame oil

1 medium shallot, peeled and diced

½ pound carrots, peeled and diced

¼ pound parsnips, peeled and diced

¼ pound butternut squash, peeled, seeded, and diced

2 cups low-sodium gluten-free chicken broth

1 teaspoon salt

1 teaspoon ground black pepper

2 teaspoons grated fresh gingerroot

2 tablespoons low-fat plain Greek yogurt

1 tablespoon chopped mint leaves

1. Heat oil in a large saucepan over medium-high heat. Add shallots and cook until softened, about 2 minutes. Stir in carrots, parsnips, and squash and cook until soft, about 8 more minutes.

2. Pour broth over vegetables and add salt and pepper. Bring mixture to a boil. Reduce heat and simmer for about 15 minutes.

3. Transfer mixture to a food processor or blender. Add ginger and pulse on low until mixture is smooth.

4. Pour mixture into soup bowls and garnish with Greek yogurt and mint leaves. Serve warm.

PER SERVING Calories: 289 | Fat: 12g | Protein: 10g | Sodium: 1,300mg | Fiber: 8g | Carbohydrates: 39g | Sugar: 14g

Simple Radish and Lentil Stew

This summery radish stew is a health-food lover's dream! The lentils give this stew a generous helping of fiber, while the radishes help to eliminate toxins and aid digestion. You can easily make this stew on the weekend for an easy and good-for-you dinner option all week long.

INGREDIENTS | SERVES 4

2 cups dried red lentils

2 tablespoons extra-virgin olive oil

1 medium onion, peeled and chopped

1 large leek, trimmed and chopped

3 large carrots, peeled and diced

2 medium sweet potatoes, peeled and diced

1 pound radishes, sliced with tops removed

1 (32-ounce) carton gluten-free vegetable broth

1 tablespoon herbes de Provence

Zest and juice of 1 large lemon

½ teaspoon salt

¼ teaspoon pepper

Preparing Lentils

Soaking your lentils overnight will quickly speed up your cooking time, making it easier to make this on a busy weeknight. However, if you can't soak overnight, bring them to a rapid boil on the stove for at least an hour, or until softened.

1. In a large bowl, cover the lentils with water. Soak overnight in water. Rinse thoroughly and drain. Set aside.

2. In a large stockpot, heat the olive oil over medium-high heat. Add onions and leeks. Cook until aromatic and tender, about 4–5 minutes. Add in carrots, sweet potatoes, and radishes. Cook until vegetables start to soften, about 6–8 minutes.

3. Stir in lentils, broth, herbes de Provence, lemon juice, zest, salt, and pepper.

4. Increase heat to high and bring the mixture to a rapid boil. Reduce heat to low and cover pot. Simmer for about 25–30 minutes, or until vegetables are fully cooked and lentils are soft.

PER SERVING Calories: 548 | Fat: 8g | Protein: 28g | Sodium: 1,323mg | Fiber: 36g | Carbohydrates: 93g | Sugar: 14g

Chilled Blackberry, Blueberry, and Mint Gazpacho

If you're a soup lover but can't bring yourself to eat a steaming bowl of your favorite during the hot summer months, why not give this chilled blackberry and blueberry gazpacho a try? It's served chilled, so you can enjoy even when the temperatures are in the triple digits.

INGREDIENTS | SERVES 4 | 10 MINUTES

1 (6-ounce) package blackberries
1 (16-ounce) package blueberries
1 cup dry white wine
2 tablespoons pure clover honey
2 tablespoons brown sugar
Juice and zest of 1 lemon
2 cups whipped cream
2 tablespoons chopped fresh mint

1. Pour blackberries, blueberries, wine, honey, brown sugar, and lemon juice into a blender. Pulse on low until mixture is thick and smooth.

2. Pour berry mixture into 4 soup bowls. Top each bowl with a dollop of fresh whipped cream, ½ tablespoon mint, and lemon zest.

PER SERVING Calories: 544 | Fat: 38g | Protein: 4g | Sodium: 48mg | Fiber: 5g | Carbohydrates: 42g | Sugar: 30g

Creamy Pumpkin Soup

Nothing says fall like pumpkin. This creamy soup is the perfect harvest recipe that can be made with either fresh or canned pumpkin purée.

INGREDIENTS | SERVES 5 | 20 MINUTES

2 tablespoons unsalted butter
¼ cup chopped red onion
2 cloves garlic, minced
2½ cups low-sodium gluten-free chicken broth
¼ tablespoon water
2 cups pumpkin purée
2½ tablespoons chopped sage
1 teaspoon salt
½ teaspoon ground black pepper
½ cup light cream
¼ cup whole milk
2¼ ounces soft goat cheese
1 teaspoon pumpkin pie spice

1. In a large stockpot, heat butter over medium-high heat. Add onions and cook about 2 minutes. Add in garlic and cook another 2–3 minutes, or until fragrant.

2. Stir in broth and water and bring to a boil. Add pumpkin purée, sage, salt, and pepper; heat for about 2–3 minutes, stirring constantly until pumpkin is incorporated into the broth.

3. Pour mixture into a food processor and blend on low until smooth. While blending, carefully pour in cream and milk. Add goat cheese and blend until mixture is completely smooth.

4. Stir in pumpkin pie spice and serve hot.

PER SERVING Calories: 204 | Fat: 15g | Protein: 7g | Sodium: 550mg | Fiber: 3g | Carbohydrates: 13g | Sugar: 5g

Spicy Black Bean and Corn Soup

If you're craving something with some spice and texture, look no further than this Mexican-inspired spicy black bean and corn soup! Jalapeño, habanero, and chipotle peppers give each bite a perfect kick.

INGREDIENTS | SERVES 5

1 medium red bell pepper, halved and seeded

½ poblano pepper, seeded

1 jalapeño pepper, halved and seeded

1 habanero pepper, halved and seeded

1 tablespoon extra-virgin olive oil

1 shallot, peeled and diced

3 cloves garlic, diced

½ cup diced celery

1 (7-ounce) can fire-roasted diced tomatoes

1½ cups corn kernels

2 cups gluten-free chicken broth

2 (15-ounce) cans black beans, undrained, divided

¾ teaspoon gluten-free Mexican seasoning

¾ teaspoon salt

¼ teaspoon cracked black pepper

Juice of 1 medium lime

4 ounces grated queso blanco cheese

2 (6-inch) corn tortillas, sliced into strips

1 medium ripe avocado, peeled, pitted, and diced

¼ cup chopped cilantro

1. Preheat broiler. Line a broiling pan with foil and spray with gluten-free nonstick cooking spray. Place all peppers on the pan, cut-side down, and cook for about 6 minutes on each side, or until the skin has darkened but isn't burnt. Place peppers in a bowl and set aside for 15–20 minutes. Carefully peel the skins off the peppers and dice. Set aside.

2. In a Dutch oven, heat olive oil over medium-high heat. Add shallots, garlic, and celery. Cook until just softened, about 5 minutes. Stir in tomatoes, corn, reserved peppers, broth, 1 can beans, Mexican seasoning, salt, and black pepper. Bring the mixture to a boil.

3. In a medium bowl, gently smash the remaining black beans. Stir into the boiling soup. Reduce heat to low and simmer for 40 minutes. Remove from heat and stir in lime juice.

4. Divide into 4 bowls and garnish with cheese, tortillas, avocado, and cilantro.

PER SERVING Calories: 450 | Fat: 19g | Protein: 20g | Sodium: 1,458mg | Fiber: 15g | Carbohydrates: 54g | Sugar: 8g

Broccoli Cheddar Soup

If you're in love with the broccoli Cheddar soup at Panera, you'll love this recipe even more. Made from all-natural ingredients, this gluten-free variety is even tastier (and cheesier) than the one you buy.

INGREDIENTS | SERVES 4 | 35 MINUTES

4 cups broccoli florets

1¼ teaspoons salt, divided

¼ cup unsalted butter

1 small yellow onion, peeled and diced

3 cloves garlic, minced

2 carrots, peeled and chopped

2 cups low-sodium gluten-free chicken broth

1 cup water

1 cup almond milk

1 cup heavy cream

¼ cup cornstarch

2 tablespoons Italian seasoning

8 ounces shredded Cheddar cheese

1 teaspoon cracked black pepper

1. Prepare an ice bath: fill a large bowl with cold water and ice cubes. Set aside.

2. Bring a large pot of water to a rapid boil and add broccoli and ¼ teaspoon salt. Cook until crisp-tender, about 3 minutes. Remove broccoli from the water and place in the ice bath.

3. Melt the butter in a large stockpot over medium-high heat. Add the onion, garlic, and carrots. Cook until vegetables are softened, about 6 minutes. Whisk in the chicken broth, water, almond milk, and cream. Heat another 3–4 minutes.

4. Whisk in the cornstarch, Italian seasoning, and remaining salt. Reduce heat to low and cook, stirring constantly, until thick and smooth, about 3 minutes.

5. Remove from heat and stir in cheese and half the broccoli florets. Continue stirring until cheese melts. Pour the mixture into a blender and pulse until puréed.

6. Return soup to the stockpot and stir in the remaining broccoli. Pour into bowls and garnish with cracked black pepper.

PER SERVING Calories: 563 | Fat: 45g | Protein: 18g | Sodium: 1,377mg | Fiber: 3g | Carbohydrates: 25g | Sugar: 5g

Slow Cooker Brunswick Stew `SC`

Brunswick stew is a Southern classic, often served in Virginia, West Virginia, and Tennessee. Although the traditional recipe is made with gamey meats, like rabbit or deer, subbing in chicken makes it easier to make. Plus, this slow cooker recipe can be made up to a week ahead of time!

INGREDIENTS | SERVES 8

14 ounces gluten-free chicken broth

1 (14-ounce) can green chilies and diced tomatoes

1 pound boneless, skinless chicken breasts

3 cloves garlic, minced

1 medium onion, peeled and finely chopped

¾ cup chopped parsnips

¾ cup chopped carrots

2 cups sliced mushrooms

1 cup corn kernels

½ cup cooked white cannellini beans

¼ cup cooked black beans

¼ cup cooked red kidney beans

1 teaspoon salt

½ teaspoon ground black pepper

1 tablespoon crushed red pepper

1 bay leaf

¼ cup chopped fresh basil

¼ cup chopped parsley

1. Place all ingredients, except basil and parsley, in a 4–6-quart slow cooker. Heat on low for about 6 hours, or until the chicken is fully cooked. Discard the bay leaf.

2. Remove the chicken breasts from the slow cooker and place into a bowl. Using two forks, shred chicken into bite-sized pieces. Place the shredded chicken back into the stew.

3. Heat another 30 minutes, and serve garnished with basil and parsley.

PER SERVING Calories: 173 | Fat: 3g | Protein: 17g | Sodium: 691mg | Fiber: 4g | Carbohydrates: 21g | Sugar: 4g

CHAPTER 5

Salads

Waldorf-Inspired Quinoa Salad MA

This salad is tasty, but also very healthy. It can be served as a side dish, dessert, or even breakfast!

INGREDIENTS | SERVES 6

1 cup water

1 cup apple juice

½ teaspoon ground cinnamon

1 cup quinoa, well rinsed and drained

1 large red apple, cored and diced

1 cup chopped celery

½ cup dried cranberries

½ cup chopped walnuts

1 cup vanilla yogurt

1. Place water, apple juice, cinnamon, and quinoa in a medium saucepan and bring to a boil. Reduce heat and simmer for 15 minutes, or until the liquid is absorbed. Cool, cover, and refrigerate quinoa for at least 1 hour.

2. Add diced apple, celery, cranberries, and walnuts to cooled quinoa. Mix well. Fold in the yogurt. Refrigerate until ready to serve.

PER SERVING Calories: 274 | Fat: 9g | Protein: 8g | Sodium: 48mg | Fiber: 4g | Carbohydrates: 44g | Sugar: 20g

Sweet Rainbow Coleslaw

Eating a "rainbow" of colorful foods allows you to enjoy a variety of good nutrition. All the different colors contribute different nutrients to your diet. You can make this up to one day ahead of time.

INGREDIENTS | SERVES 4 | 15 MINUTES

1 (16-ounce) package cut-up coleslaw mix with carrots

¼ cup chopped green bell pepper

¼ cup chopped red bell pepper

6 tablespoons white vinegar

¼ cup granulated sugar

3 tablespoons oil

2 tablespoons water

1. In a large bowl, combine coleslaw mix and chopped peppers.

2. In a small bowl, combine vinegar, sugar, oil, and water. Mix well.

3. Pour dressing over coleslaw and stir to mix well. Place in the refrigerator until ready to serve. Stir again before serving.

PER SERVING Calories: 175 | Fat: 10g | Protein: 1g | Sodium: 22mg | Fiber: 3g | Carbohydrates: 20g | Sugar: 17g

Colorful Grilled Corn Salad

*Although this salad is great paired with beef, chicken, or fish,
it is also terrific just eaten with gluten-free tortilla chips.*

INGREDIENTS | SERVES 8 | 25 MINUTES

6 ears corn, shucked and cleaned

1 (19-ounce) can black beans, drained and rinsed

1 medium red bell pepper, seeded and chopped

½ cup diced red onion

½ cup chopped fresh cilantro

1 jalapeño pepper, seeded and finely diced

½ cup olive oil

½ cup red wine vinegar

2 tablespoons lime juice

1 tablespoon agave nectar or sugar

1 teaspoon salt

1 clove garlic, minced

½ teaspoon ground cumin

½ teaspoon ground black pepper

1 teaspoon chili powder

⅛ teaspoon hot pepper sauce

1. Grill corn over medium heat for 15 minutes, turning occasionally, until slightly blackened in areas. Allow to cool and cut off corn kernels into a bowl. Add black beans, red pepper, red onion, cilantro, and jalapeño pepper.

2. In a small bowl, whisk to combine the olive oil, red wine vinegar, lime juice, agave nectar, salt, garlic, cumin, black pepper, chili powder, and hot sauce.

3. Pour over corn mixture and stir to coat.

4. Serve immediately or refrigerate until ready to serve.

PER SERVING Calories: 293 | Fat: 15g | Protein: 7g |
Sodium: 505mg | Fiber: 7g | Carbohydrates: 37g | Sugar: 8g

Great for Parties and Potlucks

This salad is the perfect dish to bring to the next barbecue or potluck that you are invited to. The dish is not only gluten-free, but also free from dairy, peanuts, tree nuts, fish and shellfish, eggs, and soy.

Classic Caesar Salad with Gluten-Free Croutons

Caesar salad has become unbelievably popular—it is served with fried calamari, grilled chicken, shrimp, fish, and vegetables.

INGREDIENTS | SERVES 4 | 10 MINUTES

1 large egg, beaten

1 large egg yolk, beaten

Juice of ½ large lemon

2 cloves garlic, minced

1 teaspoon gluten-free English mustard

1" anchovy paste or 2 canned anchovies, packed in oil, mashed

¾ cup extra-virgin olive oil

½ teaspoon salt

½ teaspoon freshly ground black pepper

1 head romaine lettuce, chopped into bite-sized pieces

6 tablespoons freshly grated Parmesan cheese

24 Fresh Gluten-Free Croutons (see recipe in this chapter)

1. Whisk together the egg, egg yolk, lemon juice, garlic, mustard, anchovy paste, and olive oil in a large bowl until very smooth. Add salt and pepper. Add the lettuce and toss.

2. Sprinkle with Parmesan cheese and croutons, and serve.

PER SERVING Calories: 662 | Fat: 70g | Protein: 4g | Sodium: 919mg | Fiber: 4g | Carbohydrates: 7g | Sugar: 2g

Not That Caesar

According to the JNA Institute of Culinary Arts in Philadelphia, Caesar salad was originally created in 1924 by Caesar Cardini, an Italian restaurateur in Tijuana, Mexico. The salad is named after its creator—a chef—not Julius Caesar of the Roman Empire.

Fresh Gluten-Free Croutons

*These can be made in advance and stored in the refrigerator,
then crisped up at the last moment. Double the recipe for extras.*

**INGREDIENTS | MAKES 24 CROUTONS |
30 MINUTES**

½ cup olive oil

2 cloves garlic, minced or put through a
garlic press

4 slices gluten-free bread, thickly cut,
crusts removed

1 teaspoon salt

½ teaspoon freshly ground black pepper

For the Love of Garlic
Garlic will give you various degrees of
potency depending on how you cut it.
Finely minced garlic, or that which has
been put through a press, will be the strongest. When garlic is sliced, it is less strong,
and when you leave the cloves whole, they
are even milder.

1. Preheat the broiler to 350°F.

2. In a small bowl, mix together the oil and garlic. Brush both sides of the bread with the garlic oil. Sprinkle with salt and pepper.

3. Cut each slice of bread into 6 cubes, to make 24 cubes. Spray a cookie sheet with gluten-free nonstick spray. Place the cubes on the sheet and broil until well browned on both sides, about 6 minutes.

4. Put the cookie sheet on the bottom rack of the oven. Turn off the oven and leave the croutons to dry for 20 minutes.

5. Store in an airtight container until ready to use.

PER SERVING (6 CROUTONS) | Calories: 334 | Fat: 27g |
Protein: 4g | Sodium: 798mg | Fiber: 1g | Carbohydrates: 19g |
Sugar: 1g

Avocado Egg Salad

You will not miss the mayonnaise that traditional egg salads have when you taste the creaminess of the avocado in this recipe. Serve it on a bed of lettuce or wrapped up in a wheat-free tortilla.

INGREDIENTS | SERVES 6 | 15 MINUTES

7 large hard-cooked eggs, peeled

1 avocado, peeled, pitted, and cut into 1" pieces

2 tablespoons plain low-fat Greek yogurt

2 tablespoons lemon juice

1 scallion, finely chopped

1 celery stalk, finely chopped

1 teaspoon paprika

½ teaspoon salt

½ teaspoon ground black pepper

1. Separate the whites and the yolks of the eggs. Set aside 3 yolks for another use.

2. Dice the egg whites.

3. In a large bowl, combine the avocado, egg yolks, and yogurt. Mash until the mixture is creamy and smooth.

4. Mix in the lemon juice, scallion, celery, paprika, salt, and pepper.

5. Gently add the chopped egg whites and stir to combine. Refrigerate or serve immediately.

PER SERVING Calories: 144 | Fat: 11g | Protein: 9g | Sodium: 290mg | Fiber: 3g | Carbohydrates: 4g | Sugar: 1g

Red Cabbage Slaw

This simple and tasty slaw is not only great on its own; it is a perfect accompaniment to tacos, chili, enchiladas, and even burgers.

INGREDIENTS | SERVES 4 | 10 MINUTES

1 (12-ounce) package red cabbage slaw

1 cup chopped artichoke hearts

1 medium red apple, peeled and chopped

4 ounces fresh mozzarella, cubed

2 tablespoons olive oil

2¼ tablespoons lemon juice

¼ teaspoon sugar

¼ teaspoon dried oregano

1 garlic clove, minced

1 teaspoon salt

½ teaspoon ground black pepper

1. Mix cabbage slaw, artichoke hearts, and apple together in a large bowl. Add in the mozzarella and stir to mix.

2. In a small bowl, whisk together the oil, lemon juice, sugar, oregano, garlic, salt, and pepper until fully combined. Add additional sugar or lemon to taste.

3. Pour dressing over salad and serve immediately.

PER SERVING Calories: 211 | Fat: 13g | Protein: 9g | Sodium: 807mg | Fiber: 6g | Carbohydrates: 17g | Sugar: 8g

Grilled Pear-Kale Salad with Feta Cheese

These grilled pears are wonderful along with the crisp texture of kale.
Kale is known for its tremendous health benefits and delicious taste.

INGREDIENTS | SERVES 6 | 25 MINUTES

Juice of 1 small lemon

5 tablespoons grapeseed oil, divided

½ teaspoon coarse salt

½ teaspoon ground black pepper

4 large Bartlett or Bosc pears, halved and cored

4 cups finely chopped curly kale leaves

¼ small red onion, peeled and finely chopped

1 tablespoon dried cranberries, unsweetened

¼ cup walnuts

¼ cup feta cheese

Super Kale

Did you know that one serving of kale has 200 percent of your vitamin C daily requirement? Kale has even more vitamin C per serving than an orange! Kale is packed with fiber, vitamins, minerals, and antioxidants.

1. For the dressing, whisk together the lemon juice, 4 tablespoons oil, salt, and pepper in a small bowl. Set aside.

2. Prepare a grill to medium-high heat (you should be able to hold you hand an inch over the cooking grate for 2–3 seconds). Make sure the cooking grate is well oiled.

3. Brush cut sides of pears with remaining grapeseed oil. Put pears, cut-side down, on the grill. Cover and cook until pear halves are grill-marked and heated through, about 10 minutes. Let them cool and slice into strips.

4. In a large bowl, add the kale, onion, cranberries, and walnuts. Stir to combine. Top with pears, feta cheese, and dressing.

PER SERVING Calories: 266 | Fat: 16g | Protein: 4g | Sodium: 288mg | Fiber: 6g | Carbohydrates: 31g | Sugar: 16g

Apple, Walnut, Cranberry, and Spinach Salad

The wonderful combination of fruit and nuts makes this salad perfect any time of year.
The dressing can be used for any salad or as a marinade for chicken or vegetables.

INGREDIENTS | SERVES 4 | 15 MINUTES

Dressing

½ cup extra-virgin olive oil

½ cup balsamic vinegar

1 clove garlic, crushed

1 teaspoon ground mustard

1 teaspoon honey

1 teaspoon salt

½ teaspoon ground black pepper

Salad

1 (6-ounce) bag organic baby spinach

2 tablespoons chopped walnuts

2 tablespoons dried, unsweetened cranberries

1 medium Fuji apple, cored and chopped

½ medium orange bell pepper, seeded and chopped

2 large plum tomatoes, chopped

½ cup kidney beans, thoroughly rinsed and drained

1 tablespoon chia seeds

1. Whisk all the dressing ingredients together in a small bowl. You can also pour into a small, airtight container and shake vigorously.

2. In a large bowl, mix the salad ingredients. Add the dressing and toss before serving.

PER SERVING Calories: 130 | Fat: 3g | Protein: 4g | Sodium: 600mg | Fiber: 5g | Carbohydrates: 21g | Sugar: 12g

Tricolor Tomato-Bean Salad MA

Take advantage of local summer produce to create this perfect, light salad.

INGREDIENTS | SERVES 6

3 large plum tomatoes, seeded and chopped

1 medium green tomato, seeded and chopped

1 medium yellow tomato, seeded and chopped

1 small cucumber, peeled and chopped into 1" wedges

1 (15-ounce) can small white beans, thoroughly rinsed and drained

½ small red onion, peeled and finely chopped

3 tablespoons extra-virgin olive oil

2 tablespoons balsamic vinegar

2 garlic cloves, crushed

1 teaspoon gluten-free Dijon mustard

1. Place the tomatoes, cucumber, beans, and onion in a medium-sized bowl.

2. In a small bowl, whisk together the oil, vinegar, garlic, and mustard until completely blended.

3. Pour oil and vinegar mixture over chopped vegetables. Stir to thoroughly combine. Refrigerate for at least 1 hour or overnight.

PER SERVING Calories: 149 | Fat: 7g | Protein: 5g | Sodium: 225mg | Fiber: 5g | Carbohydrates: 17g | Sugar: 5g

Visit Your Local Farmers' Markets

If available, your local farmers' market is the best place to buy the freshest fruit and veggies. Shopping at your local farmers' markets will not only support local farmers, but it will also stimulate your town's economy.

Fresh Tomato and Basil Bruschetta over Portobellos

Don't use canned tomatoes or dried basil for this recipe. The fresh tomato and basil really make a difference. Serve as an appetizer, as a side dish, or in a salad.

INGREDIENTS | SERVES 12 | 15 MINUTES

6 medium plum (Roma) tomatoes, seeded and chopped

2 tablespoons extra-virgin olive oil

½ small red onion, peeled and chopped finely

4 cloves garlic, minced

2 tablespoons balsamic vinegar

3 tablespoons fresh basil, torn

1 tablespoon Parmesan cheese

½ teaspoon salt

½ teaspoon ground black pepper

6 large portobello mushroom caps, wiped clean, stems removed

Extra-virgin olive oil in Misto sprayer

8 ounces fresh mozzarella, thinly sliced

1. Preheat the oven to 425°F.

2. In a large bowl, combine the tomatoes, olive oil, onion, garlic, vinegar, basil, and Parmesan cheese. Add salt and pepper and mix well.

3. Slice each mushroom cap in half, leaving two half circles, and place on a baking sheet sprayed with gluten-free nonstick cooking spray. Lightly spray each portobello mushroom cap using a Misto sprayer filled with olive oil. Bake for 5 minutes. Remove from oven.

4. Spoon bruschetta mixture on each mushroom half. Top with mozzarella and bake for 2–3 minutes more, until cheese is melted. Serve warm.

PER SERVING Calories: 100 | Fat: 7g | Protein: 6g | Sodium: 235mg | Fiber: 1g | Carbohydrates: 4g | Sugar: 2g

Wild Rice Salad

This is just as good on a summer picnic as it is for a wintry side dish. It's filling and delightful.

INGREDIENTS | SERVES 6 | 45 MINUTES

4 cups water

¾ cup wild rice

1 teaspoon salt

½ teaspoon freshly ground black pepper

1 small red onion, peeled and chopped

3 stalks celery, rinsed and chopped finely

1 cup drained and chopped water chestnuts

1 cup peeled and chopped jicama

1 small apple, cored and chopped

⅔ cup olive oil

⅓ cup gluten-free raspberry vinegar

½ cup chopped fresh Italian flat-leaf parsley

6 ounces fresh raspberries, rinsed and set on paper towels to dry

1. Bring water to a boil and add the rice; return to a rolling boil and then reduce heat to a simmer and cover tightly. After 30 minutes, add salt and pepper.

2. Cook for another 5–10 minutes, until the rice grains open up slightly. Remove from heat and add onion, celery, water chestnuts, jicama, and apple.

3. In a small bowl, mix the olive oil and vinegar together with the parsley. Combine with the rice mixture. Place in a large serving dish and serve warm or chilled. Sprinkle with raspberries at the last minute.

PER SERVING Calories: 350 | Fat: 25g | Protein: 4g | Sodium: 424mg | Fiber: 6g | Carbohydrates: 30g | Sugar: 6g

Pork and Pomegranate Salad

Forget boring chicken salads—add a new variety of meat to your favorite leafy greens. This pork tenderloin salad is not only hefty and filling, but it's low in calories, too! The sweet, crunchy, and tart pomegranate seeds add a healthier crunch than croutons.

INGREDIENTS | SERVES 4 | 40 MINUTES

1¼ cups pomegranate arils, divided

1 teaspoon gluten-free Dijon mustard

1 teaspoon honey

¼ cup plus 1 tablespoon olive oil, divided

1 tablespoon aged balsamic vinegar

1½ teaspoons salt, divided

1½ teaspoons ground black pepper, divided

1 teaspoon garlic powder

2 teaspoons Italian seasoning

1 pound pork tenderloin

4 cups shaved Brussels sprouts

1 cup chopped apples

½ cup chopped pistachios

¼ cup grated Parmesan cheese

1. Place ¾ cup pomegranate arils, mustard, honey, ¼ cup olive oil, vinegar, ½ teaspoon salt, and ½ teaspoon pepper in a blender or food processor. Pulse until blended. Set dressing aside.

2. Preheat oven to 425°F. Grease a standard roasting pan with gluten-free nonstick cooking spray.

3. In a small bowl, mix together garlic powder, Italian seasoning, 1 teaspoon salt, and 1 teaspoon pepper. Rub liberally over the pork tenderloin. Heat 1 tablespoon olive oil in a large skillet over medium heat. Place the pork in the skillet and cook until browned on all sides, about 6 minutes. Transfer the meat to the prepared roasting pan.

4. Roast for about 15 minutes or until the pork registers 150°F in the middle. Transfer pork to a plate and let rest for about 10 minutes. Slice into ¼" slices.

5. In a large bowl, mix the Brussels sprouts, apples, and pistachios together. Sprinkle in the remaining arils and carefully mix.

6. Transfer the salad to 4 large bowls. Top each with a few slices of pork and Parmesan cheese. Drizzle with dressing and serve.

PER SERVING Calories: 495 | Fat: 29g | Protein: 33g | Sodium: 1,079mg | Fiber: 8g | Carbohydrates: 29g | Sugar: 15g

Balsamic Fruit Salad

This grilled salad is a sophisticated take on a summertime favorite.

INGREDIENTS | SERVES 3 | 20 MINUTES

1 medium cucumber, peeled and sliced horizontally, about ¼" thick

2 large peaches, peeled and halved

1 tablespoon butter

½ small red onion, peeled and chopped

2 large stalks rhubarb, thickly sliced

4 strawberries, sliced

2 tablespoons balsamic vinegar

2 tablespoons honey

1 teaspoon salt

½ teaspoon ground black pepper

¼ cup chopped fresh mint

1. Preheat a gas or charcoal grill to medium. Spray grate with gluten-free nonstick cooking spray. Add cucumbers and grill until just soft, about 2–3 minutes. Add peaches and grill for about 2 more minutes. Remove cucumbers and peaches from heat.

2. Melt butter in a medium skillet over medium heat. Add onions and cook until fragrant, about 2 minutes. Add rhubarb and cook until soft but not mushy, about 2 more minutes. Remove from heat.

3. Combine cucumbers, peaches, rhubarb mixture, and strawberries in a large bowl.

4. Heat vinegar and honey in a small saucepan over medium heat for 3 minutes. Remove from heat, add salt and pepper, and whisk until slightly thick. Drizzle salad with dressing and sprinkle with chopped mint.

PER SERVING Calories: 168 | Fat: 4g | Protein: 3g | Sodium: 795mg | Fiber: 4g | Carbohydrates: 33g | Sugar: 26g

Greek Chicken and Red Quinoa Salad

Quinoa is a powerful grain, loaded with fiber, iron, and magnesium. Here, red quinoa is paired with juicy chicken and fresh vegetables for a healthy, protein- and fiber-loaded salad.

INGREDIENTS | SERVES 8 | 25 MINUTES

4 cups gluten-free chicken broth

2 cloves garlic, minced

2 cups uncooked red quinoa

3 pounds cooked chicken breast, shredded

2 large red onions, peeled and diced

1 medium orange bell pepper, peeled and chopped

1 medium yellow bell pepper, peeled and chopped

1 medium cucumber, peeled and diced

1 pint cherry tomatoes, halved

1 cup pitted kalamata olives

½ cup chopped parsley

½ cup chopped cilantro

1 cup fat-free feta cheese

½ cup extra-virgin olive oil

2 tablespoons white wine vinegar

1½ tablespoons gluten-free Greek seasoning

1 cup fresh lemon juice

1. Bring chicken broth and garlic to a boil in a large saucepan over high heat. Reduce to medium-low and stir in quinoa. Cover and cook until all of the liquid has been absorbed, about 15 minutes. Scrape the quinoa into a large bowl.

2. Mix in chicken, onions, bell peppers, cucumber, tomatoes, olives, parsley, cilantro, and cheese.

3. In a small bowl, whisk the olive oil, vinegar, Greek seasoning, and lemon juice together. Pour over the salad and serve immediately.

PER SERVING Calories: 710 | Fat: 24g | Protein: 65g | Sodium: 875mg | Fiber: 5g | Carbohydrates: 48g | Sugar: 5g

Red Quinoa

There's no real difference between red and regular quinoa besides the color. Both have the same taste and texture, so either can be used in this recipe.

Lobster Deviled Egg Salad

This salad combines the popular flavor of deviled eggs with the sweet richness of fresh lobster. The lobster provides a protein boost without adding a lot of extra fat.

INGREDIENTS | SERVES 6 | 15 MINUTES

6 cups chopped romaine lettuce

2 small red onions, peeled and chopped

2 large tomatoes, sliced

1 medium ripe avocado, peeled, pitted, and chopped

4 large hard-cooked eggs, peeled and chopped

⅓ pound fresh lobster tail meat, chopped

2 tablespoons mayonnaise

¾ teaspoon white wine vinegar

⅛ teaspoon ground mustard

¼ teaspoon paprika

1 teaspoon salt

1 teaspoon cracked black pepper

2 radishes, sliced, for garnish

1. In a large bowl, mix lettuce, onion, tomatoes, and avocado.

2. In another bowl, carefully combine eggs, lobster, mayonnaise, vinegar, mustard, paprika, and salt.

3. Separate the salad into 6 bowls. Top each salad with a dollop of the lobster-egg mixture and top with cracked black pepper and sliced radishes.

PER SERVING Calories: 177 | Fat: 12g | Protein: 11g | Sodium: 550mg | Fiber: 4g | Carbohydrates: 8g | Sugar: 2g

Roasted Beet, Goat Cheese, and Cherry Salad

*The marriage of beets, goat cheese, and fresh, tart summer cherries
makes this one of the best salads you'll ever make. You could eat this on its own,
or even serve it topped with chicken or pork for a beautiful main entrée.*

INGREDIENTS | SERVES 8 | 40 MINUTES

4 medium red beets

4 medium yellow beets

3 tablespoons olive oil

2 teaspoons salt, divided

1½ teaspoons ground black pepper, divided

12 cups mixed greens

½ cup dried cherries

2 large heirloom tomatoes, sliced

¾ cup honey mustard roasted walnuts

6 ounces herb soft goat cheese

½ cup balsamic vinegar

2 tablespoons honey

1 tablespoon gluten-free Dijon mustard

1 minced garlic clove

6 tablespoons chopped shallots

1. Preheat oven to 400°F. Grease a 9" × 13" baking dish with gluten-free nonstick cooking spray.

2. Place beets in dish and toss with olive oil, 1 teaspoon salt, and 1 teaspoon pepper. Roast for about 30 minutes, or until softened. Carefully remove the skin and cut beets into ½" slices.

3. In a large bowl, mix the greens, cherries, tomatoes, walnuts, roasted beets, and goat cheese together.

4. In a small bowl, whisk the vinegar, honey, mustard, garlic, shallots, and remaining salt and pepper. Drizzle the salad with the dressing and toss to coat.

PER SERVING Calories: 305 | Fat: 20g | Protein: 11g | Sodium: 778mg | Fiber: 5g | Carbohydrates: 23g | Sugar: 16g

Roasted Jalapeño Chicken Taco Salad

Although you don't have to roast the jalapeños to make this a delicious salad, the roasting process brings out more of the pepper's natural flavors and spice. Add some crunch to this Mexican-inspired salad by topping it with crispy strips of corn tortillas.

INGREDIENTS | SERVES 6 | 20 MINUTES

3 jalapeño peppers, seeded and halved

¾ cup sour cream

Juice of 2 limes

⅓ cup fresh cilantro

2 teaspoons gluten-free Mexican seasoning

1 teaspoon salt

½ teaspoon ground black pepper

3 cups torn iceberg lettuce

1 cup canned black beans, drained and rinsed

1 cup cooked corn kernels

16 gluten-free tortilla chips

1 pound chicken breast, cooked and shredded

1 cup sliced red onion

1 large ripe avocado, peeled, pitted, and chopped

1. Preheat broiler. Place the jalapeños, cut-side down, on a grill pan. Broil for about 5–7 minutes, or until blackened. Remove from heat and chop into bite-sized pieces.

2. In a small bowl, whisk the sour cream, lime juice, cilantro, Mexican seasoning, salt, and pepper. Set aside.

3. Mix the lettuce, black beans, corn, tortilla chips, chicken, jalapeños, onion, and avocado in a large bowl.

4. Drizzle the salad with the sour cream dressing and serve immediately.

PER SERVING Calories: 281 | Fat: 13g | Protein: 21g | Sodium: 661mg | Fiber: 7g | Carbohydrates: 23g | Sugar: 5g

Blue Cheese, Grilled Pears, and Arugula Salad

If you've never paired blue cheese and pears together, you're missing out on a wonderful flavor combination! Mild pears complement the bold, strong cheese perfectly. Tossed over a bed of spicy arugula, it's a unique and luscious summer salad.

INGREDIENTS | SERVES 4 | 20 MINUTES

2 large Bartlett pears, cored and halved

3 tablespoons honey

¼ cup blue cheese

4 cups fresh salad greens

⅓ cup gluten-free dried cranberries

½ cup candied pecans

¼ cup balsamic vinegar

2 tablespoons molasses

¾ cup extra-virgin olive oil

½ teaspoon garlic salt

¼ teaspoon cracked black pepper

1. Preheat a gas or charcoal grill to medium-high.

2. Place the pears, cut-side down, onto the grill and cook for about 4–5 minutes, or until softened. Flip and cook another 3 minutes on the other side.

3. While the pears are still hot, fill the cavities of each with honey and blue cheese. Set aside.

4. In a large bowl, mix the greens, cranberries, and pecans together. Divide among 4 small plates. Top each salad with a grilled pear half.

5. In a small bowl, whisk the vinegar, molasses, olive oil, garlic salt, and pepper. Drizzle each salad with dressing and serve.

PER SERVING Calories: 680 | Fat: 53g | Protein: 5g | Sodium: 446mg | Fiber: 6g | Carbohydrates: 53g | Sugar: 40g

CHAPTER 6

Beef and Lamb

Beef and Broccoli Stir-Fry

Ordering in Chinese food can be difficult when you are on a gluten-free diet. But you can still make some of your favorite recipes at home, and it really doesn't take very long. Serve this stir-fry with white or brown rice.

INGREDIENTS | SERVES 4 | 45 MINUTES

1¼ cups cold water, divided

½ cup gluten-free soy sauce, divided

2 cloves garlic, minced

¼ teaspoon ground black pepper

1 pound stir-fry beef (or boneless round steak, cut into thin 3" strips)

2 tablespoons peanut oil

½ cup chopped onion

½ cup thinly sliced carrots

4 cups broccoli florets

¼ cup brown sugar

1½ teaspoons ground ginger

1 teaspoon sesame oil

¼ teaspoon red pepper flakes

¼ cup cornstarch

2 teaspoons toasted sesame seeds

1. In a glass bowl, whisk together ¼ cup water, ¼ cup soy sauce, minced garlic, and black pepper. Add beef and marinate for 30 minutes.

2. In a large frying pan or wok, heat peanut oil over medium-high heat. Add the beef and marinade, and stir-fry until the meat is no longer pink, about 3–5 minutes.

3. Add the onions and carrots. Stir-fry for another 2 minutes. Add the broccoli and continue stirring and frying for an additional minute.

4. In a small bowl, whisk together 1 cup cold water, ¼ cup soy sauce, brown sugar, ginger, sesame oil, red pepper flakes, and cornstarch. Pour this mixture over the beef and broccoli mixture, and cook until sauce thickens, about 2–3 more minutes.

5. Sprinkle with toasted sesame seeds before serving.

PER SERVING Calories: 400 | Fat: 17 | Protein: 29g | Sodium: 1,903mg | Fiber: 4g | Carbohydrates: 34g | Sugar: 17g

Gascony-Style Pot Roast MA

Although pot roast is often served on holidays and special occasions, you can still enjoy it on a regular Tuesday night, too. Simply make on a Sunday or Saturday, and save the leftovers for use all week long!

INGREDIENTS | SERVES 6

1 (4-pound) top or bottom round beef roast

4 cloves garlic, slivered

1 teaspoon salt

1 teaspoon freshly ground black pepper

Pinch cinnamon

Pinch nutmeg

1 slice bacon, cut into pieces

4 shallots, peeled and halved

2 medium red onions, peeled and quartered

2 large carrots, peeled and sliced

¼ cup cognac

2 cups red wine

1 cup rich gluten-free beef broth

1 teaspoon thyme

4 whole cloves

¼ cup cornstarch mixed with ⅓ cup cold water, until smooth

A Hearty, Delectable Pot Roast

Slow cookers are excellent for cooking a pot roast. Either a top or bottom round is great. Chuck tends to be stringy. Trim the roast well but do leave a bit of fat on it. You can also marinate a pot roast overnight in red wine and herbs. That will give you a deliciously tender piece of meat.

1. Preheat the oven to 250°F.

2. Make several cuts in the meat and put slivers of garlic in each. Rub the roast with salt, pepper, and pinches of cinnamon and nutmeg.

3. Heat the bacon on the bottom of a Dutch oven over medium-high heat. Remove the bacon before it gets crisp, and add the roast to the Dutch oven. Brown the roast for 3–4 minutes on each side.

4. Surround the roast with shallots, onions, and carrots. Add the cognac, wine, beef broth, thyme, and cloves.

5. Place in the oven, covered, for 5–6 hours. When the meat is done to your liking, place the roast on a warm platter.

6. Add the cornstarch and water mixture to the pan juices and bring to a boil. Remove from heat. Slice the roast. Serve the sauce over the pot roast with the vegetables surrounding the meat.

PER SERVING Calories: 598 | Fat: 16g | Protein: 71g | Sodium: 783mg | Fiber: 5g | Carbohydrates: 21g | Sugar: 3g

Ginger-Teriyaki Flank Steak

This Asian-inspired dish pairs perfectly with steamed vegetables and rice. This marinade can be used on a variety of meats such as chicken, pork, and other cuts of beef.

INGREDIENTS | SERVES 4

½ cup water

1 tablespoon sesame oil

½ teaspoon grated gingerroot

2 garlic cloves, minced

¼ cup wheat-free soy sauce

1 tablespoon honey

1 tablespoon cornstarch

1½ pounds beef flank steak

What Does It Mean to Slice Against the Grain?

Lines in the flank steak run from right to left down the length of the steak. By cutting across these lines, the knife will cut through the fibers, which makes it easier to chew. Slicing the steak on a 45-degree angle creates an elegant presentation.

1. In a small bowl, mix water, sesame oil, gingerroot, garlic, soy sauce, honey, and cornstarch. Stir thoroughly to ensure the cornstarch has been mixed in well.

2. Place the steak in zip-top bag and pour the marinade on top. Make sure the bag is sealed and shake until well blended. Place in refrigerator and let sit for at least 4 hours or, even better, overnight.

3. When ready to cook the steaks, remove them from the bag and discard the leftover marinade.

4. Place steaks on preheated grill or on a grill pan and cook on each side for about 6–8 minutes, until you have reached your desired degree of doneness. The internal temperature should read at least 145°F.

PER SERVING Calories: 325 | Fat: 15g | Protein: 37g | Sodium: 990mg | Fiber: 0g | Carbohydrates: 8g | Sugar: 4g

Lean Beef Stroganoff

This rich but healthy dish is wonderful for entertaining.
Serve with a salad and some gluten-free garlic bread.

INGREDIENTS | SERVES 6 | 35 MINUTES

3 tablespoons olive oil, divided

3 tablespoons potato starch, divided

½ cup milk

1 cup gluten-free beef stock

1 tablespoon lemon juice

1 pound sirloin steak

½ teaspoon salt

⅛ teaspoon ground black pepper

½ cup chopped onion

3 cloves garlic, minced

1 (8-ounce) package sliced mushrooms

½ teaspoon dried thyme leaves

1 (12-ounce) package gluten-free rice noodles

1 tablespoon gluten-free Dijon mustard

Stroganoff

Beef stroganoff is a dish from Russia that is typically made of steak or other beef cuts simmered in sour cream, served over noodles. Adding vegetables adds nutrition, texture, and flavor to this classic recipe.

1. In a small saucepan heat 2 tablespoons of olive oil over medium heat. Add 2 tablespoons potato starch; cook and stir with a wire whisk until bubbly. Add milk, beef stock, and lemon juice and bring to a simmer. Reduce heat to low and simmer 5 minutes, stirring frequently, until thick. Set aside.

2. Cut steak into ¼" × 4" strips. Toss with 1 tablespoon potato starch, salt, and pepper. In a large skillet, heat 1 tablespoon olive oil over medium heat. Add steak to the skillet and brown it, stirring occasionally, about 4–5 minutes. Add onion, garlic, mushrooms, and thyme; cook and stir for 5–6 minutes.

3. Cook rice noodles as directed on package until al dente. Add the milk/stock mixture and mustard to the skillet and simmer for 5–6 minutes to blend flavors. When noodles are cooked, drain and add to skillet. Stir to coat noodles. Serve immediately.

PER SERVING Calories: 420 | Fat: 12g | Protein: 21g | Sodium: 465mg | Fiber: 2g | Carbohydrates: 56g | Sugar: 3g

Barbecue Western Ribs SC

At the end of the 8-hour cooking time, the meat will be tender and falling off of the bones. You can stretch this recipe to 8 servings if you serve barbecue beef sandwiches instead of 4 servings of beef. Add potato chips and coleslaw for a delicious, casual meal.

INGREDIENTS | SERVES 4

1 cup gluten-free hickory barbecue sauce

½ cup orange marmalade

½ cup water

3 pounds beef Western ribs

1. Add the barbecue sauce, marmalade, and water to a greased 4–6-quart slow cooker. Stir to mix.

2. Add the ribs, ladling some of the sauce over the ribs. Cover and cook on low for 8 hours.

3. To thicken the sauce, use a slotted spoon to remove the meat and bones; cover and keep warm. Skim any fat from the sauce in the cooker; increase the heat setting to high and cook uncovered for 15 minutes or until the sauce is reduced and coats the back of a spoon.

PER SERVING Calories: 1495 | Fat: 122g | Protein: 49g | Sodium: 886mg | Fiber: 1g | Carbohydrates: 49g | Sugar: 40g

Herb-Stuffed Veal Chops

This recipe calls for thick-cut chops. You can use double rib chops with a pocket for the aromatic herbs and vegetables. These can be grilled or sautéed.

INGREDIENTS | SERVES 4 | 25 MINUTES

2 tablespoons unsalted butter

½ cup minced shallots

2 tablespoons chopped fresh rosemary

2 teaspoons dried basil or 1 tablespoon chopped fresh basil

½ teaspoon ground coriander

2 teaspoons salt, divided

1½ teaspoons ground black pepper, divided

4 veal rib chops, 1½–2" thick, a pocket cut from the outside edge toward the bone in each

¼ cup olive oil

1. Heat butter in a small skillet over medium heat. Sauté the shallots, rosemary, basil, and coriander in butter for 3–5 minutes. Remove from heat and add 1 teaspoon salt and ½ teaspoon pepper. Cool for 5 minutes.

2. Stuff the chops with herb mixture. Rub chops with olive oil and remaining salt and pepper.

3. Using an outdoor grill or broiler, sear the chops over high heat. Then, reduce heat to medium and cook for 4–5 minutes per side for medium chops or rare chops, depending on the thickness.

PER SERVING Calories: 727 | Fat: 36g | Protein: 90g | Sodium: 1,600mg | Fiber: 1g | Carbohydrates: 4g | Sugar: 0g

Lamb with Garlic, Lemon, and Rosemary SC

You can use the spice rub in this recipe as a marinade by applying it to the leg of lamb the day before cooking. The red wine in this dish can be replaced with chicken or beef stock.

INGREDIENTS | SERVES 4

4 cloves of garlic, crushed
1 tablespoon fresh rosemary, chopped
1 tablespoon olive oil
½ teaspoon salt
1 teaspoon ground black pepper
1 (3-pound) leg of lamb
1 large lemon, cut into ¼" slices
½ cup red wine

1. In a small bowl mix together garlic, rosemary, olive oil, salt, and pepper. Rub this mixture onto the leg of lamb.

2. Place a few lemon slices in the bottom of a greased 4–6-quart slow cooker. Place spice-rubbed lamb on top of lemon slices.

3. Add remaining lemon slices on top of lamb. Pour wine around the lamb.

4. Cook on low heat for 8–10 hours, or on high for 4–6 hours.

PER SERVING Calories: 615 | Fat: 34g | Protein: 65g | Sodium: 600mg | Fiber: 1g | Carbohydrates: 4g | Sugar: 0g

Herbed Lamb Chops SC

This simple herb rub would make a fun Christmas gift to give to friends or family members who enjoy cooking! Include this recipe with a small jar of the rub.

INGREDIENTS | SERVES 4

1 medium onion, peeled and sliced
1 teaspoon dried oregano
½ teaspoon dried thyme
½ teaspoon garlic powder
¼ teaspoon salt
⅛ teaspoon ground black pepper
2 pounds (about 8) lamb loin chops
1 tablespoon olive oil

1. Place onion on the bottom of a greased 4–6-quart slow cooker.

2. In a small bowl mix together oregano, thyme, garlic powder, salt, and pepper. Rub herb mixture over the lamb chops.

3. Place herb-rubbed lamb chops over the sliced onions. Drizzle olive oil over the lamb chops.

4. Cook on high for 3 hours or on low for 6 hours, until tender.

PER SERVING Calories: 401 | Fat: 22g | Protein: 45g | Sodium: 330mg | Fiber: 1g | Carbohydrates: 3g | Sugar: 1g

Slow Cooker Hamburgers SC

Here's another one of those "I didn't know you could make that in the slow cooker" recipes! By cooking hamburgers in the slow cooker you can prepare them as soon as you get home from work, and they are ready to eat 60–90 minutes later with no mess or babysitting!

INGREDIENTS | SERVES 4

1 pound ground beef

1 large egg

2 tablespoons finely diced onion

½ teaspoon garlic powder

1 tablespoon gluten-free Worcestershire sauce

¼ teaspoon salt

¼ teaspoon ground black pepper

Make Mine with Cheese Please!

If you would like to make cheeseburgers, or even bacon cheeseburgers, add the cheese and precooked bacon to each patty 20 minutes prior to serving. Serve burgers on gluten-free buns, over a fresh salad, or even on top of baked French fries!

1. Make a 2–3" foil rack in the bottom of a 4–6-quart slow cooker by placing rolled strips of aluminum foil in the bottom of the greased stoneware insert. Make a grill pattern with the strips. This will allow the burgers to cook above the juices while sitting on the rack.

2. In a medium-sized bowl, mix together all ingredients. Shape mixture into 4 flat, round burger patties.

3. Place burgers on the foil rack.

4. Cook on high for 1–1½ hours or on low for 2–2½ hours, until the juices run clear when a knife or fork is inserted in the middle of each burger. Try not to overcook the burgers as they can quickly dry out.

PER SERVING Calories: 221 | Fat: 12g | Protein: 24g | Sodium: 281mg | Fiber: 0g | Carbohydrates: 2g | Sugar: 1g

Spicy Beef-Stuffed Mushrooms

The mushrooms should be 2½" across. You can sprinkle them with chopped fresh herbs of your choice when done.

INGREDIENTS | SERVES 4 | 45 MINUTES

2 tablespoons vegetable oil

½ pound chopped sirloin

½ cup minced onion

2 cloves garlic, minced

1" piece ginger, peeled and minced

1 teaspoon ground oregano

1 tablespoon wheat-free Worcestershire sauce

½ teaspoon salt

¼ teaspoon pepper

1 egg, slightly beaten

12 large mushroom caps, stems removed

1. Preheat the oven to 350°F.

2. Heat oil in a large skillet over medium-high heat. Sauté the sirloin, onion, garlic, ginger, and oregano for 5–8 minutes, mixing constantly to break up lumps. When the meat turns pink (but not gray or brown), remove from the heat and add Worcestershire sauce, salt, and pepper. Cool for 5 minutes, then stir in egg.

3. Place mushrooms in a single layer in a large baking pan. Divide the stuffing among the mushrooms. Pour enough water around the mushrooms to come ¼" up the sides in the pan.

4. Bake the mushrooms for 25 minutes.

PER SERVING Calories: 186 | Fat: 11g | Protein: 16g | Sodium: 390mg | Fiber: 1g | Carbohydrates: 6g | Sugar: 2g

French Cheese–Filled Veal Roulades

Be creative—you can use any number of stuffings. The stuffing of Boursin cheese and oregano is very spicy, a nice counterpoint to the creamy sauce.

INGREDIENTS | SERVES 4 | 40 MINUTES

8 veal scallops, pounded very thin

6 ounces pepper-flavored Boursin cheese

1 teaspoon dried oregano or 2 teaspoons fresh

1 large egg, beaten

2 tablespoons butter

½ cup dry white wine

1 cup light cream

¼ cup finely grated Parmesan cheese

¼ teaspoon ground nutmeg or paprika

Pounding Veal

A five-pound barbell works great for pounding the meat. Whether scallops or chops, place between slices of waxed paper and, working from the center to the edges, pound away! The meat will be very tender after this process.

1. Trim the pounded veal to resemble rectangles. In a medium bowl, combine Boursin cheese, oregano, and egg to make the stuffing. Spread stuffing on veal. Roll and tie with kitchen string.

2. Melt butter in a large skillet over medium-high heat and lightly brown veal. Add wine and bring to a boil. Reduce heat to low, cover, and cook for 30 minutes.

3. Transfer veal to a platter. To the sauce in the pan add the cream, Parmesan cheese, and nutmeg and raise heat to medium. Stir sauce and cook until heated through, about 5 minutes. Pour sauce over veal.

PER SERVING Calories: 515 | Fat: 37g | Protein: 34g | Sodium: 395mg | Fiber: 0g | Carbohydrates: 5g | Sugar: 2g

Turkish Veal Roulades

Stuffing the veal with a nice tapenade of olives and parsley is another excellent choice.

INGREDIENTS | SERVES 4 | 40 MINUTES

8 veal scallops, pounded very thin with a mallet

10 pimiento-stuffed green olives, minced

8 black olives (Spanish or Greek), pitted and minced

6 scallions, minced

½ cup minced parsley

2 tablespoons olive oil

Juice of ½ lemon

1 egg, beaten

4 tablespoons butter

½ cup dry white wine

1. Trim the pounded veal to resemble rectangles. Lay the veal out flat.

2. In a medium bowl, mix the olives, scallions, parsley, olive oil, and lemon juice with the beaten egg. Spread mixture on veal scallops. Roll the veal and tie with kitchen string.

3. Melt butter in a large skillet over medium-high heat and lightly brown veal. Add wine and bring to a boil. Reduce heat to low, cover, and cook for 30 minutes.

4. Transfer veal to serving platter and pour wine in pan over the veal.

PER SERVING Calories: 355 | Fat: 25g | Protein: 25g | Sodium: 295mg | Fiber: 1g | Carbohydrates: 4g | Sugar: 2g

Marinated Spicy Beef and Baby Spinach MA

After you have marinated the beef, the dish takes but a few minutes to cook. Serve with gluten-free soy sauce and chopped scallions on the side and slices of lemon or lime.

INGREDIENTS | SERVES 4

2 cloves garlic, minced

2 tablespoons, plus 2 teaspoons sugar, divided

½ teaspoon salt

1 teaspoon red pepper flakes

4 tablespoons canola oil, divided

1½ pounds filet mignon, trimmed and cut into ½" slices

¼ cup dry white wine

¼ cup white wine vinegar

2 tablespoons fish sauce

4 cups fresh baby spinach, stems removed

1 tablespoon butter

Fish Sauce

Fish sauce, available at Asian markets, is an important ingredient in Southeast Asian, Chinese, and Indonesian cuisines.

1. In a large bowl or glass baking dish, mix together the garlic, 2 tablespoons sugar, salt, pepper flakes, and 2 tablespoons oil. Add the slices of filet mignon, turning to coat. Cover and refrigerate for 2 hours.

2. In a small bowl, mix together the wine, vinegar, 2 teaspoons sugar, and fish sauce; set aside.

3. Heat a large nonstick pan over very high heat and add 2 tablespoons oil. Quickly sauté the filet mignon slices until browned on both sides, about 2 minutes per side. Arrange the meat over a bed of spinach.

4. Add the wine mixture and butter to the pan and deglaze, reducing quickly. Pour over the spinach and meat.

PER SERVING Calories: 625 | Fat: 48g | Protein: 34g | Sodium: 1,100mg | Fiber: 1g | Carbohydrates: 11g | Sugar: 9g

Spicy Steak Fajitas

Skirt steak rubbed with spicy seasoning and chopped peppers and served with warmed corn tortillas makes for the perfect family meal.

INGREDIENTS | SERVES 8 | 20 MINUTES

1 tablespoon cornstarch

2 teaspoons chili powder

1 teaspoon salt

1 teaspoon paprika

½ teaspoon red pepper flakes

1 teaspoon wheat-free Worcestershire sauce

1 teaspoon fresh lime juice

1 teaspoon turbinado sugar

¼ teaspoon cumin

3 pounds skirt steak

4 garlic cloves, minced

2 tablespoons canola oil

½ medium onion, peeled and chopped

1 large green bell pepper, seeded and sliced

1 large red or yellow bell pepper, seeded and sliced

½ bunch fresh cilantro

16 corn tortillas

10 ounces shredded Monterey jack cheese

1. In a small bowl, mix the cornstarch, chili powder, salt, paprika, red pepper flakes, Worcestershire sauce, lime juice, sugar, and cumin.

2. Rub the steaks with the garlic and the prepared seasoning mixture and then cut it into strips.

3. Heat oil in a large skillet over medium heat. Cook the onion, bell peppers, and cilantro for 3–4 minutes. Add steak strips and cook, stirring frequently, until cooked through, about 7 minutes.

4. Remove from heat and spoon the meat into a corn tortilla. Top with cheese and roll them up.

PER SERVING Calories: 580 | Fat: 37g | Protein: 44g | Sodium: 615mg | Fiber: 3g | Carbohydrates: 17g | Sugar: 2g

Red Wine–Braised Beef Short Ribs with Mushrooms `SC`

Short ribs are one of the most elegant dishes you can prepare, and are actually one of the easiest, too. The short ribs, combined with dry red wine and mushrooms, create a luscious sauce to serve with your favorite mashed potatoes.

INGREDIENTS | SERVES 4

1½ tablespoons unsalted butter

1 large yellow onion, peeled and chopped

1 large leek, chopped

3 medium carrots, peeled and diced

3 cloves garlic, minced

2 cups sliced mushrooms

3 pounds English-cut beef short ribs

1½ tablespoons cornstarch

3 tablespoons honey

1 cup low-sodium gluten-free beef broth

2½ cups dry red wine

1 teaspoon salt

1 teaspoon ground black pepper

1 bay leaf

¼ cup chopped fresh parsley

1. Heat butter in a large skillet over medium heat. Add onion, leek, carrot, garlic, and mushrooms. Cook, stirring occasionally, until softened and caramelized, about 8 minutes. Transfer vegetables to a 4–6-quart slow cooker.

2. Add ribs to the same skillet and cook until browned on all sides. Put the ribs into the slow cooker with the vegetables.

3. In a small bowl, whisk together cornstarch, honey, and broth. Pour over the short ribs. Stir in wine, salt, pepper, and bay leaf.

4. Cook on low for about 9–10 hours, or until meat is fork-tender. Remove and discard bay leaf. Garnish with parsley.

PER SERVING Calories: 865 | Fat: 39g | Protein: 67g | Sodium: 600mg | Fiber: 3g | Carbohydrates: 32g | Sugar: 19g

Types of Short Ribs

There are three types of short ribs you can buy: boneless, English cut, and flanken style. English-cut ribs are bone-in ribs with lots of marbling and are best slow cooked or braised.

California Burgers

Avocado, arugula, and goat cheese adorn these sophisticated burgers. If you don't like the spicy sauce, substitute your favorite creamy topping to make this your dream burger.

INGREDIENTS | SERVES 8 | 30 MINUTES

¼ cup mayonnaise (not low-fat)

3 tablespoons sriracha chili sauce

2 pounds lean ground beef

1 large egg

¾ cup gluten-free panko bread crumbs

2 tablespoons olive oil

2 tablespoons gluten-free Worcestershire sauce

¼ teaspoon crushed red pepper

1 teaspoon salt

½ teaspoon ground black pepper

8 gluten-free hamburger buns

1 cup crumbled soft goat cheese

1 cup baby arugula

8 slices red onion

1 large ripe avocado, peeled, pitted, and cut into 8 slices

1. In a small bowl, mix mayonnaise and sriracha. Cover and refrigerate while you make the burgers.

2. In a large bowl, mix ground beef, egg, bread crumbs, olive oil, Worcestershire sauce, crushed red pepper, salt, and pepper with your hands. Shape mixture into 8 patties and place them on a baking sheet lined with parchment paper. Refrigerate for at least 15 minutes.

3. Preheat a grill pan or large skillet over medium heat. Add burgers and cook about 5 minutes on each side.

4. Spread 1 tablespoon sriracha-mayonnaise mixture on the bottom halves of the buns and top each with a burger patty. Top with goat cheese, arugula, onion, and avocado. Cover with top halves of the buns.

PER SERVING Calories: 620 | Fat: 20g | Protein: 39g | Sodium: 680mg | Fiber: 5g | Carbohydrates: 54g | Sugar: 3g

Spicy Moroccan Lamb Stew

If you've never had Moroccan food, you are in for a spicy, flavorful treat! Moroccan dishes are often spiced with harissa, a sauce or paste that is a blend of spicy North African chilies. You can serve this lamb stew over rice (to help mellow out the spice) or couscous for an even more authentic dish.

INGREDIENTS | SERVES 4 | 25 MINUTES

2 tablespoons extra-virgin olive oil

½ medium onion, peeled and chopped

1 medium carrot, peeled and chopped

½ large parsnip, peeled and chopped

¼ cup chopped fresh parsley

1 teaspoon salt

½ teaspoon ground black pepper

4 medium-sized lamb chops

1 (14.5-ounce) can diced tomatoes

1 (19-ounce) can chickpeas, drained and rinsed

3 tablespoons spicy harissa

1 tablespoon Moroccan spice

1. Heat the olive oil in a Dutch oven over medium-high heat. Add the onion, carrot, parsnip, parsley, salt, and pepper. Cook 4–6 minutes, or until softened. Add the lamb chops and cook until browned on both sides, about 2 minutes. Add the tomatoes, chickpeas, harissa, and Moroccan spice.

2. Reduce to low and simmer until most of the liquid has evaporated, about 10 minutes. Serve hot.

PER SERVING Calories: 620 | Fat: 27g | Protein: 53g | Sodium: 1,200mg | Fiber: 9g | Carbohydrates: 40g | Sugar: 5g

Coriander Meatballs

These aren't your ordinary meatballs. These luscious Coriander Meatballs are tart with a hint of Middle Eastern spice. They'd be great in a fluffy gluten-free pita.

INGREDIENTS | SERVES 4 | 25 MINUTES

½ pound ground lamb

2 tablespoons chopped red onion

1 tablespoon chopped fresh mint

½ garlic clove, minced

½ teaspoon coriander

½ teaspoon ground cinnamon

1 teaspoon salt

½ teaspoon ground black pepper

1 cup Creamy Tzatziki (see recipe in Chapter 3)

1. Preheat oven to 375°F. Grease a 9" × 13" glass baking dish with gluten-free nonstick cooking spray.

2. In a large mixing bowl, combine the lamb, onion, mint, garlic, coriander, cinnamon, salt, and pepper with your hands.

3. Form the mixture into about 16 medium-sized balls. Place meatballs in the greased baking dish in one layer.

4. Bake for about 15 minutes, or until golden brown. Serve with Creamy Tzatziki on the side for dipping.

PER SERVING Calories: 280 | Fat: 21g | Protein: 13g | Sodium: 830mg | Fiber: 1g | Carbohydrates: 10g | Sugar: 6g

Herb-Crusted Grilled Lamb

Easy, flavorful, and simple, this herb-crusted lamb recipe is elegant, sophisticated, and quick to prepare. Although it's perfect on its own, a little zest of fresh lemon juice will add a beautiful pop of flavor.

INGREDIENTS | SERVES 6 | 40 MINUTES

2 racks of trimmed lamb (3 pounds total)

1 tablespoon plus 1 teaspoon salt, divided

2½ teaspoons ground black pepper, divided

3 cloves garlic, minced

2 tablespoons chopped fresh parsley

2 tablespoons chopped fresh basil

2 tablespoons chopped fresh rosemary

1 cup cornmeal

¼ cup extra-virgin olive oil, divided

½ cup spicy gluten-free mustard

1. Position oven rack in the middle of the oven and preheat to 450°F. Rub lamb with 1 tablespoon salt and 2 teaspoons pepper.

2. In a large bowl, mix garlic, parsley, basil, rosemary, cornmeal, 1 teaspoon salt, and ½ teaspoon pepper together. Add ⅛ cup olive oil and mix until mixture forms a paste.

3. Heat remaining oil in a large skillet over medium-high heat. Put one rack of lamb, meat-side down, into the skillet and hold against the heat for about 4 minutes, or until it has a nice crust. Repeat with second rack.

4. Using a brush, paint the meaty side of both racks with mustard and press the herb mixture on top of it.

5. Bake for about 20 minutes, or until medium rare (130°F–140°F). Let rest about 10 minutes before serving.

PER SERVING Calories: 540 | Fat: 28g | Protein: 48g | Sodium: 1,900mg | Fiber: 2g | Carbohydrates: 20g | Sugar: 0g

Juicy Steak with Hawaiian Salsa

This juicy and tender steak is topped with a sweet and boozy salsa that adds a wonderful taste of the tropics.

INGREDIENTS | SERVES 4 | 35 MINUTES

2 cups chopped pineapple

½ cup halved cherry tomatoes

½ cup chopped red and orange bell peppers

4 tablespoons chopped red onion

⅔ cup blueberries

Juice of ½ lime

½ cup shredded coconut

¼ cup chopped cilantro

½ teaspoon table salt

½ teaspoon ground black pepper

2 tablespoons rosemary-infused (or regular) olive oil

2 (1-pound) New York boneless rib eye steaks

2 teaspoons sea salt

2 teaspoons cracked black pepper

1. In a large bowl, combine pineapple, tomatoes, peppers, onion, blueberries, lime juice, coconut, cilantro, table salt, and ground black pepper. Refrigerate for about 15 minutes.

2. Preheat broiler to high. Coat a grill pan with olive oil.

3. Sprinkle steaks with sea salt and cracked pepper on both sides. Place them on the grill pan and broil for about 5–6 minutes on each side for a medium-rare steak (145°F). Remove from the oven, and let rest for about 10 minutes.

4. Cut steaks into thick slices and top them with salsa.

PER SERVING Calories: 525 | Fat: 28g | Protein: 47g | Sodium: 1,600mg | Fiber: 4g | Carbohydrates: 20g | Sugar: 12g

Pork

Orange Honey–Glazed Ham `SC`

Many people are intimidated by making ham. Using the slow cooker makes it super easy, and the homemade orange honey glaze is a breeze to mix up.

INGREDIENTS | SERVES 6

1 (4-pound) bone-in gluten-free ham (discard glaze or seasoning packet)

½ cup seltzer water

½ cup orange juice

¼ cup honey

1–2 tablespoons orange zest

1 teaspoon ground cloves

¼ teaspoon cinnamon

1. Place ham, seltzer water, and orange juice in a greased 4–6-quart slow cooker. Cook on low for 6–8 hours or on high for 3–4 hours.

2. In a small bowl mix together honey, orange zest, ground cloves, and cinnamon. Spread over ham. Cook for an additional 45–60 minutes, venting the slow cooker lid with a chopstick or spoon handle. The ham should become golden brown and glazed. If necessary, finish off ham in a 350°F oven for 15–20 minutes to get a shiny glaze.

PER SERVING Calories: 580 | Fat: 28g | Protein: 67g | Sodium: 2,000mg | Fiber: 0g | Carbohydrates: 16g | Sugar: 14g

Tomato-Braised Pork `SC`

In this recipe pork is gently cooked in tomatoes to yield incredibly tender meat. Serve this pork and sauce over cooked rice or polenta with a salad on the side.

INGREDIENTS | SERVES 4

1 (28-ounce) can crushed tomatoes

3 tablespoons tomato paste

1 cup loosely packed fresh basil

½ teaspoon freshly ground black pepper

½ teaspoon marjoram

1¼ pounds boneless pork roast

1. Place the tomatoes, tomato paste, basil, pepper, and marjoram into a greased 4–6-quart slow cooker. Stir to create a uniform sauce. Add the pork.

2. Cook on low for 7–8 hours or until the pork easily falls apart when poked with a fork.

PER SERVING Calories: 224 | Fat: 5g | Protein: 34g | Sodium: 445mg | Fiber: 3g | Carbohydrates: 10g | Sugar: 6g

Italian Pork with Cannellini Beans `SC`

This is an incredibly simple one-dish meal that is packed with flavor.

INGREDIENTS | SERVES 4

1½ pounds pork loin

1 (28-ounce) can crushed tomatoes

1 head roasted garlic

1 medium onion, peeled and minced

2 teaspoons Italian seasoning

2 tablespoons capers

1 (15-ounce) can cannellini beans, drained and rinsed

1. Place the pork loin into a 4–6-quart slow cooker. Add the tomatoes, garlic, onion, Italian seasoning, and capers. Cook on low for 7–8 hours.

2. One hour before serving, add the cannellini beans and continue to cook on low for the remaining time.

PER SERVING Calories: 330 | Fat: 4g | Protein: 43g | Sodium: 500mg | Fiber: 9g | Carbohydrates: 28g | Sugar: 8g

Fruit and Corn-Crusted Pork Tenderloin

The colorful filling makes this a very pretty presentation. It also is delicious—and perfect for entertaining. If you have time, soak the dried fruits in a cup of warm water and the juice of half a lemon for 3–4 hours.

INGREDIENTS | SERVES 8 | 35 MINUTES

2 pork tenderloins, about ¾ pound each

6 dried apricots, chopped

½ cup dried cranberries

¼ cup white raisins (sultanas)

2 tablespoons wheat-free Worcestershire sauce

1 cup cornmeal

1 teaspoon salt

½ teaspoon freshly ground black pepper

½ cup extra-virgin olive oil

1. Preheat the oven to 350°F.

2. Make a tunnel through each tenderloin using a fat knitting needle or the handle of a blunt knife. Stuff the fruit into the tunnels.

3. Sprinkle both roasts with Worcestershire sauce.

4. In a small bowl, make a paste with the cornmeal, salt, pepper, and olive oil. Spread it on the pork.

5. Roast for 30 minutes. The crust should be golden brown and the pork pink.

PER SERVING Calories: 328 | Fat: 15g | Protein: 19g | Sodium: 380mg | Fiber: 2g | Carbohydrates: 28g | Sugar: 11g

Slow Cooker Pulled Pork SC

You will love how your house smells when this is slow cooking. Feel free to use chicken if you don't eat pork. Serve this pork warm in wheat-free buns or tortillas.

INGREDIENTS | SERVES 6

2 medium yellow onions, peeled and chopped

5 garlic cloves, minced

1 cup gluten-free beef broth

1 tablespoon brown sugar

1 tablespoon chili powder

2 teaspoons kosher salt

1 teaspoon cumin

½ teaspoon cinnamon

½ teaspoon dried oregano

1 (5-pound) pork shoulder, boneless or bone-in

1 cup wheat-free barbecue sauce

1 teaspoon wheat-free soy sauce

1. Place the onions, garlic, and broth in a 4–6-quart slow cooker.

2. In a small bowl, combine the sugar, chili powder, salt, cumin, cinnamon, and oregano and mix well.

3. Pat the pork with a paper towel and rub the prepared mixture all over it. Place pork on top of broth in slow cooker.

4. In the same small bowl, mix the barbecue sauce and the soy sauce. Stir to combine. Pour on top of pork, making sure the mixture is spread evenly on top. Cover and cook on low for 8 hours.

5. Remove pork from slow cooker and allow to cool slightly. If using bone-in pork, discard bone. Place pork in 9" × 13" casserole dish.

6. Shred the pork using a fork. Add additional barbecue sauce and slow cooker mixture if you'd like.

PER SERVING Calories: 590 | Fat: 20g | Protein: 71g | Sodium: 1,600mg | Fiber: 2g | Carbohydrates: 22g | Sugar: 14g

Stuffed Pork Chops

Ask the butcher for thick rib chops, and to slit a pocket in each. The pears become part of the sauce.

INGREDIENTS | SERVES 4 | 40 MINUTES

4 thick-cut pork rib chops (1½ pounds)

¾ cup olive oil, divided

1 tart apple, peeled, cored, and chopped

2 large onions, peeled and chopped, divided

1 tablespoon dried rosemary, crumbled, or 2 tablespoons chopped fresh

¼ cup finely chopped Italian flat-leaf parsley

½ cup gluten-free cornbread crumbs

1 teaspoon salt

½ teaspoon freshly ground black pepper

4 garlic cloves, chopped

½ cup gluten-free chicken broth

½ cup dry white wine

Zest and juice of ½ lemon

2 large ripe pears, peeled, cored, and quartered

2 teaspoons cornstarch mixed with 2 ounces cold water

1. Cut a pocket into each of the chops. Set aside.

2. Heat ½ cup olive oil in a large skillet over medium heat. Sauté the apple, ½ cup onion, rosemary, and parsley until softened, about 5 minutes. Add the cornbread crumbs, salt, and pepper. When cool enough to handle, stuff into the chops and secure with toothpicks.

3. Add ¼ cup olive oil to the pan and brown the chops on medium-high. Add garlic, broth, wine, lemon zest, lemon juice, pears, and remaining onion. Bring to a boil. Reduce heat to low, cover, and simmer for 30 minutes.

4. Place the chops on a warm platter and add the cornstarch and water mixture to the liquid in the pan. Cook and stir 5 minutes, until thickened. Pour gravy over the chops.

PER SERVING Calories: 800 | Fat: 52g | Protein: 38g | Sodium: 900mg | Fiber: 7g | Carbohydrates: 40g | Sugar: 20g

Tenderloin of Pork with Spinach and Water Chestnuts

For convenience, use fresh baby spinach, prewashed and packed in a bag. Serve this dish with rice.

INGREDIENTS | SERVES 4 | 20 MINUTES

2 (¾-pound) pork tenderloins

¼ cup potato flour

¼ teaspoon nutmeg

¼ teaspoon ground cloves

1 teaspoon salt

½ teaspoon freshly ground black pepper

¼ cup olive oil

2 tablespoons lemon juice

1 teaspoon gluten-free Worcestershire sauce

1 (8-ounce) bag fresh baby spinach or 1 (10-ounce) box frozen chopped spinach, thawed

½ cup sliced water chestnuts

1. Trim the pork and cut into serving pieces. On a sheet of waxed paper, mix together the flour and seasonings. Dredge the pork in the mixture.

2. Heat the olive oil in a medium skillet over medium heat, add the pork, and sauté for about 6 minutes per side; it should be medium.

3. Add the lemon juice, Worcestershire sauce, spinach, and water chestnuts. Stir and cook until spinach is wilted, about 5 minutes. Sprinkle with more olive oil, if the pan is dry.

PER SERVING Calories: 370 | Fat: 17g | Protein: 38g | Sodium: 740mg | Fiber: 2g | Carbohydrates: 15g | Sugar: 2g

Buying Pork

You can get "heirloom" or "heritage" pork on the Internet. Or you can get pork tenderloin in almost any supermarket. The tenderloin is about the best and juciest cut available.

Ricotta Torte with Serrano Ham and Parmesan

If you can't find Serrano ham, substitute prosciutto.
Do not, however, use low-fat ricotta—it just doesn't do the trick.

INGREDIENTS | SERVES 6 | 40 MINUTES

2 shallots, peeled and minced
2 tablespoons butter
3 large eggs
1 pound whole-milk ricotta cheese
½ cup grated Parmesan cheese
¼ cup finely chopped Serrano ham
4 tablespoons butter, melted
1 teaspoon dried oregano
⅛ teaspoon nutmeg
1 teaspoon salt
½ teaspoon freshly ground black pepper

1. Preheat the oven to 325°F.

2. In a small skillet over medium heat, sauté the shallots in butter for 3–5 minutes, until they are softened. Place contents of skillet into a pie pan you have prepared with gluten-free nonstick spray. Set aside.

3. In a medium bowl, beat the eggs and then add the rest of the ingredients, beating continuously. Pour mixture into pie pan and bake for 35 minutes, or until set and golden. Cut into wedges and serve.

PER SERVING Calories: 316 | Fat: 26g | Protein: 16g | Sodium: 700mg | Fiber: 0g | Carbohydrates: 3g | Sugar: 0g

Greek Pork-Stuffed Eggplants MA

You can do most of this recipe in advance, refrigerate, and then put it in the oven for 10 minutes. This is wonderful over a bed of greens, garnished with plain yogurt and finely chopped tomato.

INGREDIENTS | SERVES 4 | 40 MINUTES

½ cup extra-virgin olive oil
8 small eggplants, about 4–5" in length
½ cup minced onion
4 cloves garlic, minced
½ pound lean ground pork
1 teaspoon salt
½ teaspoon freshly ground black pepper
½ cup finely chopped fresh tomato
¼ teaspoon ground coriander
Juice of ½ lemon

1. Preheat oven to 400°F.

2. In a large skillet over medium-high heat, heat olive oil. Fry the whole eggplants for 5 minutes. Remove from pan and when cool enough to handle, make a slit from top to bottom but do not cut through.

3. In the same pan over medium heat, sauté onion, garlic, pork, salt, pepper, tomato, and coriander for 10 minutes, or until pork is no longer pink. Keep stirring to blend and break up the pork. Add the lemon juice.

4. Set aside to cool for 15 minutes.

5. Place the eggplants on a baking sheet that has been covered with aluminum foil. Spread the eggplants open, scoop the seeds out, and fill with pork stuffing.

6. Bake for 10 minutes. Serve warm.

PER SERVING Calories: 600 | Fat: 40g | Protein: 18g | Sodium: 600mg | Fiber: 29g | Carbohydrates: 51g | Sugar: 20g

Grilled Chops with Strawberries and Basil

This dish has all of the savory flavors of traditional pork chops, with the added saltiness and fat you get from bacon. Pair the chops with a sweet strawberry, bacon, and basil compote, and you have a truly mouthwatering dish.

INGREDIENTS | SERVES 4 | 20 MINUTES

5 slices thick-cut bacon

4 (6-ounce) bone-in pork chops

1½ teaspoons salt

1 teaspoon ground black pepper

½ cup chopped strawberries

6 large basil leaves, chopped

1 tablespoon lemon juice

1. Heat a large skillet over medium-high heat. Cook bacon for 5–7 minutes, or until crispy. Remove bacon from the pan, drain on paper towels, and chop it into bite-sized pieces. Set aside. Pour off all but 2–3 tablespoons of the bacon drippings.

2. Season pork chops with salt and pepper. Heat bacon drippings over medium-high heat and add chops to the skillet. Cook about 3–4 minutes on each side. Remove from heat.

3. Mash strawberries in a medium bowl using a fork. Stir in basil and lemon juice until the mixture has a jam-like consistency. Add bacon.

4. Serve the strawberry compote over the pork chops.

PER SERVING Calories: 350 | Fat: 20g | Protein: 40g | Sodium: 1,200mg | Fiber: 1g | Carbohydrates: 2g | Sugar: 1g

Barbecue Pulled Pork and Cheesy Spaghetti sc

This recipe was inspired by Brandy of Nutmeg Nanny. Her recipe for pulled pork macaroni and cheese is made heartier with a thicker sauce and store-bought, gluten-free spaghetti noodles.

INGREDIENTS | SERVES 8

1 pound gluten-free spaghetti

1 (4½-pound) boneless pork shoulder

12 ounces gluten-free chicken broth

3 teaspoons salt, divided

2 teaspoons ground black pepper, divided

2 cups Sticky and Spicy Barbecue Sauce (see recipe in Chapter 3)

2 tablespoons unsalted butter

2 tablespoons gluten-free all-purpose flour

1 cup heavy cream

1 cup 2% milk

3 cups shredded Cheddar cheese

1 cup shredded mozzarella cheese

1. Bring a large pot of salted water to a boil. Add spaghetti and cook until softened, about 8 minutes. Drain, rinse in cold water, and set aside.

2. Place the pork shoulder, broth, 2 teaspoons salt, and 1½ teaspoons pepper in a 4–6-quart slow cooker. Cook on low for 6–8 hours, or until fork-tender. Remove pork from slow cooker and shred with two forks. Stir in barbecue sauce.

3. Melt butter in a large skillet over medium heat. Add flour and whisk until a thick paste is formed. Gradually stir in cream and milk. Reduce heat to medium-low and cook until thick and coats the back of a spoon.

4. Remove from heat and stir in cheeses and remaining salt and pepper.

5. In a large bowl, mix the cheese sauce with the spaghetti and pour into a large serving dish or casserole. Top the spaghetti with the pulled pork.

PER SERVING Calories: 1,154 | Fat: 50g | Protein: 73g | Sodium: 2,200mg | Fiber: 3g | Carbohydrates: 103g | Sugar: 40g

Adobo Pork with Chimichurri Sauce

Adobo is simply a blend of spices that are commonly found in Mexico and the Caribbean. It's typically served with chicken, but here it seasons a juicy pork tenderloin. A spicy chimichurri sauce adds even more flavor.

INGREDIENTS | SERVES 6

5 tablespoons plus 1 teaspoon salt, divided

5 tablespoons minced garlic

4 tablespoons dried oregano

2 tablespoons dried turmeric

2 tablespoons onion powder

1 teaspoon cracked black pepper

1 large pork tenderloin

1 tablespoon saffron oil

2 cups fresh cilantro

4 cloves garlic

2 tablespoons minced onion

½ cup extra-virgin olive oil

2 tablespoons Mexican oregano

2 tablespoons white wine vinegar

1 tablespoon lime juice

1 teaspoon ground black pepper

Chimichurri

Chimichurri is a Spanish and Argentinean green sauce that is best paired with grilled and roasted meat. It's traditionally made with parsley, garlic, olive oil, oregano, and white vinegar, but cilantro is used here instead for a stronger taste. You can also replace the cilantro with basil and make a pesto instead.

1. In a small bowl, mix 5 tablespoons salt, minced garlic, oregano, turmeric, onion powder, and cracked black pepper.

2. Coat the pork with saffron oil. Rub seasoning mix into the pork. Cover, refrigerate, and marinate for about 1 hour.

3. Preheat oven to 450°F. Grease a 9" × 13" baking dish with gluten-free nonstick cooking spray and place the pork in the dish.

4. Bake pork for about 28–38 minutes, or until the internal temperature is 145°F. Let rest for at least 15 minutes.

5. Pulse cilantro, garlic cloves, onion, olive oil, Mexican oregano, vinegar, lime juice, 1 teaspoon salt, and ground pepper in a blender or food processor. Pulse until mixture is slightly puréed.

6. Serve the tenderloin with chimichurri sauce.

PER SERVING Calories: 380 | Fat: 24g | Protein: 33g | Sodium: 4,000mg | Fiber: 2g | Carbohydrates: 8g | Sugar: 1g

Sausage and Caramelized Onion Pita Pizza

This easy sausage pizza is the perfect quick supper. It's a great, healthier version of regular pizza.

INGREDIENTS | SERVES 2 | 10 MINUTES

1 large gluten-free pita bread

¼ cup tomato sauce

½ cup cooked and crumbled gluten-free pork sausage

2 ounces soft goat cheese

¼ cup shredded Parmesan cheese

¼ cup chopped scallions

¼ cup chopped fresh cilantro, for garnish

Pizza Crust Options

Gluten-free pitas can be hard to find in regular supermarkets, so you may need to check out your specialty health-food stores or whole-foods markets. If you can't find them, it's easy enough to make your own gluten-free pizza dough. Try making the crust in the recipe for Barbecue Chicken Pizza in Chapter 8.

1. Preheat broiler. Place the pita bread on a large baking sheet coated with gluten-free nonstick cooking spray.

2. Top pita with tomato sauce, then add sausage, cheeses, and scallions.

3. Broil for about 5–6 minutes or until the cheese is browned and bubbly. Slice into bite-sized pieces and garnish with cilantro.

PER SERVING Calories: 400 | Fat: 24g | Protein: 25g | Sodium: 900mg | Fiber: 1g | Carbohydrates: 20g | Sugar: 3g

Crispy Pork Belly Pizza

This luscious recipe for pizza will soon become a favorite in your house, even if you have some seriously picky pizza eaters. The juicy pork belly makes a great addition to the creamy white pizza sauce and fresh herbs.

INGREDIENTS | SERVES 8 | 25 MINUTES

1 pound gluten-free pizza dough

1 tablespoon unsalted butter

1 garlic clove, minced

1½ tablespoons gluten-free all-purpose flour

½ cup 1% milk

1 teaspoon salt

½ teaspoon ground black pepper

¼ cup Parmesan cheese

½ pound cooked, chopped pork belly

1 cup diced fresh mozzarella cheese

1 medium red onion, peeled and chopped

¼ cup chopped fresh basil

1. Preheat oven to 425°F. Grease a large pizza pan with gluten-free nonstick cooking spray.

2. Roll pizza dough out into a large circle (about ¼" thick) and set aside.

3. In a small saucepan, melt butter over medium heat and add garlic. Add flour and stir. Gradually add milk and stir after each addition. Heat until sauce starts to thicken, about 5 minutes. Add salt, pepper, and Parmesan. Remove from heat and cool for about 1 minute (sauce will thicken as it cools).

4. Spread sauce over pizza dough. Top sauce with pork belly bits, mozzarella, and onion.

5. Bake pizza for about 12–14 minutes, or until crust is golden brown and cheese is bubbly. Remove from oven and cut into 8 slices. Top each slice with chopped basil before serving.

PER SERVING Calories: 480 | Fat: 37g | Protein: 10g | Sodium: 680mg | Fiber: 2g | Carbohydrates: 27g | Sugar: 2g

Crispy Egg Rolls

Many people living a gluten-free lifestyle have to cut out Chinese food because of the gluten found in the sauces, mixes, and wrappers. Instead of forgoing your favorite Chinese, make it yourself with gluten-free, all-natural ingredients. These egg rolls taste even better than take-out!

INGREDIENTS | SERVES 10 | 35 MINUTES

1 tablespoon olive oil

3 ounces chopped mushrooms

1 medium carrot, peeled and shredded

2 scallions, diced

½ head napa cabbage, chopped

½ teaspoon gluten-free five-spice powder

2 cups cooked ground pork

½ tablespoon cornstarch

2 tablespoons gluten-free soy sauce

¾ teaspoon sesame oil

10 gluten-free rice papers

1 large egg white, beaten with 2 tablespoons water

1. Heat the olive oil in a large skillet over medium heat. Add the mushrooms, carrot, scallions, and cabbage. Cook until vegetables are soft, about 6 minutes. Sprinkle with five-spice powder. Mix in the ground pork.

2. Dissolve the cornstarch in the soy sauce and stir in sesame oil. Drizzle the soy sauce mixture over the pork and vegetables and cook 1–2 minutes more. Remove from heat.

3. Place about 1½ tablespoons of the mixture into the center of each of the rice paper wrappers. Roll the corner up and over the filling, fold each side in, and then roll up the rest of the way. Repeat with the remaining egg rolls.

4. Preheat oven to 425°F. Grease a large cookie sheet with gluten-free nonstick cooking spray. Place egg rolls, seam-side down, onto the cookie sheet. Brush with egg white mixture.

5. Bake for about 20 minutes, or until crispy and golden brown.

PER SERVING Calories: 180 | Fat: 11g | Protein: 13g | Sodium: 235mg | Fiber: 1g | Carbohydrates: 7g | Sugar: 1g

Broccoli Cheddar Soup (Chapter 4)

Adobo Pork with Chimichurri Sauce (Chapter 7)

Barbeque Pulled Pork and Cheesy Spaghetti (Chapter 7)

Barbeque Chicken Pizza (Chapter 8)

Chilled Blackberry, Blueberry, and Mint Gazpacho
(Chapter 4)

Quinoa Fried "Rice" (Chapter 11)

Cioppino (Chapter 15)

Slow Cooker Butter Chicken Wings (Chapter 8)

Ahi Tuna and Melon Spring Rolls (Chapter 9)

Sesame-Glazed Plank Salmon (Chapter 9)

Chocolate Chip Peanut Butter Sandwich Cookies
(Chapter 16)

Gluten-Free Chicken and Waffles (Chapter 10)

Red Wine-Braised Beef Short Ribs
with Mushrooms (Chapter 6)

Sticky and Spicy Barbecue Sauce (Chapter 3)

Four-Cheese Baked Penne with Prosciutto (Chapter 12)

Baked Spaghetti Squash Boats (Chapter 11)

Bourbon, Brown Sugar, and Peach Sauce
(Chapter 3)

Black Bean Cakes with Avocado and Cilantro Cream (Chapter 13)

Tomato and Mozzarella Baked Eggs (Chapter 10)

Lobster Deviled Egg Salad (Chapter 5)

Fresh Corn and Sweet Pepper Muffins (Chapter 14)

Fresh Berry Pie (Chapter 16)

Strawberry Guacamole (Chapter 2)

Orange Chicken (Chapter 8)

Bacon and Egg Mini Quiches

Quiche is one of those dishes that work just as well for dinner as for breakfast.
These bite-sized tarts are perfect for a light dinner or as a side dish to any grilled poultry or fish.

INGREDIENTS | SERVES 6 | 35 MINUTES

6 slices gluten-free sandwich bread

1 cup frozen chopped spinach, defrosted and squeezed dry

½ medium onion, peeled and finely chopped

1 garlic clove, finely chopped

½ cup grated fresh mozzarella cheese

2 large eggs

½ cup light cream

1 teaspoon sea salt

½ teaspoon freshly ground black pepper

½ teaspoon dried parsley

4 slices turkey bacon, cooked and crumbled

1. Preheat oven to 375°F. Grease a muffin tin liberally with gluten-free cooking spray.

2. Using a round cookie cutter that equals the size of the bottom of the muffin tin, cut out a hole in the middle each bread slice. Place the circle of bread on the bottom of 6 muffin cavities.

3. Evenly distribute spinach, onion, garlic, and cheese among the 6 pieces of bread.

4. In a medium bowl, mix eggs, cream, salt, pepper, and parsley. Pour egg mixture evenly over the spinach cups, being careful not to overflow. Sprinkle crumbled bacon on top and bake for at least 20 minutes.

5. Let quiches cool (they will sink in a bit) about 5 minutes before removing from muffin tin. Serve hot or at room temperature.

PER SERVING Calories: 220 | Fat: 13g | Protein: 11g | Sodium: 1,000mg | Fiber: 1g | Carbohydrates: 15g | Sugar: 1g

Sausage and Asparagus Risotto

This flavorful one-pot meal will leave you asking for a second helping.
You can use turkey or chicken sausage as well.

INGREDIENTS | SERVES 6 | 45 MINUTES

4 tablespoons extra-virgin olive oil

1 scallion, chopped

2 cloves garlic, minced

1 pound gluten-free mild Italian sausage links, casings removed

2 cups shiitake mushrooms, wiped clean and stems removed

2 cups Arborio rice

½ cup dry white wine or vermouth

5¼ cups gluten-free low-sodium chicken broth, warmed

1 pound asparagus stalks, stems removed and cut into 2" pieces

1 teaspoon ground oregano

1 teaspoon ground basil

⅓ cup freshly grated Parmesan cheese

1. In a large skillet over medium heat, cook the oil, scallion, and garlic for 2–3 minutes.

2. Add the sausage links and cook while breaking them apart with a spoon. Once the sausages are browned, about 5–7 minutes, add mushrooms and stir for 1–2 minutes to combine.

3. Add rice and wine, and continue to stir and cook until liquid is completely absorbed, about 3 minutes.

4. Add chicken broth, 1 cup at a time, while making sure all the liquid is absorbed before adding another cup.

5. After adding all the broth, add chopped asparagus and herbs, and continue to stir. When risotto is firm, yet creamy, it is finished. Top with grated Parmesan.

PER SERVING Calories: 650 | Fat: 32g | Protein: 25g | Sodium: 400mg | Fiber: 5g | Carbohydrates: 67g | Sugar: 5g

CHAPTER 8

Poultry

Biscuit-Topped Chicken Pie

This creamy chicken-and-vegetable pie topped with homemade gluten-free buttermilk drop biscuits is pure comfort food! To make the pie extra rich, drizzle a few tablespoons of melted butter over the biscuit topping right before cooking.

INGREDIENTS | SERVES 6 | 45 MINUTES

4 tablespoons brown rice flour

4 tablespoons butter

1 cup milk

1 cup gluten-free chicken broth

1 teaspoon salt

½ teaspoon ground black pepper

2 cups cooked chicken, cut or torn into bite-sized pieces

1 (12-ounce) can mixed vegetables, drained

½ recipe prepared Fluffy Buttermilk Biscuits dough (see recipe in Chapter 11)

Gluten-Free Baking Mixes

Instead of the biscuit dough recipe, you can use your favorite homemade baking mix. It must be an all-purpose mix that includes xanthan gum and a leavening ingredient such as baking powder or baking soda. Use a recipe on the package that will make 8–10 gluten-free biscuits as a topping for chicken pie.

1. Preheat oven to 350°F. Grease a 3- or 4-quart baking dish with gluten-free nonstick cooking spray or olive oil.

2. In a small saucepan whisk together brown rice flour and butter. When butter has melted slowly stir in milk, chicken broth, salt, and pepper. Cook on medium heat for 5–10 minutes, whisking constantly until mixture is the consistency of cream soup or gravy.

3. Add cooked chicken and drained vegetables to baking dish. Pour cream soup mixture into the baking dish and mix with chicken and vegetables.

4. Using an ice cream scoop, drop biscuit dough over chicken, vegetables, and sauce.

5. Cover dish with foil and bake for 35 minutes, until sauce is bubbling up around the biscuits, and the biscuits are cooked through. Remove foil in the last 10 minutes of baking to allow the biscuits to brown.

PER SERVING Calories: 400 | Fat: 22g | Protein: 20g | Sodium: 1,000mg | Fiber: 3g | Carbohydrates: 31g | Sugar: 5g

Chicken in Apple Cider and Brandy

You can prepare this dish in advance. Reheat when you're ready to serve, adding the cream at the last minute.

INGREDIENTS | SERVES 6 | 45 MINUTES

4 tablespoons butter

2 whole (3-pound) chickens, cut into quarters

1 cup chopped onion

1 tablespoon cornstarch

¼ cup apple brandy or applejack

1¼ cups apple cider

1 teaspoon salt

½ teaspoon ground black pepper

½ cup heavy cream or half-and-half

1 teaspoon dried rosemary

1. Heat the butter in a large skillet over medium heat. Add the chicken pieces and brown for 5 minutes per side.

2. Add the onion and cook until softened, about 2–3 minutes. Stir in the cornstarch.

3. Add the brandy and flame it by setting it on fire with a long match. (Be careful not to burn yourself.) After the flames die out, add the cider, salt, and pepper. Cover and simmer for 25 minutes.

4. Just before serving, remove the chicken to a platter. Add the cream to the sauce in the pan, and heat for 2 minutes. Spoon sauce over chicken, sprinkle with rosemary, and serve.

PER SERVING Calories: 460 | Fat: 21g | Protein: 48g | Sodium: 550mg | Fiber: 1g | Carbohydrates: 10g | Sugar: 6g

Chicken Mushroom Marinara Bake

Combine chicken, marinara sauce, and mushrooms with your favorite gluten-free pasta for an easy one-pot meal.

INGREDIENTS | SERVES 4 | 45 MINUTES

1 pound fresh button mushrooms, sliced

2 tablespoons butter or olive oil

1 (16- or 18-ounce) jar marinara sauce

1 cup cooked and diced chicken breast

8 ounces gluten-free pasta, cooked according to package directions

1 teaspoon dried basil

½ teaspoon garlic salt

1 cup shredded mozzarella cheese

1. Preheat oven to 350°F. Grease a medium-sized casserole baking dish; set aside.

2. In a medium-sized sauté pan over medium heat, cook mushroom slices in butter or olive oil for 4–5 minutes until tender.

3. In a medium bowl, mix together marinara sauce, chicken, sautéed mushrooms, and cooked pasta. Pour into casserole dish. Sprinkle basil and garlic salt evenly over casserole. Top with mozzarella cheese.

4. Bake for 30–35 minutes until cheese is slightly browned and sauce is bubbly. Allow to cool for 5 minutes before serving.

PER SERVING Calories: 620 | Fat: 25g | Protein: 36g | Sodium: 1,000mg | Fiber: 6g | Carbohydrates: 64g | Sugar: 15g

Tasty Turkey Parmesan

You can doctor your sauce with extra herbs, some lemon zest, and/or red wine.

INGREDIENTS | SERVES 4 | 35 MINUTES

1¼ pounds boneless, skinless turkey breast, sliced thinly

1 cup gluten-free cornbread crumbs

1 cup Parmesan cheese, divided

1 cup corn flour

1 teaspoon salt

½ teaspoon freshly ground black pepper

1 large egg, beaten

1 cup vegetable oil

2 cups tomato sauce

½ pound whole-milk mozzarella, shredded or thinly sliced

What's in the Stuffing?

The key to buying gluten-free food is reading every label carefully. Store-bought cornbread stuffing may have wheat flour mixed in with the corn flour and cornmeal. Corn muffins, also a favorite in making homemade stuffing, can have a mixture of wheat flour and cornmeal. In the long run, the safest way to provide gluten-free stuffing is to make the cornbread yourself.

1. Flatten the turkey pieces with a meat pounder. Cut into 4 serving pieces.

2. In a shallow bowl, mix the cornbread crumbs with ½ cup Parmesan cheese. In another bowl combine the flour with the salt and pepper. In a third bowl add the beaten egg. Dip the turkey in the flour, then in the egg, and finally in the crumb mixture.

3. Preheat oven to 350°F.

4. In a deep skillet, heat the oil over medium-high heat. Add the turkey pieces and fry in the oil until golden brown; drain on paper towels.

5. Treat a baking dish with gluten-free nonstick spray. Pour a little tomato sauce into the baking dish. Add the turkey pieces. Sprinkle with remaining ½ cup Parmesan cheese. Cover with remaining tomato sauce. Spread the mozzarella over the top.

6. Bake in oven until hot and bubbling, about 20 minutes. Serve hot.

PER SERVING Calories: 900 | Fat: 53g | Protein: 73g | Sodium: 2,000mg | Fiber: 4g | Carbohydrates: 47g | Sugar: 8g

Balsamic Chicken with Sun-Dried Tomatoes and Roasted Red Peppers

This tangy chicken dish can be served over rice or quinoa for a perfect, balanced meal.

INGREDIENTS | SERVES 6 | 35 MINUTES

3 (5-ounce) boneless, skinless chicken breasts, rinsed and sliced in half

½ teaspoon salt

½ teaspoon pepper

1 tablespoon vegetable oil

1 small onion, peeled and chopped

2 garlic cloves, chopped

¼ cup balsamic vinegar

½ teaspoon brown sugar

¼ cup gluten-free low-sodium chicken broth

1 teaspoon dried rosemary

1 teaspoon dried basil

1 teaspoon dried oregano

1 (6-ounce) bag sun-dried tomatoes, sliced in quarters

1 (12-ounce) jar roasted red peppers, drained and sliced

1. Season the chicken breasts with salt and pepper.

2. Heat the oil in a medium skillet over medium heat. Add the onion and garlic and sauté for 2–3 minutes, until tender. Add chicken and brown about 5 minutes per side.

3. In a small bowl, combine the balsamic vinegar, brown sugar, chicken broth, rosemary, basil, and oregano.

4. Add the tomatoes and red pepper to the chicken in the skillet. Pour the balsamic mixture over the chicken and vegetables. Turn heat to high and let the liquid come to a boil. Reduce heat to medium-low and simmer for about 15 minutes, or until the chicken is no longer pink inside.

PER SERVING Calories: 215 | Fat: 5g | Protein: 20g | Sodium: 500mg | Fiber: 5g | Carbohydrates: 25g | Sugar: 16g

What Kind of Balsamic Vinegar Do You Use?

All balsamic vinegars are not the same. Just like fine wine, balsamic vinegar tastes better when aged. The longer it ages, the thicker and sweeter it becomes. Although the aged balsamic vinegars may be more expensive, you have to remember that a little goes a long way.

Elegant Duckling and Fruit-Filled Corn Crepes

The sweetness of the duck works with the fruit—a marriage made in heaven.
Serve these crepes over fresh salad greens or sautéed baby spinach.

INGREDIENTS | SERVES 4 | 45 MINUTES

½ cup gluten-free chicken broth

1 tablespoon cornstarch

3 tablespoons unsalted butter

⅔ pound boneless, skinless duck breasts

½ cup corn flour

½ teaspoon salt

2 teaspoons freshly ground black pepper

½ cup dried cranberries soaked in ⅔ cup apple juice or wine

¼ cup dried cherries soaked in ½ cup orange juice

¼ cup chopped celery tops

24 pearl onions, peeled (frozen is fine)

1 tablespoon dried rosemary

½ cup apple brandy (such as Calvados)

8 large Corn Crepes (see recipe in Chapter 10)

2 tablespoons olive oil

1. Mix the chicken broth and the cornstarch in a small bowl and set aside.

2. Heat butter in a medium skillet over medium heat. Place the corn flour in a shallow bowl and then dredge the duck breasts in it. Add the duck to the skillet and sauté until browned, about 5 minutes per side. Add the salt and pepper and the chicken broth mixture to the pan, stirring to make a sauce.

3. Add the cranberries, cherries, celery tops, onions, rosemary, and apple brandy. Reduce heat to low, cover, and cook for 20 minutes.

4. Preheat oven to 350°F.

5. Remove the duck from the pan. Cut duck into small pieces and return to the sauce. Stir to combine.

6. Divide the duck mixture between the 8 crepes. Roll the crepes, place them seam-side down in a greased baking dish, and drizzle with olive oil. Heat them in the oven for 10 minutes.

PER SERVING Calories: 750 | Fat: 37g | Protein: 24g | Sodium: 1,000mg | Fiber: 4g | Carbohydrates: 71g | Sugar: 22g

Classic Southern Fried Chicken

A great fried chicken is a perfectly delicious dinner, but it's not often a gluten-free friendly option. Don't worry! This amazingly juicy and crispy chicken works well next to your favorite potatoes or chips!

INGREDIENTS | SERVES 8

1 (4-pound) chicken, cut into 8 pieces (drumsticks, thighs, breasts, and wings)

1 cup buttermilk

1½ cups corn flour

1 teaspoon salt

1 teaspoon ground black pepper

1 teaspoon baking powder

1 large egg, beaten

½ cup gluten-free buckwheat beer

1½ cups cornmeal

2 cups vegetable oil

Frying with Corn Flour

When you use corn flour or cornmeal for frying, you can mix it with either rice flour or potato flour for good results. For a light, tempura-like crust, try cornstarch mixed with water and egg. Gluten-free cooking does require a whole new chemistry.

1. Rinse the chicken pieces and dry on paper towels, then place in a resealable plastic bag with the buttermilk and marinate for 2–3 hours.

2. In a large paper bag, mix together the corn flour, salt, pepper, and baking powder. Add the chicken pieces to the corn flour mixture one at a time, then close the bag and shake until the chicken is well coated.

3. In a small bowl, whisk the egg and beer together. Spread the cornmeal on a large piece of waxed paper. Dip the chicken in the beaten egg/beer mixture. Then roll in the cornmeal, pressing it all together.

4. Bring 1" of oil to 365°F in a fryer, or ½" of oil in a frying pan. Fry the chicken for 20–25 minutes; turn every 4 or 5 minutes. Watch the chicken carefully to make sure that it doesn't burn.

PER SERVING Calories: 650 | Fat: 37g | Protein: 35g | Sodium: 450mg | Fiber: 1g | Carbohydrates: 42g | Sugar: 2g

Chicken Piccata

This zesty, traditional Italian dish is packed with flavor and has become extremely popular in restaurants. Serve it with rice or wheat-free pasta.

INGREDIENTS | SERVES 8 | 25 MINUTES

1 cup gluten-free low-sodium chicken broth

½ cup dry white wine or vermouth

2 tablespoons lemon juice

4 skinless, boneless chicken breasts, sliced in half

½ teaspoon salt

½ teaspoon ground black pepper

1 tablespoon butter

½ medium onion, peeled and chopped

4 garlic cloves, minced

1 (13.75-ounce) can artichoke hearts, rinsed and drained

4 tablespoons gluten-free capers

2 tablespoons freshly minced flat-leaf parsley

½ large lemon, thinly sliced

1. In a small bowl, whisk together the broth, wine, and lemon juice. Set it aside.

2. Place a halved chicken breast between two pieces of plastic wrap. Using the flat side of a mallet, pound each breast until about ¼" thick.

3. Remove the top of the plastic wrap and sprinkle one side of the chicken with half of the salt and pepper.

4. Heat butter in a large skillet over medium heat. Place chicken in the skillet with the salt and pepper side down. Add remaining salt and pepper to the other side.

5. Cook chicken about 4 minutes per side, until no longer pink in the middle. Remove chicken from the skillet and place on a plate. Keep warm.

6. Add broth mixture, onion, and garlic to the same skillet; cover and reduce heat to low. Let simmer for 5–10 minutes until liquid reduces to about half.

7. Add browned chicken, artichoke hearts, and capers. Let simmer on low heat, uncovered, for a few minutes so sauce thickens. Top with parsley and lemon slices.

PER SERVING Calories: 205 | Fat: 5g | Protein: 27g | Sodium: 500mg | Fiber: 5g | Carbohydrates: 10g | Sugar: 1g

Parmesan–Chia Seed Crusted Chicken

Chia seeds pack a nutritional punch in this chicken dish. You won't even miss the bread crumbs in this fantastic entrée.

INGREDIENTS | SERVES 8 | 40 MINUTES

1 cup wheat-free, all-purpose flour

1 tablespoon finely shredded Parmesan cheese

1 garlic clove, finely chopped

1 teaspoon dried basil

3 tablespoons ground chia seeds

1 large egg

3 large egg whites

4 boneless, skinless organic chicken breasts

1. Preheat the oven to 350°F.

2. Place the flour, cheese, garlic, basil, and chia seeds in a shallow bowl. Stir until well blended.

3. In another shallow bowl, whisk the egg and egg whites until well blended.

4. Dip each chicken breast in egg mixture first, then dredge in flour/chia seed mixture until completely covered. Place in a 9" × 13" casserole dish.

5. Bake for 30–35 minutes, turning over halfway through the cooking time, until chicken is no longer pink.

PER SERVING Calories: 230 | Fat: 6g | Protein: 30g | Sodium: 175mg | Fiber: 1g | Carbohydrates: 13g | Sugar: 0g

Hot and Spicy Turkey Meatballs

Meatball recipes usually include bread crumbs as a filler and sometimes for an outside coating. This recipe uses ground potato chips. The eggs will hold the meatballs together, and who doesn't love potato chips?

INGREDIENTS | SERVES 6 | 25 MINUTES

1 pound ground turkey

2 large eggs

2 cloves garlic, minced

1 teaspoon dried oregano

1 teaspoon dried basil

½ teaspoon cinnamon

½ teaspoon fennel seeds

½ cup finely grated Parmesan cheese

2 cups crushed low-salt potato chips, divided

½ teaspoon salt

½ teaspoon ground black pepper

4 tablespoons canola oil

1. In a large bowl, mix the turkey, eggs, garlic, oregano, basil, cinnamon, fennel seeds, cheese, 1 cup potato chip crumbs, salt, and pepper.

2. Place a large sheet of waxed paper on the counter. Sprinkle remaining cup of chip crumbs on it.

3. Form 1" meatballs from the turkey mixture. Roll meatballs in crumbs to coat.

4. Heat oil in a large skillet over medium-high heat. Fry meatballs until well browned, about 5 minutes. Drain on paper towels and then either refrigerate, freeze, or serve with the marinara sauce of your choice.

PER SERVING Calories: 315 | Fat: 23g | Protein: 18g | Sodium: 450mg | Fiber: 1g | Carbohydrates: 8g | Sugar: 0g

Kick Up Those Meatballs

You can add flavor to your meatballs by grinding up some sweet or hot Italian sausage and mixing it with the ground turkey or beef. A truly great Italian sausage has aromatics like garlic and herbs, and spices such as anise seeds.

Ginger, Soy, and Kale Chicken

This recipe has a wonderful combination of ginger and soy. Marinate it the night before to let the chicken thoroughly absorb the flavors.

INGREDIENTS | SERVES 4

4 tablespoons low-sodium wheat-free soy sauce

1 tablespoon toasted sesame oil

1 tablespoon honey

½ teaspoon fresh grated gingerroot

2 garlic cloves, crushed

2 boneless, skinless organic chicken breasts, cut into 1" cubes

1 tablespoon extra-virgin olive oil

2 cups kale

Kale Is a Nutritional Powerhouse

Kale is a powerhouse of nutrition as well as being a member of the cabbage family. Kale is packed with fiber, calcium, vitamin B_6, vitamin A, vitamin K, and vitamin C. Kale can be eaten raw or cooked and can replace your other leafy greens in all varieties of recipes.

1. In a small bowl, whisk together the soy sauce, sesame oil, honey, gingerroot, and garlic.

2. Place chicken in a zip-top plastic bag and pour half of the soy mixture into bag. Make sure the bag is closed and shake it up so all the chicken is covered. Let marinate for at least a half-hour or overnight.

3. Remove chicken from the marinade. Heat olive oil in a medium skillet over medium-high heat. Sauté the chicken for 5–8 minutes, until fully cooked and no longer pink.

4. Add the kale and cook until it is still bright green and only a little soft, about 2 minutes. Add remaining soy mixture and mix well.

PER SERVING Calories: 237 | Fat: 10g | Protein: 27g | Sodium: 200mg | Fiber: 1g | Carbohydrates: 9g | Sugar: 5g

Turkey Drumsticks with Gluten-Free Stuffing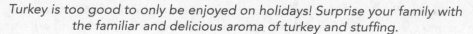

Turkey is too good to only be enjoyed on holidays! Surprise your family with the familiar and delicious aroma of turkey and stuffing.

INGREDIENTS | SERVES 4

1 medium onion, peeled and chopped

½ cup chopped celery

2 tablespoons butter

2 teaspoons gluten-free poultry seasoning

4 cups gluten-free bread, toasted and cubed

½ cup gluten-free chicken broth

¼ cup dried, gluten-free cranberries

2 large (1½-pound) turkey drumsticks

½ teaspoon salt

½ teaspoon ground black pepper

2 slices bacon

Turkey Isn't Just for Thanksgiving

Turkey drumsticks can be found at many grocery stores year round and are an extremely budget-friendly protein. While many people prefer white turkey meat over dark, drumsticks and thighs can hold up well during long cooking periods. They stay moist and are a perfect meat for the slow cooker.

1. In a large glass bowl place onion, celery, butter, and poultry seasoning. Cook in microwave on high for 2 minutes until vegetables have softened.

2. Add bread cubes and broth to the softened vegetables. Stir in the dried cranberries. Pour stuffing into the bottom of a greased 4–6-quart slow cooker.

3. Place turkey drumsticks on top of stuffing. Sprinkle salt and pepper evenly over turkey. Place a piece of bacon on each drumstick.

4. Cook on high for 3 hours or on low for 6 hours. Each turkey drumstick makes 2 servings.

5. Cut turkey off of the bone and serve over stuffing.

PER SERVING Calories: 550 | Fat: 17g | Protein: 24g | Sodium: 1,000mg | Fiber: 4g | Carbohydrates: 78g | Sugar: 9g

Creole Chicken and Vegetables sc

This recipe is extremely quick to assemble, as none of the ingredients require chopping or slicing. The unique blend of spices in Creole seasoning gives this dish its signature flavor that will remind you of vacations in New Orleans.

INGREDIENTS | SERVES 4

8 boneless, skinless chicken thighs

2 tablespoons gluten-free Creole seasoning

1 (14-ounce) package frozen mixed vegetables such as broccoli, cauliflower, and carrots (you can also use Steamfresh vegetables)

1 (15-ounce) can diced tomatoes

½ teaspoon ground black pepper

1 cup brown rice, uncooked

1. Place chicken thighs in the bottom of a 4–6-quart greased slow cooker.

2. Sprinkle Creole seasoning over chicken.

3. Add frozen vegetables, tomatoes, and pepper to the slow cooker.

4. Cook on high for 3 hours or on low for 6 hours. An hour before serving stir in the brown rice.

PER SERVING Calories: 415 | Fat: 7g | Protein: 35g | Sodium: 315mg | Fiber: 7g | Carbohydrates: 54g | Sugar: 2g

Buffalo Chicken Sandwich Filling sc

Serve on toasted gluten-free bread with crumbled blue cheese or gluten-free ranch dressing on top of each sandwich. This also makes a great topping for baked potatoes and pizza!

INGREDIENTS | SERVES 4

6 boneless, skinless chicken thighs

¼ cup diced onion

1 clove garlic, minced

½ teaspoon freshly ground black pepper

½ teaspoon salt

2 cups gluten-free buffalo wing sauce

1. Place all ingredients in a greased 4–6-quart slow cooker. Stir to combine. Cook on high for 2–3 hours or on low for 4–6 hours or until the chicken is easily shredded with a fork. If the sauce is very thin, continue to cook on high uncovered for 30 minutes or until thickened.

2. Shred the chicken and toss with the sauce.

PER SERVING Calories: 140 | Fat: 5g | Protein: 21g | Sodium: 2,000mg | Fiber: 1g | Carbohydrates: 3g | Sugar: 2g

Orange Chicken MA

Orange chicken is one of the most popular Chinese takeout dishes.
It's also one of the easiest to whip up at home. Serve this over brown rice or quinoa.

INGREDIENTS | SERVES 6

¾ cup low-sodium, gluten-free chicken broth

¾ cup orange juice

3 tablespoons grated orange zest, divided

4½ tablespoons apple cider vinegar

¼ cup low-sodium gluten-free soy sauce

¼ cup dark brown sugar

¼ cup honey

2 cloves garlic, minced

½ teaspoon cayenne pepper

1½ pounds boneless, skinless chicken breast

1½ tablespoons cornstarch

1½ tablespoons water

1 teaspoon salt

½ teaspoon ground black pepper

2 tablespoons olive oil

¼ cup chopped chives

Crispy Orange Chicken

For crispier orange chicken, cut the chicken into bite-sized pieces. Dip the pieces into beaten egg and then dredge them in your favorite gluten-free, all-purpose flour blend mixed with a few teaspoons of orange zest.

1. In a medium bowl, mix together broth, orange juice, 1 tablespoon zest, vinegar, soy sauce, brown sugar, honey, garlic, and cayenne pepper. Reserve ½ cup of the marinade and pour the rest into a gallon-sized zip-top plastic bag. Add chicken, seal bag, and shake to combine. Marinate in the refrigerator for at least 1 hour.

2. Bring the reserved marinade to a rapid boil in a small saucepan over high heat. Whisk in cornstarch, water, salt, and pepper. Reduce heat to low and simmer until mixture is thick, about 5 minutes.

3. Remove from heat and stir in remaining orange zest. Set aside and keep warm.

4. Heat oil in a large wok over medium-high heat. Remove chicken from marinade and cook in hot oil until browned on each side, about 6–8 minutes. Pour orange sauce over the chicken once it is on the plate, and garnish with chives.

PER SERVING Calories: 290 | Fat: 7g | Protein: 25g | Sodium: 600mg | Fiber: 0g | Carbohydrates: 30g | Sugar: 24g

Slow Cooker Butter Chicken Wings SC

Slow cooking chicken wings results in a more tender, fall-off-the-bone variety than the fried ones you're probably used to eating. These can be made a few days in advance and store well in the freezer.

INGREDIENTS | SERVES 12

4 tablespoons butter

4 pounds chicken wings

1 medium onion, peeled and diced

3 garlic cloves, chopped

2 teaspoons gluten-free curry powder

1 tablespoon curry paste

1 teaspoon gluten-free garam masala

16 ounces tomato paste

1 teaspoon ginger powder

1 teaspoon cumin

2 teaspoons gluten-free tandoori masala

1 teaspoon salt

1 teaspoon ground black pepper

1 cup 2% plain Greek yogurt

1 (13.5-ounce) can coconut milk

1. Melt butter in a large skillet over medium-high heat. Add chicken, onions, and garlic and cook until chicken is browned on both sides and onions are soft, about 8–10 minutes. Stir in curry powder, curry paste, garam masala, tomato paste, ginger, cumin, tandoori masala, salt, and pepper.

2. Pour the mixture into a 4–6-quart slow cooker and stir in yogurt and coconut milk.

3. Cook the mixture on low for 4–6 hours, until the chicken is tender and the sauce has reduced.

PER SERVING Calories: 334 | Fat: 17g | Protein: 36g | Sodium: 500mg | Fiber: 2g | Carbohydrates: 11g | Sugar: 6g

Potato Chip–Crusted Chicken Breasts

Spruce up the standby chicken dinner by making this crispy and delicious sweet potato chip–crusted chicken breast topped with a spicy mustard-mayo sauce.

INGREDIENTS | SERVES 4 | 40 MINUTES

1 large egg, beaten

¼ cup gluten-free all-purpose flour

4 cups crushed gluten-free sweet potato chips

4 (5-ounce) boneless, skinless chicken breasts

½ cup Creamy Mustard-Mayo Sauce (see recipe in Chapter 3)

1. Preheat oven to 375°F. Grease a 9" × 13" baking dish with gluten-free nonstick cooking spray and set aside.

2. Place egg, flour, and crushed chips into three separate shallow bowls. Dip chicken breasts in flour, dredge in egg, and then liberally cover in chips. Place in the baking dish. Repeat until all of the chicken is coated.

3. Bake for about 35 minutes or until no longer pink in the middle (a meat thermometer should reach 170°F).

4. Drizzle with Creamy Mustard-Mayo Sauce before serving.

PER SERVING Calories: 430 | Fat: 16g | Protein: 35g | Sodium: 650mg | Fiber: 5g | Carbohydrates: 34g | Sugar: 5g

Barbecue Chicken Pizza

Gluten-free pizza crusts often fall apart, flake, or turn into mush after baking. But this crust bakes golden brown and crispy on the outside and fluffy on the inside. Paired with a buffalo chicken topping, it's the pizza to beat.

INGREDIENTS | SERVES 8 | 40 MINUTES

2 tablespoons cornmeal

1 package active dry yeast

1 cup warm water (110°F)

1 tablespoon sugar

2½ cups gluten-free all-purpose flour

2 tablespoons olive oil

1⅓ cups Sticky and Spicy Barbecue Sauce (see recipe in Chapter 3)

2 (5-ounce) chicken breasts, cooked and shredded

¾ cup diced red onion

1 cup sliced orange bell pepper

2 cups shredded Cheddar cheese

½ cup chopped fresh herbs (oregano, basil, parsley, or a combination)

1. Preheat a pizza stone in the oven at 450°F. Dust a pizza peel or large cutting board with cornmeal and set aside.

2. In a large bowl, mix yeast, water, and sugar together. Let sit until foamy, about 10 minutes. Stir in flour and oil.

3. Place the dough onto a floured surface and knead with your hands until smooth and soft. Roll out to a circle about ¼" thick. Transfer dough to pizza peel and then to hot pizza stone.

4. Bake for about 12 minutes, or until lightly browned. Remove crust from oven.

5. Spread 1 cup barbecue sauce over the crust. Top with chicken, onion, and peppers. Drizzle with the remaining barbecue sauce.

6. Cover the toppings with the shredded cheese. Return to pizza stone and bake for about 13–15 minutes, or until cheese is melted. Garnish with herbs before serving.

PER SERVING Calories: 460 | Fat: 15g | Protein: 20g | Sodium: 800mg | Fiber: 3g | Carbohydrates: 67g | Sugar: 22g

Mini Turkey Meatloaves

The classic diner favorite is made healthier and more flavorful with ground turkey and tart, fresh cranberries. Forming the mixture into smaller loaves means dinner is on the table in no time. You can also make one larger meatloaf in a loaf pan. It will need about 50–60 minutes in the oven.

INGREDIENTS | SERVES 8 | 40 MINUTES

½ pound 98% fat-free ground turkey

1 large white onion, peeled and chopped

2 garlic cloves, finely minced

1½ tablespoons gluten-free Worcestershire sauce

1 tablespoon gluten-free ketchup

⅓ cup gluten-free low-sodium vegetable broth

2 large eggs

¾ cup gluten-free bread crumbs

1 teaspoon salt

1 teaspoon ground black pepper

1 tablespoon crushed red pepper

1 teaspoon oregano

4 cups fresh cranberries

⅓ cup raw cane sugar

⅓ cup water

1 cup no-sugar-added cranberry juice

1 teaspoon cinnamon

2 tablespoons freshly grated orange peel

1. Preheat oven to 375°F. Line a large baking sheet with aluminum foil. Liberally grease foil with gluten-free cooking spray and set aside.

2. In a large bowl, mix ground turkey, onion, garlic, Worcestershire sauce, ketchup, and broth. Thoroughly mix in eggs.

3. Stir in bread crumbs, salt, black pepper, crushed red pepper, and oregano.

4. Form mixture into 8 small ovals and place on prepared baking sheet. Bake for 25–30 minutes, or until a meat thermometer registers 170°F. Let cool 5 minutes before removing from foil.

5. While meatloaf is cooking, bring cranberries, sugar, water, and cranberry juice to a boil in a medium saucepan over high heat, stirring constantly. Reduce heat to medium-low and cook an additional 5–8 minutes, or until cranberries have popped (they will literally make popping noises!). Stir in cinnamon and orange zest.

6. Top each mini loaf with a spoonful of cranberry sauce or serve the sauce on the side.

PER SERVING Calories: 280 | Fat: 10g | Protein: 20g | Sodium: 450mg | Fiber: 3g | Carbohydrates: 28g | Sugar: 3.5g

Turkey-Stuffed Sweet Potatoes

This easy dinner is like Thanksgiving in one delicious bite.
Make this when you have leftover baked sweet potatoes and turkey.

INGREDIENTS | SERVES 2 | 25 MINUTES

2 large baked sweet potatoes
2 tablespoons butter
4 tablespoons heavy cream
½ teaspoon salt
½ teaspoon ground black pepper
¾ cup shredded cooked turkey
2 tablespoons shredded white Cheddar cheese
3 tablespoons cranberry sauce
2 tablespoons chopped arugula

Make Your Own Crumbs!

Gluten-free bread crumbs can be made at home very easily with crusty gluten-free bread or toast. Simply pour into a blender and pulverize until fine like a bread crumb! If you want flavors, add in your favorite cheeses, spices, and salt and pepper.

1. Preheat oven to 375°F.

2. Cut sweet potatoes lengthwise and scoop out the insides (carefully so as not to break the skin) and place in a medium bowl. Place skins on a baking sheet lined with foil and set aside.

3. Add butter and cream to sweet potatoes. Purée with an electric mixer. Add salt and pepper.

4. Scoop about 2–3 tablespoons mashed sweet potatoes back into each potato skin. Top with turkey. Bake for about 10 minutes.

5. Remove potatoes from oven and top with cheese. Return to oven and bake for another 5 minutes or until cheese is melted. Transfer sweet potatoes to a serving dish.

6. Top each sweet potato with cranberry sauce and garnish with arugula. Serve immediately.

PER SERVING Calories: 465 | Fat: 26g | Protein: 20g | Sodium: 700mg | Fiber: 4g | Carbohydrates: 37g | Sugar: 15g

CHAPTER 9

Fish and Seafood

Beer-Battered Fish

When it comes to deep-fried foods, most fryers in restaurants are contaminated with gluten. However, you can still treat yourself to the occasional deep-fried meal at home, like this restaurant-style beer-battered fish.

INGREDIENTS | SERVES 8 | 25 MINUTES

Enough vegetable oil for deep-frying, about 2" in your pot/fryer

8 (4-ounce) cod or tilapia fillets

3 teaspoons salt, divided

2 teaspoons freshly ground black pepper, divided

1 cup brown rice flour

¼ cup plus 2 tablespoons potato starch

2 tablespoons tapioca starch

2 tablespoons garlic powder

2 tablespoons paprika

1 large egg, beaten

12 ounces gluten-free beer

1. Heat the oil in a heavy-bottomed pot or a deep fryer until it reaches 365°F. Rinse fish, pat dry, and season with 1 teaspoon salt and ½ teaspoon pepper.

2. In a medium bowl, whisk together the brown rice flour, potato starch, and tapioca starch and place ½ cup of the flour mixture into a shallow dish. Lay fish fillets in ½ cup of the flour mixture, just to coat them on both sides. Shake off excess.

3. Combine the remaining gluten-free flour mixture, garlic powder, paprika, and remaining salt and pepper. Stir egg into dry ingredients. Gradually mix in beer until a thin batter is formed. You should be able to see the fish through the batter after it has been dipped.

4. Dip fish fillets into batter, then gently drop one at a time into hot oil. Fry fish, turning once, until both sides are a golden brown. Drain on paper towels, and serve while still warm.

PER SERVING Calories: 290 | Fat: 8g | Protein: 23g | Sodium: 900mg | Fiber: 1g | Carbohydrates: 27g | Sugar: 0g

Lobster with Sherry Sauce

*This might become your new favorite way to serve up lobster. The sherry adds
a great flavor without weighing down the fish with butters or creams.*

INGREDIENTS | SERVES 4 | 30 MINUTES

4 chicken lobsters, 1–1¼ pounds each

1 teaspoon gluten-free Asian five-spice powder

1 clove garlic, minced

1 teaspoon parsley

¼ cup sesame seed oil

¼ cup sherry

Juice of ½ lemon

2 tablespoons minced gingerroot

1. Boil the lobsters for 20 minutes, then split them and crack the claws. Place the lobsters in a baking dish. Leave in the shell.

2. Preheat the broiler to 500°F.

3. In a medium saucepan, mix the rest of the ingredients together to make the sauce. Bring to a boil and then spoon over the lobsters.

4. Broil for 3 minutes. Serve.

PER SERVING Calories: 650 | Fat: 18g | Protein: 105g | Sodium: 1,500mg | Fiber: 0g | Carbohydrates: 6g | Sugar: 1g

Chinese Shrimp Balls

*These Chinese favorites make the perfect party apps. Serve with your favorite
dipping sauce for an easy snack or appetizer!*

INGREDIENTS | SERVES 8 | 20 MINUTES

1 pound raw shrimp, peeled and deveined

1 large egg

1 tablespoon dry sherry

2 teaspoons gluten-free soy sauce

1 teaspoon sugar

1 tablespoon cornstarch

1 cup lean ground pork

2 scallions, chopped

3 cups vegetable oil

1. Place all ingredients, except the vegetable oil, in a food processor. Pulse until thoroughly mixed, scraping the sides often.

2. Heat the oil to 360°F. Carefully place the shrimp mixture by the teaspoonful into the oil. When golden, after about 3–4 minutes, place the balls on a serving platter lined with paper towels or napkins to drain. Serve and enjoy.

PER SERVING Calories: 190 | Fat: 12g | Protein: 17g | Sodium: 180mg | Fiber: 0g | Carbohydrates: 2g | Sugar: 1g

Red Snapper in White Wine Sauce

This sauce can be used with any fish or meat, mashed potatoes, or rice. Feel free to adjust the amount of herbs or add some sliced mushrooms, olives, capers, or green peppercorns.

INGREDIENTS | SERVES 2 | 30 MINUTES

2 (8-ounce) red snapper fillets

1 teaspoon salt

1 teaspoon ground black pepper

½ cup minced sweet onion

1 garlic clove, minced

2 tablespoons unsalted butter

2 tablespoons extra-virgin olive oil, divided

3 tablespoons cornstarch

1 cup gluten-free chicken broth, warmed

½ cup dry white wine or white vermouth

½ teaspoon prepared gluten-free Dijon mustard

¼ cup chopped parsley

1 teaspoon shredded fresh basil

½ teaspoon dried tarragon or rosemary

1. Season the fillets with salt and pepper on both sides.

2. In a medium skillet over medium heat, sauté the onion and garlic for 4 minutes in the butter and 1 tablespoon oil. Whisk in the cornstarch and cook for 3–4 minutes.

3. Whisk in the warm chicken broth, stirring until smooth. Then add the wine or vermouth. Swirl in the mustard and herbs. Simmer over low heat for 10 minutes, stirring occasionally.

4. While sauce is simmering, place remaining 1 tablespoon olive oil in another medium skillet over medium heat. Add fish and cook approximately 3–4 minutes on each side. Move the fish to a plate. Pour the sauce over the top and serve hot.

PER SERVING Calories: 600 | Fat: 30g | Protein: 50g | Sodium: 1,500mg | Fiber: 1g | Carbohydrates: 23g | Sugar: 2g

Fish Tacos with Tropical Fruit Salsa

These folded tacos can be stuffed with a number of different toppings. Although tacos originated in Mexico, fish tacos are said to have been born in Southern California. Serve these tacos with shredded lettuce, sliced avocado, sour cream, and extra cilantro.

INGREDIENTS | SERVES 6 | 30 MINUTES

½ teaspoon gluten-free chili powder

1 teaspoon oregano, dried

2 cloves garlic, minced

1 teaspoon cumin

1 teaspoon cilantro, minced

½ teaspoon red pepper flakes

1 pound boneless cod fillets, fresh, or frozen and thawed

Juice of 1 medium lime

1 teaspoon salt

½ teaspoon freshly ground black pepper

12 corn tortillas, warmed

Tropical Fruit Salsa (see recipe in Chapter 3)

1. Preheat oven to 375°F.

2. In a small bowl, mix chili powder, oregano, garlic, cumin, cilantro, and red pepper flakes.

3. Place cod fillets on a large sheet of aluminum foil and squeeze lime juice over top of them. With a spoon, sprinkle prepared seasonings on each side of the fillets. Season with salt and pepper. Fold the foil around the fish, and seal top to create a pouch. Place pouch on a baking tray.

4. Bake in the oven for 20 minutes or until fish easily flakes with a fork. Divide fish among the corn tortillas and top with Tropical Fruit Salsa.

PER SERVING Calories: 215 | Fat: 2g | Protein: 17g | Sodium: 600mg | Fiber: 5g | Carbohydrates: 33g | Sugar: 9g

Marseille Whipped Cod and Potatoes

You can use either salt cod or fresh cod in this dish. If you use salt cod, you'll need to soak overnight in 2 cups cold water, changing the water once or twice. You can also substitute half-and-half for the milk or cream if you would like to lighten it up.

INGREDIENTS | SERVES 4 | 40 MINUTES

4 medium potatoes (2 pounds)
2 tablespoons extra-virgin olive oil
½ cup light cream
1 teaspoon salt
½ teaspoon freshly ground black pepper
1 teaspoon dried basil
1¼ pounds fresh cod
¼ cup chopped chives
¼ cup chopped parsley

1. Boil the potatoes in their skins until a knife slides into the flesh easily, about 20 minutes.

2. Using a long-handled fork, spear the boiled potatoes and peel them. Put the potatoes through a ricer and into a bowl. Whisk in the olive oil and the cream, then add salt, pepper, and basil and keep warm.

3. Steam the cod about 15 minutes, until very tender. Make sure there are no bones.

4. Place the cod in a food processor and process until smooth.

5. Fold the cod into the potatoes and mix in the chives and parsley. Blend with a fork until fluffy. Serve hot.

PER SERVING Calories: 390 | Fat: 14g | Protein: 30g | Sodium: 600mg | Fiber: 6g | Carbohydrates: 37g | Sugar: 3g

Poached Monkfish in Caper Butter Sauce

*Monkfish is a mild, sweet fish that is wonderful cooked in many ways.
It is delicious poached, broiled, or baked.*

INGREDIENTS | SERVES 4 | 25 MINUTES

2 tablespoons olive oil

½ cup potato flour

1½ pounds monkfish, cut in 4 serving pieces

¼ cup dry white wine

¼ cup gluten-free chicken broth

1 tablespoon butter

2 tablespoons gluten-free capers

½ teaspoon salt

½ teaspoon freshly ground black pepper

1 teaspoon paprika

4 lemon wedges

1. Heat olive oil in a large skillet over medium-high heat. Place the flour in a shallow bowl, dredge the fish in flour, then sauté it in hot skillet, about 4 minutes per side.

2. Add the wine, broth, butter, and capers. Bring liquid just to a boil. Reduce heat to low and simmer for about 8 minutes, or until the fish is cooked through. Remove fish from skillet and keep warm. Increase heat to medium-high and cook liquid until reduced by half, about 5 minutes. Pour sauce over fish.

3. Sprinkle with salt, pepper, and paprika. Serve with lemon wedges.

PER SERVING Calories: 250 | Fat: 6g | Protein: 26g | Sodium: 500mg | Fiber: 2g | Carbohydrates: 20g | Sugar: 1g

Maryland-Style Crab Cakes with Country Ham

The addition of country ham balances the sweetness of the crabmeat.

INGREDIENTS | SERVES 4 | 20 MINUTES

½ cup mayonnaise

2 large eggs

1 teaspoon gluten-free Dijon-style mustard

1 teaspoon gluten-free Worcestershire sauce

1 teaspoon salt

1 teaspoon red pepper flakes

1 tablespoon fresh lemon juice

1 cup gluten-free cornbread crumbs, divided

1¼ pounds lump blue crabmeat

2 cups vegetable oil

4 lemon wedges

1. In a large bowl, mix the mayonnaise, eggs, mustard, Worcestershire sauce, salt, pepper flakes, and lemon juice. Stir until well mixed.

2. Add half the cornbread crumbs and gently toss in the crabmeat. Form 8 cakes and coat with more cornbread crumbs.

3. Over medium heat, bring the oil to 300°F. Fry the cakes, turning after 5 minutes, until golden brown. Serve with lemon wedges.

PER SERVING Calories: 490 | Fat: 35g | Protein: 30g | Sodium: 1,200mg | Fiber: 2g | Carbohydrates: 13g | Sugar: 3g

Sole Florentine

Sole is an adaptable fish; mild and sweet, it goes with many different flavors.
Frozen spinach works fine in this recipe.

INGREDIENTS | SERVES 4 | 30 MINUTES

3 tablespoons unsalted butter

1 shallot, minced

3 tablespoons cornstarch

2 (10-ounce) packages frozen chopped spinach, thawed, moisture squeezed out

⅔ cup heavy cream

¼ teaspoon nutmeg

4 sole fillets (1½ pounds)

1 large egg, beaten

½ cup rice or potato flour

1 teaspoon salt

½ teaspoon freshly ground black pepper

⅔ cup olive oil

¼ cup Parmesan cheese

1. Melt the butter in a large skillet over medium heat, and sauté the shallot until softened, about 5 minutes. Blend in the cornstarch, cooking until smooth.

2. Add the spinach, cream, and nutmeg. Cook and stir until thickened, about 10 minutes. Pour into a baking dish treated with gluten-free nonstick spray and set aside.

3. Dip the pieces of sole in beaten egg. Then, on a sheet of waxed paper, mix the flour, salt, and pepper. Dredge the sole in the flour mixture.

4. Sauté the sole in the olive oil until lightly browned, about 4 minutes per side. Arrange over the spinach mixture. Sprinkle with cheese. Run under the broiler until very brown and hot, about 3 minutes.

PER SERVING Calories: 670 | Fat: 42g | Protein: 42g | Sodium: 800mg | Fiber: 4g | Carbohydrates: 32g | Sugar: 1g

Cod Broiled on a Bed of Paper-Thin Potatoes

Cod is one of the world's most beloved and versatile fish. It can be baked, broiled, steamed, poached, salted, or cooked with milk in a stew. This dish is simple yet delicious.

INGREDIENTS | SERVES 4 | 45 MINUTES

2 pounds Idaho or Yukon gold potatoes, peeled and sliced paper-thin

¼ cup extra-virgin olive oil

2 tablespoons butter, melted

1 teaspoon salt

½ teaspoon freshly ground black pepper

4 (5-ounce) cod fillets or steaks

1 tablespoon butter

¼ cup chopped parsley

4 lemon wedges

1. Preheat the oven to 400°F.

2. In a baking pan that has been treated with gluten-free nonstick spray, toss the thinly sliced potatoes with oil and melted butter, salt, and pepper.

3. Bake the potatoes for 30 minutes or until the top is brown and crisp and the inside soft.

4. When the potatoes are done, lay the fish on top, dot with butter, and turn the oven to broil.

5. Broil until the fish is done—8–10 minutes, depending on the thickness of the fish. If the potatoes start to burn, move the pan to a lower shelf in the oven.

6. Sprinkle with chopped parsley and serve with lemon wedges.

PER SERVING Calories: 470 | Fat: 23g | Protein: 29g | Sodium: 600mg | Fiber: 6g | Carbohydrates: 36g | Sugar: 3g

Southern Fried Oysters

These are so crunchy on the outside and succulent on the inside, you will probably have to make an extra batch. Fried oysters are best when served with a squeeze of fresh lemon juice.

INGREDIENTS | SERVES 4 | 20 MINUTES

1 quart shucked oysters

½ cup corn flour

1 cup cornmeal

1 teaspoon baking powder

¼ teaspoon nutmeg

½ teaspoon dried parsley

½ teaspoon salt

½ teaspoon freshly ground black pepper

2 large eggs, beaten

2 cups vegetable oil

1. Place the oysters in a colander to drain.

2. In a large bowl, thoroughly mix the flour, cornmeal, baking powder, nutmeg, parsley, salt, and pepper.

3. Dip the oysters in the beaten egg and then in the flour-and-cornmeal mixture.

4. Bring the oil in a pot to 375°F and fry oysters for about 3–4 minutes or until browned.

5. Remove with a slotted spoon. Drain on paper towels.

PER SERVING Calories: 430 | Fat: 14g | Protein: 24g | Sodium: 900mg | Fiber: 2g | Carbohydrates: 51g | Sugar: 1g

Savory Shark and Bacon

Shark is a melt-in-your-mouth kind of fish—and it really deserves to be cooked more often. It is sweet and tender.

INGREDIENTS | SERVES 4 | 20 MINUTES

2 tablespoons chili sauce

1 tablespoon concentrated orange juice

1 tablespoon gluten-free Worcestershire sauce

Juice of ½ large lemon

1 teaspoon Tabasco sauce

1¼ pounds boneless shark steak, cut into serving pieces

1 teaspoon salt

½ teaspoon freshly ground black pepper

4 strips bacon

1. Preheat broiler. In a small bowl, mix the chili sauce, orange juice, Worcestershire sauce, lemon juice, and Tabasco sauce.

2. Rinse and pat the shark steaks dry. Sprinkle with salt and pepper. Paint them with the sauce mixture.

3. Place them on a broiler pan that you have treated with gluten-free nonstick spray. Arrange the bacon on top of the shark and broil for 3 minutes. Turn the bacon and broil for 2 more minutes. Turn off the broiler and close the door to let the shark cook through, about 6 minutes.

PER SERVING Calories: 300 | Fat: 16g | Protein: 32g | Sodium: 1,000mg | Fiber: 1g | Carbohydrates: 4g | Sugar: 2g

Parmesan-Crusted Tilapia

Tilapia is a mild-mannered fish that makes a great accompaniment to many different flavors. We love this crunchy Italian version made with Parmesan cheese and fresh herbs.

INGREDIENTS | SERVES 2 | 30 MINUTES

2 tablespoons extra-virgin olive oil, divided

¼ cup wheat-free bread crumbs or cornmeal

¼ cup grated Parmesan cheese

1 teaspoon dried basil

½ teaspoon dried oregano

½ teaspoon onion powder

½ teaspoon red pepper flakes

½ teaspoon dried rosemary

2 garlic cloves, minced

½ teaspoon salt

¼ teaspoon ground black pepper

1 tablespoon freshly squeezed lemon juice

3 or 4 tilapia fillets, depending on their size, washed and dried

1. Preheat oven to 425°F.

2. In a medium bowl, combine 1 tablespoon olive oil, bread crumbs, Parmesan cheese, seasonings, garlic, salt, and pepper. Stir to combine.

3. On a medium-size plated, pour lemon juice.

4. Dip each fillet in lemon juice and then in the bread crumb mixture to coat evenly on both sides. Place in baking dish that is well oiled. Sprinkle with remaining 1 tablespoon olive oil and additional Parmesan cheese, if you desire. Cover with aluminum foil so fish remains moist.

5. Bake for 20 minutes, or until the edges are browning. Take baking dish out of the oven and put the broiler on. Broil on medium for about 2 minutes so fillets get crispy.

PER SERVING Calories: 420 | Fat: 21g | Protein: 46g | Sodium: 900mg | Fiber: 1g | Carbohydrates: 13g | Sugar: 1g

Mussels Mariniere

This is a thick, creamy stew that can be made regardless of the season.
Serve with pasta or rice for an easy, fresh dish.

INGREDIENTS | SERVES 8 | 30 MINUTES

2 tablespoons butter

½ cup finely chopped onion

2 tablespoons cornstarch

1 cup dry white wine

½ cup celery tops, chopped

4 pounds mussels, scrubbed and tapped

1 cup heavy cream

1 teaspoon salt

½ teaspoon freshly ground black pepper

Juice of ½ large lemon

½ cup chopped fresh Italian flat-leaf parsley

Check Your Mussels

You must be sure that your mussels are alive. This means they are shut tightly, and when you tap two together, you get a sharp click, not a hollow thump. Often, they will be slightly open but will close when tapped—that's fine. Just don't use any that are cracked, open, or hollow-sounding. The same is true for clams. Always scrub clams and mussels with a stiff brush under cold running water.

1. Heat butter in a large, high-sided frying pan over medium-high heat. Sauté the onion until soft, about 5 minutes. Stir in the cornstarch and mix until smooth. Whisk in the white wine and add the celery tops. Increase heat to high and bring to a boil.

2. Pour in the prepared mussels. Cover and continue to boil for 2 minutes, stirring to bring the bottom ones to the top.

3. Have a large serving bowl on the side of the pot. Remove mussels as they open.

4. When all of the mussels are open and removed from the pot, reduce heat to medium-low and add the cream. Heat for 5 minutes, but do not boil. Add salt and pepper.

5. Pour sauce over the mussels; sprinkle with lemon juice and parsley. Serve in warm bowls with a big bowl for the shells.

PER SERVING Calories: 360 | Fat: 19g | Protein: 27g | Sodium: 400mg | Fiber: 0.5g | Carbohydrates: 13g | Sugar: 1g

Seafood à la King MA

You can make the sauce the day before and add the seafood at the last minute.
Serve with rice or stuffed into crepes.

INGREDIENTS | SERVES 4 | 25 MINUTES

¼ cup unsalted butter

½ cup minced shallots

20 small white mushrooms, cut in half

20 pearl onions, fresh or frozen, cut in half

2 tablespoons cornstarch

2 ounces cold water

1 tablespoon tomato paste

2 tablespoons brandy

1½ cups cream

1 teaspoon salt

½ teaspoon freshly ground black pepper

½ pound shrimp, cleaned and deveined

½ pound bay scallops

2 tablespoons red salmon caviar

Long Live the King!

This dish was created at the Brighton Beach Hotel on Long Island, New York, by Chef George Greenwald for his boss, E. Clarke King, II. It became very popular when Campbell's came out with canned cream of mushroom soup, used as a base.

1. Heat butter in a medium skillet over medium heat. Sauté the shallots for 5 minutes. Add the mushrooms and pearl onions. Stir, cooking for 2 more minutes.

2. Mix the cornstarch with cold water and add to the pan, stirring to blend. Blend in the tomato paste and brandy. Warm the cream slightly, then stir it into the sauce in the pan. (You can prepare this dish in advance up to this point. Store in the refrigerator until ready to serve.)

3. Reheat the sauce but do not boil. Add salt, pepper, shrimp, and scallops. When the shrimp turns pink (about 10 minutes), the dish is done. Garnish with caviar and serve.

PER SERVING Calories: 570 | Fat: 41g | Protein: 27g | Sodium: 800mg | Fiber: 2g | Carbohydrates: 21g | Sugar: 5g

Sesame-Glazed Planked Salmon

This flavor-packed salmon is cooked on a plank over an open flame, which ensures the fish is cooked thoroughly without burning. It's best topped with fresh herbs, like cilantro, and served with rice.

INGREDIENTS | SERVES 2

2½ tablespoons extra-virgin olive oil

1½ tablespoons gluten-free soy sauce

1 tablespoon sesame oil

1 tablespoon molasses

1½ tablespoons gluten-free Dijon mustard

1½ teaspoons minced garlic

2 tablespoons chopped crystalized ginger

2 tablespoons chopped fresh chives

2 tablespoons chopped fresh cilantro

2 (5-ounce) skin-on salmon fillets

1 large wooden plank, soaked in water overnight

2 teaspoons sesame seeds

Preparing Planks for the Grill

Use only untreated cedar, alder, hickory, or maple for grilling. It's important to soak the plank for at least 1 hour in cold water. This adds moisture and prevents the plank from burning. You can season your plank if it's being used for the first time by cooking on a preheated grill to get a smoky flavor.

1. Whisk olive oil, soy sauce, sesame oil, molasses, mustard, garlic, ginger, chives, and cilantro in a medium bowl. Pour the mixture into a large baking dish and add the salmon. Turn fillets to coat. Cover dish with plastic wrap and marinate in the refrigerator for at least 2 hours. Remove salmon from dish and reserve marinade.

2. Preheat one side of a gas or charcoal grill to medium-high heat. Place the plank directly over the heat source for about 2 minutes.

3. Move the plank to the indirect heat side of the grill and place salmon on top. Drizzle with the reserved marinade; sprinkle with sesame seeds. Close the grill and cook until salmon is fully cooked, about 10 minutes.

PER SERVING Calories: 380 | Fat: 20g | Protein: 29g | Sodium: 600mg | Fiber: 1g | Carbohydrates: 21g | Sugar: 10g

Ahi Tuna and Melon Spring Rolls

These spring rolls are an easy, healthy, and gluten-free appetizer or dinner option for spring and summer.

INGREDIENTS | SERVES 5 | 30 MINUTES

2 ounces brown rice noodles

10 large rice paper spring roll wrappers

4 ounces ahi tuna fillet, diced

5 ounces extra-firm tofu, pressed, drained, and diced

1 cup diced cantaloupe

½ cup chopped chives

5 large basil leaves, cut in half

⅓ cup chopped wasabi peas

1 teaspoon cracked black pepper

½ cup gluten-free spicy chili sauce

1. Bring a small pot of water to a rapid boil over high heat. Add the rice noodles and immediately remove pot from heat. Let sit for about 15 minutes, or until noodles have softened. Drain noodles and set aside.

2. Dampen a tea towel with water and place over a cutting board. Fill a medium bowl with cold water and set it beside the cutting board. Working with one rice paper at a time, soak each wrap in the cold water for about 10–15 seconds or until pliable. Remove from the water and place on the damp tea towel.

3. Layer a few pieces of tuna on the half of the paper closest to you. Add a few slices of tofu, cantaloupe, noodles, and chives on top of the tuna. Add a basil leaf half and a sprinkle of chopped wasabi peas, leaving about 1½" free on either side. Top with cracked pepper.

4. Working carefully, fold the roll up like you would an egg roll, folding the sides into the roll. Set aside and cover with another damp towel. (Be sure to keep the rolls covered while you make the rest. Otherwise, the rice paper will harden.)

5. Repeat with the remaining spring roll wrappers. Serve with chili sauce for dipping.

PER SERVING Calories: 315 | Fat: 3g | Protein: 16g | Sodium: 800mg | Fiber: 4g | Carbohydrates: 54g | Sugar: 6g

Open-Faced Lobster Sandwiches with Hollandaise

*Lobster is one of the most elegant and sophisticated types of seafood,
and it quickly jazzes up any of your favorite sandwiches. Soft, buttery lobster meat
is paired with low-fat hollandaise sauce for a fun breakfast-for-dinner sandwich.*

INGREDIENTS | SERVES 4 | 25 MINUTES

2 tablespoons butter

½ cup light cream

2 tablespoons cornstarch

1 teaspoon salt

½ teaspoon ground black pepper

2 large eggs, beaten

1 cup nonfat buttermilk

2 tablespoons lemon juice

5 tablespoons finely diced lobster meat

4 gluten-free English muffins

4 pieces part-skim sliced mozzarella cheese

⅔ cup baby arugula

About ½ cup chopped lobster tail meat

4 large eggs, poached

4 tablespoons chopped tomato

Substitutions

If lobster is too expensive, you can replace it with your favorite seafood, like crab or shrimp.

1. Melt butter in a medium saucepan over medium-high heat until golden brown. Remove from heat and pour into a small bowl.

2. Return saucepan to heat and add cream, cornstarch, salt, and pepper. Whisk the mixture constantly until smooth. Reduce heat to low. Gradually whisk in beaten eggs, melted butter, and buttermilk until sauce is smooth. Remove from heat and stir in lemon juice and diced lobster meat. Set aside and keep warm.

3. Toast English muffins and immediately top 4 halves with a slice of cheese. Top with arugula, chopped lobster tail meat, and poached eggs.

4. Pour about 2 tablespoons of lobster sauce over each egg and garnish with chopped tomato. Serve immediately.

PER SERVING Calories: 515 | Fat: 22g | Protein: 31g | Sodium: 1,200mg | Fiber: 2g | Carbohydrates: 36g | Sugar: 4g

Crispy Potato Chip and Cheese Baked Shrimp

Looking for a healthy, easy, and delicious one-pot weeknight dinner? Try this healthy and flavorful crispy baked shrimp! You won't be able to have just one bite.

INGREDIENTS | SERVES 4 | 30 MINUTES

3 cloves garlic, minced

2 tablespoons extra-virgin olive oil

⅔ cup crushed gluten-free kettle-style potato chips

¼ cup gluten-free chicken broth

½ teaspoon crushed red pepper

½ teaspoon chili powder

½ teaspoon salt

½ teaspoon ground black pepper

1 pound large shrimp, peeled and deveined

⅓ cup shredded part-skim mozzarella cheese

2 tablespoons chopped fresh basil

1. Preheat oven to 375°F. Grease a large oven-safe skillet with gluten-free nonstick cooking spray.

2. In a medium bowl, mix the garlic, olive oil, kettle chips, broth, crushed red pepper, chili powder, salt, and pepper.

3. Lay shrimp in the bottom of the prepared skillet. Press the potato chip mixture over the top of the shrimp with a spatula. Sprinkle with cheese.

4. Bake for at least 20 minutes, or until cheese is melted and the shrimp is pink. Remove from oven and garnish with basil.

PER SERVING Calories: 290 | Fat: 14g | Protein: 26g | Sodium: 600mg | Fiber: 1g | Carbohydrates: 10g | Sugar: 0g

Tequila Grilled Swordfish with Pico de Gallo

Swordfish is a very thick, hearty, and meaty fish. It goes well with almost anything you put on it. Be sure to leave the skin on when you grill swordfish, but remove it before serving, since it can have a rubbery texture.

INGREDIENTS | SERVES 4

¼ cup plus 1 tablespoon extra-virgin olive oil, divided

6 teaspoons gluten-free Mexican seasoning

3 tablespoons tequila

5 tablespoons chopped fresh cilantro, divided

1 tablespoon fresh lemon juice

1 teaspoon salt

1 teaspoon ground black pepper

4 (5-ounce) swordfish steaks

¼ cup sour cream

½ cup pico de gallo

1. Preheat a gas or charcoal grill to medium-high heat.

2. In a large shallow baking dish, whisk ¼ cup olive oil, Mexican seasoning, tequila, 3 tablespoons cilantro, lemon juice, salt, and pepper. Add swordfish and toss to coat.

3. Cover dish with plastic wrap and marinate in the refrigerator for at least 1 hour.

4. Remove swordfish from marinade and brush with remaining olive oil. Grill until just cooked through, about 3 minutes on each side.

5. Top each steak with sour cream, pico de gallo, and remaining cilantro.

PER SERVING Calories: 380 | Fat: 25g | Protein: 28g | Sodium: 950mg | Fiber: 1g | Carbohydrates: 4g | Sugar: 2g

Breakfast for Dinner

Corn Crepes MA

As with the Chestnut Flour Crepes (see recipe in this chapter), you can make these in advance and store them in the refrigerator or freezer. You can stuff these with salsa, jack cheese, and sour cream, or you can stuff them with mashed fruit such as strawberries.

INGREDIENTS | MAKES 12 CREPES | 15 MINUTES

2 large eggs

1 cup milk or buttermilk

1 teaspoon salt

1 cup corn flour

2 teaspoons sugar

2 tablespoons butter, melted

2 tablespoons vegetable oil

Storing Crepes

To store crepes, simply put a bit of corn flour on sheets of waxed paper and stack the crepes individually. Then put the whole thing in a plastic bag and store.

1. Place the eggs, milk, and salt in your food processor and process until smooth. With the motor on low, slowly add the flour and spoon in the sugar. Scrape down the sides of the jar often. Add melted butter.

2. Heat a medium nonstick pan over medium heat and add a spoonful of vegetable oil. Pour in ½ cup batter. Tilt the pan to spread the batter evenly. Cook until lightly browned on both sides.

3. Place crepes on sheets of waxed paper that have been dusted with extra corn flour. Continue with remaining batter, adding more oil to the pan if needed.

4. To store, place in a plastic bag in refrigerator or freezer.

PER SERVING (2 CREPES) | Calories: 205 | Fat: 11g | Protein: 4.5g | Sodium: 400mg | Fiber: 0g | Carbohydrates: 20g | Sugar: 3g

Corn Crepes with Eggs, Cheese, and Salsa

These Mexican-style crepes make a fantastic quick supper,
especially if you have some Corn Crepes in the freezer!

**INGREDIENTS | MAKES 12 CREPES |
15 MINUTES**

1 recipe Corn Crepes (see recipe in this chapter)

12 thin slices jack or pepper jack cheese

12 large eggs, poached or fried sunny-side up

12 teaspoons salsa

12 teaspoons grated Parmesan cheese

1. Place the crepes on cookie sheets that you've prepared with gluten-free nonstick spray. Put a slice of cheese on each crepe. Place 1 egg on each piece of cheese. Spoon a bit of salsa on top of each egg.

2. Preheat the broiler to 400°F. Sprinkle the crepes with Parmesan cheese and broil for about 5 minutes, until cheese is hot and starting to melt.

3. You could also put the jack cheese on top of the eggs if you wish, and serve the salsa on the side.

PER SERVING (2 CREPES) | Calories: 575 | Fat: 39g | Protein: 32g | Sodium: 1,000mg | Fiber: 0.5g | Carbohydrates: 22g | Sugar: 5g

Ham and Asparagus Rolls with Cheese

These easy-to-make, filling rolls are packed with protein and antioxidants,
so it's a healthy and delicious meal for any day of the week.

INGREDIENTS | SERVES 6 | 30 MINUTES

1 (10-ounce) package frozen asparagus

½ pound smoked ham, thinly sliced

½ pound white American cheese, thinly sliced

1 recipe Creamy Cheddar Sauce with Ham and Sherry (see recipe in Chapter 3)

1. Preheat oven to 350°F. Drop frozen asparagus in boiling water for 1 minute and dry on paper towels. Lay out the slices of ham. Place a slice of cheese and then an asparagus spear on each ham slice. Roll up and secure with toothpicks if necessary.

2. Place the rolls in a glass baking pan that you've treated with gluten-free nonstick spray. Pour cheese sauce over the top.

3. Bake for 25 minutes or until lightly browned on top and heated through. Serve hot.

PER SERVING Calories: 390 | Fat: 26g | Protein: 25g | Sodium: 1,000mg | Fiber: 1g | Carbohydrates: 13g | Sugar: 5g

Spicy Egg-and-Cheese-Stuffed Tomatoes

This is a fine way to use up the end-of-summer tomatoes in your garden.

INGREDIENTS | SERVES 4 | 30 MINUTES

8 medium tomatoes

1 teaspoon salt

1 teaspoon ground black pepper

1 teaspoon cayenne pepper

1 teaspoon cumin powder

1 teaspoon dried oregano

4 tablespoons butter

2 cloves garlic, minced or put through a garlic press

8 large eggs

½ cup grated Monterey jack or Cheddar cheese

8 teaspoons gluten-free cornbread crumbs

Priceless Heirlooms

There are good tomatoes in the supermarket and good tomatoes in cans, but the best tomatoes are homegrown. Recently there has been a trend toward growing ancient varieties of tomato. These "heirlooms," as they are called, have more flavor, sweetness paired with acid, than ordinary tomatoes. You can buy the seeds and grow them yourself, and some greenmarkets have them, too.

1. Cut the tops off the tomatoes, core, and using a melon baller, scoop out seeds and pulp. Place the tomatoes on a baking sheet covered with parchment paper or sprayed with gluten-free nonstick spray.

2. In a small bowl, mix salt, black pepper, cayenne, cumin, and oregano together. Set aside.

3. Preheat the oven to 350°F.

4. Heat butter in a small skillet over medium heat. Add the garlic and sauté for 5 minutes. Spoon the butter and garlic mixture into the tomatoes. Sprinkle half the spice mixture on the insides of the tomatoes.

5. Break an egg into each tomato. Sprinkle with the rest of the spice mixture. Loosely spoon the cheese over the eggs, then sprinkle 1 teaspoon cornbread crumbs over each tomato. Bake for 20 minutes. The tomatoes should still be firm, the eggs soft, the cheese melted, and the bread crumbs browned.

PER SERVING Calories: 368 | Fat: 27g | Protein: 18g | Sodium: 850mg | Fiber: 3g | Carbohydrates: 14g | Sugar: 8g

Chestnut Flour Crepes

*Chestnut flour is sweet and nutty, making the most delicious crepes you can imagine.
You can stuff them with fruit and whipped cream, or with savory fillings.
Omit the sugar if you are going to fill these crepes with savory delights.*

**INGREDIENTS | MAKES 12 CREPES |
15 MINUTES**

2 large eggs

1 cup whole milk

½ teaspoon salt

½ cup chestnut flour

½ cup rice flour

2 teaspoons sugar

2 tablespoons melted butter, plus more
for pan

Using Nonstick Sauté Pans

Nonstick pans take all of the grief out of
making crepes. However, even if your pan
is quite new, it's important to use a bit of
butter for insurance and extra flavor. Keep
the pan well buttered and you have an
almost foolproof method for making perfect crepes.

1. Process the eggs, milk, and salt in your food processor.
   With the motor on low, slowly add the flours, stopping
   occasionally to scrape down the sides of the jar.

2. Add the sugar and 2 tablespoons melted butter.
   Process until well blended. Pour by ½-cupful into a
   medium nonstick sauté pan to which you've added a
   dot of butter. Tilt the pan to spread the batter thinly.

3. Fry the crepes on medium heat, turning, until browned
   on both sides; place on waxed paper and sprinkle with
   a bit of rice flour to prevent them from sticking.

4. When the crepes are done, you can fill them right
   away or store them in the refrigerator or freezer for
   later use.

PER SERVING (2 CREPES) | Calories: 195 | Fat: 12g | Protein: 5g |
Sodium: 235mg | Fiber: 1g | Carbohydrates: 15g | Sugar: 4g

Chestnut Crepes with Prosciutto and Peach Sauce

If you can't find mascarpone cheese, use cream cheese. You can make the crepes and sauce and fill the crepes in advance. Just heat everything up at the last moment.

INGREDIENT | SERVES 4 | 35 MINUTES

2 tablespoons cornstarch

¼ cup cold water

2 peaches, blanched, peeled, and sliced

Juice of ½ large lemon

1 teaspoon hot red pepper sauce

½ cup sugar

1 teaspoon freshly ground black pepper

8 small Chestnut Flour Crepes (see recipe in this chapter)

8 teaspoons mascarpone cheese

8 paper-thin slices prosciutto ham

1. Mix the cornstarch in cold water until very smooth. Place in a large saucepan with the peaches, lemon juice, hot sauce, sugar, and black pepper. You may need to add some more water if the peaches are not very juicy. Bring to a boil, stirring constantly, until very thick and syrupy. Remove from heat.

2. Preheat oven to 300°F.

3. Lay the crepes on a baking sheet and spread with the cheese. Place a slice of ham over each and roll.

4. Arrange the rolls, seam-side down, in pie pan or baking dish sprayed with gluten-free nonstick spray and bake for 10–15 minutes or until the crepe rolls are hot. Serve with the peach syrup.

PER SERVING Calories: 405 | Fat: 18g | Protein: 11g | Sodium: 460mg | Fiber: 2g | Carbohydrates: 53g | Sugar: 36g

Crustless Vegetable Quiche Cups

This protein-packed supper can be made with whatever vegetables you have on hand. It's also the perfect way to sneak in your daily dose of vegetables.

INGREDIENTS | SERVES 6 | 45 MINUTES

1 tablespoon canola oil

½ cup finely chopped onion

1 cup fresh organic spinach

1 cup fresh grape or cherry tomatoes, halved

1 cup fresh mushrooms, diced

2 large eggs, beaten

6 large egg whites, beaten

1 cup shredded Cheddar cheese

¼ teaspoon thyme

½ teaspoon sweet basil

¼ teaspoon oregano

¼ teaspoon salt

⅛ teaspoon ground black pepper

Powerful Protein

Studies show that people who consume a breakfast that contains protein tend to eat less throughout the day. One quiche cup has over 6 grams of protein!

1. Preheat the oven to 350°F. Lightly spray a 12-cup muffin tin with gluten-free nonstick cooking spray or line with cupcake liners.

2. Heat oil in a large skillet over medium-high heat. Add the onions and cook, stirring occasionally, until onions are soft, about 2–3 minutes. Stir in spinach, tomatoes, and mushrooms, and continue cooking until veggies have wilted, about 3–4 minutes.

3. In a large bowl, combine the eggs, egg whites, cheese, thyme, basil, oregano, salt, and pepper. Add spinach mixture and stir to blend. Pour into prepared muffin tins.

4. Bake in preheated oven until eggs have set, about 30 minutes. Let cool for 10 minutes before serving.

PER SERVING Calories: 160 | Fat: 10g | Protein: 11g | Sodium: 300mg | Fiber: 1g | Carbohydrates: 7g | Sugar: 5g

Shirred Eggs and Asparagus au Gratin

This is a very easy dish. Fresh asparagus is definitely better in this recipe. The trick is arranging the asparagus evenly in the pan.

INGREDIENTS | SERVES 4 | 25 MINUTES

1 pound fresh asparagus, ends trimmed, or 2 (10-ounce) packages frozen asparagus

8 large eggs

1 cup crumbled Roquefort cheese

½ teaspoon salt

½ teaspoon ground black pepper

1. Preheat oven to 350°F.

2. Blanch the asparagus in boiling water for 5 minutes. Take immediately out of the boiling water and place in ice water and drain.

3. Prepare a gratin pan or dish with gluten-free nonstick spray and arrange the asparagus in the bottom in a single layer. Break the eggs over the top. Sprinkle with Roquefort, salt, and pepper, and bake until eggs are done and cheese is hot and runny (about 12 minutes). Serve hot.

PER SERVING Calories: 180 | Fat: 13g | Protein: 12g | Sodium: 1,000mg | Fiber: 2g | Carbohydrates: 5g | Sugar: 2g

Savory Egg Burrito

Burritos are favorites for an easy dinner. Why not try an egg and cheese variation?

INGREDIENTS | SERVES 1 | 10 MINUTES

1 teaspoon oil

1 large egg, beaten

1 (6") corn tortilla

1 tablespoon shredded Cheddar cheese

1½ teaspoons salsa

1. Heat oil in a small skillet over medium heat. Add egg and cook, stirring constantly, until set, about 4 minutes.

2. Place scrambled egg in center of tortilla. Top with cheese and salsa. Roll up and eat.

3. If you want your cheese melted, you can heat the burrito with cheese in the microwave for about 15 seconds before topping with the salsa.

PER SERVING Calories: 195 | Fat: 12g | Protein: 10g | Sodium: 170mg | Fiber: 2g | Carbohydrates: 12g | Sugar: 1g

My Corn Tortilla Won't Bend

Corn tortillas stored in the fridge have a tendency to break if used cold. To make them roll nicely, either microwave between two damp paper towels for 30 seconds, or fry them for 1 minute per side in a lightly oiled pan over medium-high heat.

Eastern North Carolina Cheesy Grits Casserole SC

Cheesy grits is a favorite dish to bring to church potlucks and luncheons.
This recipe combines eggs, bacon, and cheesy grits all in one pot.

INGREDIENTS | SERVES 8

1½ cups Bob's Red Mill Gluten-Free Corn Grits (also known as "polenta style"; not quick-cooking)

4¼ cups water

1 teaspoon salt

½ teaspoon ground black pepper

4 tablespoons butter, divided

6 large eggs

1 pound bacon, cooked and crumbled

1 cup shredded Cheddar cheese

1. Pour grits, water, salt, pepper, and 2 tablespoons of butter into a greased 4–6-quart slow cooker.

2. Cover and cook on high for 3 hours or on low for 6 hours.

3. Thirty minutes before serving, whisk eggs together and cook them in a medium skillet over medium heat in the remaining 2 tablespoons of butter for 4–5 minutes until eggs are cooked through. Fold scrambled eggs into the cooked grits in the slow cooker.

4. Add crumbled bacon and cheese.

5. Cook on high an additional 30 minutes to melt cheese and heat bacon through.

PER SERVING Calories: 525 | Fat: 40g | Protein: 17g | Sodium: 900mg | Fiber: 1.5g | Carbohydrates: 25g | Sugar: 0g

Sausage and Cheese Casserole SC

A big bowl of freshly prepared fruit salad would be the perfect accompaniment to this savory casserole.

INGREDIENTS | SERVES 8

1 tablespoon extra-virgin olive oil or vegetable oil

1 large onion, peeled and diced

1 large green bell pepper, seeded and diced

1 pound gluten-free ground sausage

4 cups frozen gluten-free hash brown potatoes, thawed and drained of all liquid

8 large eggs

¼ cup water

½ teaspoon salt

½ teaspoon freshly ground black pepper

½ pound Cheddar cheese, grated

Feeding a Crowd

You can stretch this recipe to even more servings by increasing the amount of chopped peppers you sauté with the onion. In fact, a mixture of red, green, and yellow peppers makes for a delicious combo.

1. Preheat a deep 3½-quart nonstick sauté pan over medium-high heat and add the oil. Once the oil is heated, add the onion and pepper and sauté until the onion is transparent, or about 5 minutes.

2. Add the sausage and cook, browning (and crumbling), for 5 minutes. Remove any excess fat, if necessary, by carefully dabbing the pan with a paper towel.

3. Stir the hash browns into the sausage mixture, and then transfer the mixture to a 4–6-quart slow cooker treated with gluten-free nonstick spray.

4. In a medium bowl, whisk together the eggs, water, salt, and pepper. Pour over the sausage–hash brown mixture in the slow cooker. Cover and cook on low for 4 hours.

5. Turn the cooker to warm. About 45 minutes before you'll be serving the casserole, sprinkle the cheese over the cooked mixture in the slow cooker. After 30 minutes, uncover the casserole and let stand for 15 minutes before serving.

PER SERVING Calories: 430 | Fat: 30g | Protein: 23g | Sodium: 750mg | Fiber: 3g | Carbohydrates: 15g | Sugar: 3g

Cheddar Baked Hominy SC

Hominy is a wonderful, naturally gluten-free alternative to regular wheat pasta. Try it in this macaroni and cheese–inspired dish.

INGREDIENTS | SERVES 6

1½ cups whole milk

2 tablespoons cornstarch

1½ tablespoons butter

2 cups shredded Cheddar cheese, divided

1 (29-ounce) can white or yellow hominy, drained

1 large egg, beaten

½ teaspoon sea salt

1 teaspoon freshly ground black pepper

1 teaspoon garlic powder

¼ cup gluten-free bread crumbs or crushed tortilla chips

1. In a small bowl whisk together milk and cornstarch. Melt butter in a medium-sized saucepan and heat until sizzling. Add milk and cornstarch mixture to the saucepan. Whisk constantly until mixture thickens.

2. When thickened, add 1¼ cups cheese. Stir together until you have a thick, cheesy sauce. Add drained hominy and mix thoroughly into sauce. Add beaten egg. Stir in salt, pepper, and garlic powder.

3. Pour mixture into a greased 4–6-quart slow cooker and sprinkle with bread crumbs or crushed tortilla chips. Cover and vent lid with a chopstick. Cook on low for 3–4 hours or on high for 2–2½ hours.

4. Thirty minutes prior to serving, sprinkle remaining shredded cheese on top of casserole. Cover and cook for 25–30 minutes until cheese has melted.

PER SERVING Calories: 365 | Fat: 20g | Protein: 16g | Sodium: 900mg | Fiber: 3g | Carbohydrates: 35g | Sugar: 7g

Skillet Frittata

Cast-iron skillets work great for frittata making. They cook evenly and are oven-safe.

INGREDIENTS | SERVES 6 | 25 MINUTES

1 tablespoon butter

1 tablespoon olive oil

½ cup diced onion

1 pound asparagus, chopped

¼ cup fresh or frozen peas

1 cup crumbled feta cheese

1 teaspoon dried oregano

1 teaspoon dried dill

1 teaspoon dried parsley

½ teaspoon dried basil

½ teaspoon salt

½ teaspoon ground black pepper

7 large eggs

Why Use Butter and Oil in the Same Recipe?

While it seems counterintuitive to use two different kinds of fats to grease a pan, there is a good reason. Butter cannot stand up to the same high heat as oil, but adds flavor oil cannot produce. When using the two together, you can cook at a higher temperature, and still get the great flavor that the butter adds.

1. Preheat oven to 325°F. Heat the butter and oil in a 12" cast-iron skillet over medium heat. Sauté the onion, asparagus, and peas until the onions are soft, about 8–10 minutes.

2. Meanwhile, in a medium bowl, whisk together the feta, oregano, dill, parsley, basil, salt, pepper, and eggs.

3. Pour the egg mixture over the vegetables in the skillet. Tilt the skillet slightly to coat all of the ingredients with the egg mixture. Cook over medium heat until the eggs are just beginning to set, about 4 minutes.

4. Place skillet in the oven and bake for 10 minutes or until the mixture is cooked through and just beginning to brown.

5. Remove from the pan and slice. Serve immediately.

PER SERVING Calories: 210 | Fat: 15g | Protein: 13g | Sodium: 550mg | Fiber: 2g | Carbohydrates: 7g | Sugar: 4g

Cheesy Scrambled Eggs

Try combining several cheeses to create your own favorite cheesy eggs.

INGREDIENTS | SERVES 2 | 15 MINUTES

4 large eggs
¼ cup milk
½ teaspoon salt
¼ teaspoon ground black pepper
¼ cup shredded cheese, any type
1 tablespoon butter

1. Crack the eggs into a small bowl. Whisk until they are light yellow and mixed well.

2. Add the milk, salt, pepper, and cheese to the eggs.

3. Melt the butter in a medium skillet over medium heat.

4. Pour egg mixture into the heated skillet and let it cook. As the eggs start to set, use a spatula to break them up and turn them over.

5. When eggs are cooked throughout and no longer runny, about 8 minutes, remove them from the skillet and serve.

PER SERVING Calories: 270 | Fat: 21g | Protein: 17g | Sodium: 800mg | Fiber: 0g | Carbohydrates: 3g | Sugar: 2g

Ham and Cheese Slow Cooker Omelet

Eggs are one of the most affordable proteins available, and they are naturally gluten-free. If you make a large family-sized omelet one evening, the leftovers make a great lunch.

INGREDIENTS | SERVES 5

10 large eggs
½ teaspoon gluten-free ground mustard
½ teaspoon salt
½ teaspoon paprika
½ teaspoon ground black pepper
½ teaspoon dill weed
1½ cups ham, diced
1½ cups shredded Cheddar cheese
½ cup chopped scallions

1. Whisk eggs in a large bowl. Add in ground mustard, salt, paprika, ground pepper, and dill weed. Stir in diced ham.

2. Pour egg mixture into a greased 2.5-quart slow cooker.

3. Sprinkle cheese and scallions over the top of the egg mixture.

4. Cover and cook on high for 1½–2 hours or on low for 2½–3 hours.

PER SERVING Calories: 400 | Fat: 27g | Protein: 36g | Sodium: 1,000mg | Fiber: 0g | Carbohydrates: 2g | Sugar: 1g

Buffalo Chorizo Hash

This spicy hash is hearty enough to eat on its own or can be served over pasta, rice, or your favorite quinoa blend.

INGREDIENTS | SERVES 4 | 25 MINUTES

1 tablespoon olive oil
1 medium onion, peeled and diced
3 cloves garlic, minced
1 cup chopped red bell pepper
2 large (8-ounce) potatoes, peeled and cubed
1 teaspoon salt
½ teaspoon ground black pepper
2 tablespoons chopped cilantro
1½ teaspoons crushed red pepper
5 ounces buffalo chorizo
¼ cup shredded Cheddar cheese

1. Heat olive oil in a large skillet over medium heat. Add onion and cook until just fragrant, about 2 minutes. Add garlic and cook another 2 minutes. Stir in bell peppers and potatoes; cook until potatoes are soft, about 8 minutes. Add salt, pepper, cilantro, and crushed red pepper.

2. In another skillet, crumble chorizo over medium heat and cook until browned, about 6 minutes. Stir into potato mixture.

3. Sprinkle hash with cheese and serve hot.

PER SERVING Calories: 370 | Fat: 20g | Protein: 14g | Sodium: 1,000mg | Fiber: 6g | Carbohydrates: 36g | Sugar: 5g

Eggs Florentine SC

Freshly ground black pepper goes well in this dish. You can use up to a teaspoon in the recipe. If you prefer to go lighter on the seasoning to accommodate individual tastes, be sure to have a pepper grinder at the table for those who want to add more.

INGREDIENTS | SERVES 4

9 ounces (2 cups) Cheddar cheese, grated, divided

1 (10-ounce) package frozen spinach, thawed

1 (8-ounce) can sliced mushrooms, drained

1 small onion, peeled and diced

6 large eggs

1 cup heavy cream

½ teaspoon Italian seasoning

½ teaspoon garlic powder

½ teaspoon freshly ground black pepper

Make It Dairy-Free

To make egg casseroles dairy-free, replace the cream with full-fat coconut milk. For the Cheddar cheese, there are many dairy-free alternatives available now; one in particular, called Daiya, is sold in shreds and melts beautifully in dishes like this.

1. Grease a 4–6-quart slow cooker with gluten-free nonstick spray. Spread 1 cup of the grated cheese over the bottom of the slow cooker.

2. Drain the spinach and squeeze out any excess moisture; add in a layer on top of the cheese. Next add the drained mushrooms in a layer and then top them with the onion.

3. In a small bowl beat together the eggs, cream, Italian seasoning, garlic powder, and pepper. Pour over the layers in the slow cooker. Top with the remaining cup of cheese.

4. Cover and cook on high for 2 hours or until eggs are set.

PER SERVING Calories: 610 | Fat: 51g | Protein: 30g | Sodium: 800mg | Fiber: 4g | Carbohydrates: 11g | Sugar: 3g

Spanish Tortilla SC

Traditionally served as tapas or an appetizer in Spanish restaurants and bars, this version of the Spanish tortilla removes a lot of the fat and makes a healthy casserole. Conventionally, a tortilla does not contain cheese, but feel free to sprinkle some on top in the last 30 minutes of cooking.

INGREDIENTS | SERVES 6

2 small onions, peeled and finely diced

3 tablespoons olive oil

10 large eggs

1 teaspoon salt

1 teaspoon ground black pepper

3 large baking potatoes, peeled and thinly sliced

1. In a medium skillet over medium heat slowly cook onions in olive oil until lightly brown and caramelized, about 5–6 minutes.

2. In a large bowl whisk together the eggs, salt, and pepper.

3. Layer half of the potatoes and fried onions in a greased 4–6-quart slow cooker. Pour half the eggs over the layers. Repeat layers ending with the last of the whisked eggs.

4. Cover and cook on low for 6–7 hours or on high for 3½–4 hours.

PER SERVING Calories: 330 | Fat: 15g | Protein: 15g | Sodium: 500mg | Fiber: 3g | Carbohydrates: 36g | Sugar: 3g

Huevos Rancheros Taco Cups

*These cute little cups are perfect for a Cinco de Mayo dinner,
and leftovers make fabulous lunches and snacks, too.*

INGREDIENTS | SERVES 5 | 35 MINUTES

10 gluten-free wonton wrappers

1 tablespoon olive oil

¼ medium red onion, peeled and chopped

1 clove garlic, minced

2 plum tomatoes, chopped

2 tomatillos, chopped

1 (4-ounce) can chopped green chilies

1 teaspoon salt

1 teaspoon ground black pepper

1 teaspoon gluten-free chili powder

½ cup shredded Mexican cheese blend, divided

4 tablespoons chopped cilantro, divided

10 large eggs

1. Preheat oven to 350°F. Lightly grease a muffin tin with gluten-free nonstick cooking spray. Line muffin cups with wonton wrappers, folding them slightly to fit. Bake for about 8–12 minutes, or until crispy and golden brown. Remove from the pan to cool.

2. Heat olive oil in a medium skillet over medium heat. Add onion and cook until translucent, about 2 minutes. Add garlic, tomatoes, tomatillos, chilies, salt, pepper, and chili powder. Cook, stirring occasionally until most of the liquid is evaporated, about 10 minutes. Add ¼ cup cheese and 2 tablespoons cilantro and remove from heat.

3. Scoop about 1 tablespoon or so of filling into each taco cup. Top with remaining cheese and cilantro.

4. Heat a large skillet or griddle coated with gluten-free nonstick cooking spray over medium heat. In batches if necessary, cook eggs sunny-side up. Transfer eggs to a platter or cutting board. Using a sharp knife, cut most of the white off so the egg yolk fits perfectly over the cups. (Save egg whites for another use.)

5. Place eggs on top of the filling and serve immediately.

PER SERVING Calories: 280 | Fat: 17g | Protein: 18g | Sodium: 780mg | Fiber: 1.5g | Carbohydrates: 15g | Sugar: 3g

Gluten-Free Breakfast Sausage Pizza with Bacon

Breakfast pizza is the ideal alternative when your kids are tired of the same old pepperoni or cheese pizza. Serve them this protein-packed delicious pizza instead. There won't be a frown at the table.

INGREDIENTS | SERVES 8 | 35 MINUTES

1 pound gluten-free pizza dough

1 small white onion, peeled and chopped

½ medium yellow bell pepper, seeded and chopped

7 ounces gluten-free lean breakfast sausage

½ teaspoon salt

½ teaspoon ground black pepper

1 cup shredded low-fat Cheddar cheese

4 ounces fresh mozzarella, cubed

4 slices low-sodium bacon, cooked and crumbled

2 large eggs

1. Roll pizza dough out to a large circle. Place on a floured pizza pan and set aside. Preheat oven to 400°F.

2. Heat a large skillet coated with gluten-free nonstick cooking spray over medium heat. Add onion and pepper and cook until soft, about 4 minutes. Add sausage and cook about 8–10 minutes, breaking apart with a spatula as it cooks. Add salt and pepper.

3. Cover the dough with Cheddar cheese. Add the sausage mixture to the top and spread out evenly. Add mozzarella cheese and bacon.

4. Crack both eggs over the pizza. Bake for about 12 minutes, or until crust is golden brown and egg whites are fully cooked.

PER SERVING Calories: 510 | Fat: 30g | Protein: 17g | Sodium: 775mg | Fiber: 2g | Carbohydrates: 25g | Sugar: 1g

Gluten-Free Chicken and Waffles

Fried chicken and waffles are a Southern institution, and there are probably hundreds of ways to prepare them. This version is a little healthier—with baked chicken breasts instead of battered and deep-fried chicken.

INGREDIENTS | SERVES 5 | 45 MINUTES

½ cup gluten-free all-purpose flour

2 tablespoons gluten-free panko bread crumbs

½ teaspoon crushed red pepper

1 teaspoon salt

½ teaspoon ground black pepper

¼ cup buttermilk

2½ pounds chicken legs and/or thighs

1 cup brown rice flour

½ cup almond meal

¼ cup coconut flour

2 teaspoons baking powder

2 tablespoons melted butter

2 tablespoons unsweetened applesauce

2 large eggs, room temperature

1½ cups heavy cream

1 tablespoon honey

½ cup maple syrup

1. Preheat oven to 375°F. Grease a large baking dish with gluten-free nonstick cooking spray.

2. In a shallow bowl, whisk all-purpose flour, bread crumbs, red pepper, salt, and pepper. Pour buttermilk into another shallow bowl.

3. Dip the chicken into the buttermilk and then dredge in the flour mixture. Place the chicken in the prepared baking dish and bake for 20 minutes. Turn chicken and bake another 20 minutes or until golden and crispy.

4. Meanwhile, whisk brown rice flour, almond meal, and coconut flour together in a large bowl. Stir in baking powder. In another bowl, whisk butter, applesauce, eggs, cream, and honey together.

5. Make a well in the center of the flour mixture and pour in the wet mixture. Stir to combine.

6. Preheat waffle iron and lightly grease both sides. Pour the waffle mixture into waffle iron and bake until golden brown, about 4 minutes.

7. Place 1 or 2 pieces of chicken on each waffle. Drizzle with syrup.

PER SERVING Calories: 850 | Fat: 48g | Protein: 56g | Sodium: 900mg | Fiber: 6g | Carbohydrates: 50g | Sugar: 5g

Poached Eggs with Asparagus and Prosciutto

This is one of those recipes that can be made when you're in a hurry but want something elegant and filling. The poached egg and prosciutto add a touch of sophistication, while the asparagus adds fiber and lots of good-for-you antioxidants.

INGREDIENTS | SERVES 4 | 30 MINUTES

1 pound asparagus, trimmed

1 tablespoon extra-virgin olive oil

1 teaspoon lemon juice

1½ teaspoons salt, divided

1½ teaspoons ground black pepper, divided

1 tablespoon rice vinegar

4 large eggs

4 slices gluten-free French bread

4 thin slices prosciutto

½ cup shredded white Cheddar cheese

Perfect Poached Eggs

For the best poached eggs, bring the water to a rapid simmer, not a boil. Add a little rice vinegar to the water to prevent the egg from sticking to the bottom. Crack each egg in a shallow bowl before you pour into the simmering water to avoid getting bits of shell in the pan. When removing the egg, use a slotted spoon to ensure it stays together.

1. Preheat oven to 400°F. Place asparagus side by side on a rimmed baking sheet. Sprinkle with olive oil, lemon juice, 1 teaspoon salt, and 1 teaspoon pepper. Roast for 8 minutes, then flip the asparagus and roast another 8 minutes. Remove from oven.

2. Meanwhile, bring a full pot of water to a rapid simmer. Add rice vinegar. Crack eggs, one at a time, into 4 small, shallow bowls. Carefully pour 2 eggs into the simmering water. Using a slotted spoon, gently move the egg whites over the egg yolk. Turn off the heat, cover, and let sit about 4 minutes, or until egg whites are fully cooked. Using the same slotted spoon, very carefully remove eggs from the pan and place on a plate. Keep warm and repeat with remaining 2 eggs.

3. Place a few asparagus spears on each slice of bread. Top with prosciutto and cheese. Carefully place eggs over cheese and asparagus. Sprinkle with remaining salt and pepper. Serve warm.

PER SERVING Calories: 320 | Fat: 16g | Protein: 21g | Sodium: 1,200mg | Fiber: 4g | Carbohydrates: 25g | Sugar: 3g

Tomato and Mozzarella Baked Eggs

Need a quick dinner? As long as you have diced tomatoes, fresh mozzarella cheese, eggs, and any fresh herbs on hand, you can make this in a flash!

INGREDIENTS | SERVES 6 | 35 MINUTES

2 tablespoons unsalted butter

2 medium shallots, peeled and chopped

6 garlic cloves, minced

3 orange or yellow bell peppers, seeded and chopped

1 cup chopped mushrooms

1 (14.5-ounce) can diced tomatoes, lightly drained

2 tablespoons fresh oregano leaves

1½ tablespoons chopped fresh rosemary

¼ cup chopped fresh basil leaves

1 teaspoon chili powder

1 cup full-fat ricotta cheese

5 large eggs, room temperature

1 cup shredded Parmesan cheese

4 ounces fresh mozzarella cheese, diced

1. Heat the butter in a large cast-iron skillet over medium-high heat. Add the shallots, garlic, peppers, and mushrooms. Cook until softened and almost caramelized, about 6–8 minutes.

2. Stir in the tomatoes, oregano, rosemary, basil, and chili powder. Reduce heat to medium-low and cook another 10 minutes, or until the mixture starts to thicken a bit.

3. Preheat oven to 400°F.

4. Place five dollops of ricotta cheese over the tomato mixture. With a large spoon, create a well in each mound of ricotta. Crack an egg over each, careful not to let it run into the tomato mixture. Sprinkle with cheeses.

5. Bake for about 15 minutes (yolks will be slightly runny).

PER SERVING Calories: 350 | Fat: 23g | Protein: 23g | Sodium: 600mg | Fiber: 3g | Carbohydrates: 16g | Sugar: 9g

Hash Brown Waffles with Sunny-Side Up Eggs

That waffle maker isn't just for sweet waffles. These buttery hash brown waffles are made with a greased waffle maker, making them the perfect base for sunny-side up eggs and crispy bacon.

INGREDIENTS | SERVES 4 | 35 MINUTES

6 cups refrigerated gluten-free hash brown potatoes

4 slices bacon, cut in half

4 large eggs

1. Preheat a waffle iron and spray with gluten-free nonstick cooking spray.

2. Place about 1½ cups hash brown potatoes on the hot waffle iron. Close the lid and cook for about 15 minutes, or until the hash browns are crispy and a thick crust forms on them. Try not to open the waffle maker while they cook. Repeat with remaining potatoes.

3. Clean the waffle maker with a damp towel. Preheat again and place the bacon on top. Close the lid and cook bacon until crispy, about 5 minutes.

4. Spray a large skillet with gluten-free nonstick cooking spray and heat over medium heat. Add eggs and cook until whites are fully cooked, about 5 minutes. Top the waffles with eggs and bacon and serve warm.

PER SERVING Calories: 330 | Fat: 15g | Protein: 13g | Sodium: 270mg | Fiber: 5g | Carbohydrates: 35g | Sugar: 3g

CHAPTER 11

Side Dishes

Chinese Cabbage with Sesame

Chinese cabbage, also called napa cabbage, is wonderful cooked or served raw in salads. It's pale green, mild, leafy, and very good for you!

INGREDIENTS | SERVES 4 | 10 MINUTES

2 tablespoons sesame seed oil

2 tablespoons canola or other light oil

1 tablespoon sesame seeds

1 (1½-pound) head Chinese (napa) cabbage, washed and thinly sliced

Juice of ½ large lemon

2 cloves garlic, minced

½ teaspoon salt

½ teaspoon freshly ground black pepper

2 teaspoons gluten-free soy sauce

1. Place the oils in a hot wok or frying pan. Add the sesame seeds and toast for 2 minutes.

2. Stir in the cabbage, lemon juice, and garlic. Toss until just wilted, about 4 minutes. Add salt, pepper, and soy sauce before serving.

PER SERVING Calories: 165 | Fat: 15g | Protein: 3g | Sodium: 450mg | Fiber: 2g | Carbohydrates: 7g | Sugar: 2g

Snow Peas with Water Chestnuts and Ginger

This tasty side dish is very fast and good. It's a boon to the busy working person who wants fresh vegetables but has little time.

INGREDIENTS | SERVES 4 | 10 MINUTES

1 pound snow pea pods, ends trimmed

½ cup peanut oil

1 (8-ounce) can water chestnuts, drained, rinsed, and sliced

½ cup unsalted peanuts

2 tablespoons gluten-free soy sauce

1 teaspoon lemon juice

1 tablespoon minced fresh gingerroot

½ teaspoon red pepper sauce

1. Place the snow pea pods in a hot wok or frying pan with the oil. Stir to coat, then add the water chestnuts and peanuts, stirring again.

2. Continue cooking, and after 5 minutes, add the rest of the ingredients. Mix well and serve hot or at room temperature.

PER SERVING Calories: 420 | Fat: 36g | Protein: 9g | Sodium: 450mg | Fiber: 6g | Carbohydrates: 19g | Sugar: 7g

Crunchy Cornbread Squares

These can also be cut into rectangles and used as bases for dips and spreads.

INGREDIENTS | SERVES 8 | 30 MINUTES

1 cup cornmeal

1 cup corn flour

2 teaspoons baking soda

1 teaspoon cream of tartar

1 teaspoon salt

4 tablespoons sugar

1 cup sour cream

¼ cup buttermilk

2 large eggs, beaten

4 tablespoons butter, melted

1. Prepare a 9" × 13" baking pan with gluten-free nonstick spray and preheat oven to 425°F. Mix all of the dry ingredients together in a bowl. Stir in sour cream, buttermilk, eggs, and butter. (You can add various herbs and spices to change the flavors, such as oregano and garlic powder for an Italian flavor, or chili and cumin for a Mexican taste.)

2. Pour into the prepared baking pan and bake for 20 minutes or until lightly browned. Cool completely, then cut into squares.

PER SERVING Calories: 275 | Fat: 13g | Protein: 5g | Sodium: 660mg | Fiber: 1g | Carbohydrates: 35g | Sugar: 8g

Garlicky Parmesan Roasted Potatoes

This side dish is a perfect companion to any meat or poultry dish.
Using fresh herbs and Parmesan cheese is definitely better when roasting.

INGREDIENTS | SERVES 4 | 45 MINUTES

2 tablespoons extra-virgin olive oil

2 cloves garlic, minced

1 medium onion, peeled and finely chopped

1 teaspoon chopped fresh basil

1 teaspoon fresh rosemary, chopped

1 teaspoon fresh parsley, chopped

2 tablespoons fresh Parmesan cheese, grated

⅛ teaspoon crushed red pepper flakes

½ teaspoon salt

4 large red potatoes, scrubbed and sliced into cubes

1. Preheat oven to 450°F.

2. Place all the ingredients in a large resealable plastic bag. Close the bag and shake to evenly coat potatoes.

3. Spray a baking sheet with gluten-free nonstick cooking spray. Spread potato mixture in an even layer on baking sheet. Place in oven for 40 minutes, making sure to stir potatoes occasionally.

4. Place oven on broil and cook potatoes 1–2 minutes, until they become browned and crispy. Remove from oven. Serve immediately.

PER SERVING Calories: 350 | Fat: 8g | Protein: 9g | Sodium: 400mg | Fiber: 7g | Carbohydrates: 62g | Sugar: 5g

Balsamic Roasted Brussels Sprouts

Even those who do not typically like Brussels sprouts will love these!
This is a simple and tasty dish, delicious enough for a holiday dinner.

INGREDIENTS | SERVES 6 | 40 MINUTES

3 tablespoons extra-virgin olive oil

2 tablespoons balsamic vinegar

1 clove garlic, minced

1 teaspoon sweet paprika

1½ pounds Brussels sprouts, bottoms trimmed, outer leaves removed, and halved

4 shallots, peeled and thinly sliced

1 teaspoon salt

½ teaspoon freshly ground black pepper

The Many Benefits of Brussels Sprouts

Brussels sprouts are part of the cabbage family and actually look like little cabbages. Brussels sprouts were first grown in Brussels, Belgium, hence the name. These sprouts are packed with vitamins C, A, and B.

1. Preheat the oven to 400°F.

2. In a small bowl, mix together the oil, balsamic vinegar, garlic, and paprika.

3. Place Brussels sprouts, shallots, and oil/vinegar mixture in a large resealable plastic bag. Make sure the bag is closed and shake to coat sprouts evenly. Season with salt and pepper.

4. Place sprouts on a baking sheet that is coated with gluten-free nonstick cooking spray. Roast sprouts for 35 minutes, shaking pan every 5–8 minutes to make sure they are evenly browning.

5. Remove from oven when finished; season with some more salt if desired. Serve immediately.

PER SERVING Calories: 120 | Fat: 7g | Protein: 4g | Sodium: 400mg | Fiber: 4g | Carbohydrates: 13g | Sugar: 3g

Baked Spaghetti Squash Boats

*This recipe is so delicious, and makes a beautiful presentation
as each person gets their own boat to enjoy.*

INGREDIENTS | SERVES 4 | 45 MINUTES

2 medium spaghetti squashes

1 tablespoon olive oil

½ cup chopped onions

½ cup sliced and chopped mushrooms

½ cup fresh bell peppers, chopped

⅓ pound ground sausage

8 ounces diced tomatoes

6 ounces pizza sauce

1 teaspoon Italian seasoning

⅓ cup fresh mozzarella cheese

1. Cut the squashes in half lengthwise and scoop out the seeds. Place the squash, cut-side down, into a glass baking dish. Fill with water (to cover the squash up to an inch).

2. Preheat oven to 375°F. Bake for about 35–40 minutes or until soft.

3. When cool enough to handle, use a fork to loosen the "spaghetti" noodles.

4. In a medium skillet over medium heat, heat the olive oil. Add the onions, mushrooms, peppers, and sausage, and cook until sausage is browned, about 6–8 minutes. Mix in the diced tomatoes, pizza sauce, and Italian seasoning.

5. Fill the spaghetti squash halves with the filling (about ½ cup each). Top the filling with fresh mozzarella.

6. Bake, uncovered, until cheese is melted, about 6–8 minutes.

PER SERVING Calories: 325 | Fat: 15g | Protein: 13g | Sodium: 722mg | Fiber: 4g | Carbohydrates: 18g | Sugar: 8g

Polenta with Sun-Dried Tomatoes and Basil

The fascinating thing about polenta is that you can change the seasonings and/or toppings and fry, grill, or broil and have a different dish, still based on polenta, time after time.

INGREDIENTS | SERVES 8 | 30 MINUTES

1 (8-ounce) jar sun-dried tomatoes in oil, drained and chopped finely

20 basil leaves, rinsed

2 cloves garlic

½ teaspoon oregano, dried

Additional extra-virgin olive oil, if necessary

1 batch Classic Polenta with Herbs and Parmesan (see recipe in this chapter), prepared firm

1 cup grated mozzarella cheese

Polenta: A Fancy Name for Good Old Cornmeal

You can buy polenta by the ounce in the market. It is expensive and less nourishing than making it yourself. You can make polenta by the pound cheaply. It can be elegant but usually is simply fried or served in a soft, creamy mound, like mashed potatoes. It's good with any sauce or gravy; it's so very bland that you really need to spice it up.

1. Preheat oven to 350°F.

2. Blend the tomatoes, basil, garlic, and oregano in a food processor. This should be chunky, not puréed. Add extra olive oil if too dry to process. Spread the tomato mixture over the polenta and cut into squares.

3. Place the squares on a cookie sheet that you have buttered or sprayed with gluten-free nonstick spray. Bake for 20 minutes.

4. At the last minute, sprinkle the mozzarella cheese over the top and bake until melted. Serve immediately.

PER SERVING Calories: 320 | Fat: 12g | Protein: 12g | Sodium: 2,000mg | Fiber: 5g | Carbohydrates: 45g | Sugar: 11g

Classic Polenta with Herbs and Parmesan

This recipe makes soft polenta the consistency of mashed potatoes. If you're making firm polenta to cut into squares to broil, grill, or fry, use 6½ cups of water instead of 7. After it's cooked, spread the polenta in a 9" × 13" pan that has been prepared with gluten-free nonstick spray and chill for at least 3 hours.

INGREDIENTS | SERVES 8 | 30 MINUTES

7 cups water

2 tablespoons salt

2 cups yellow cornmeal

2 ounces unsalted butter

2 cloves garlic, minced

½ medium onion, peeled and finely minced

2 tablespoons dried herbs, or 1 tablespoon chopped fresh basil, rosemary, or parsley

½ cup freshly grated Parmesan cheese

½ teaspoon freshly ground black pepper

The Staple of Lombardy

Polenta has been the staple food of Lombardy, at the foot of the Italian Alps, for three centuries. You can use polenta wherever you'd use pasta, serving it with tomato, vegetable, or cream sauces, or with brown gravy and mushrooms. You can make it soft, to mound on a plate or platter, or firm and then fry it in squares.

1. Bring the water to a boil.

2. Add salt, and using your hand to drop the cornmeal into the boiling water, let the cornmeal slip slowly between your fingers to make a very slim stream. You should be able to see each grain. Don't dump the cornmeal into the water or you will get a mass of glue.

3. Stir constantly while adding the cornmeal. Reduce heat to a simmer and keep stirring for about 20 minutes as it thickens.

4. Stir in the butter, garlic, onion, herbs, Parmesan cheese, and pepper. If you're making soft polenta, serve immediately.

PER SERVING Calories: 205 | Fat: 8g | Protein: 5g | Sodium: 1,700mg | Fiber: 2g | Carbohydrates: 28g | Sugar: 1g

Lemon Rice with Toasted Pine Nuts

This dish can easily be made into a meal by simply adding chicken or sausage.
The lemon flavor is so light and can easily go alongside most entrées.

INGREDIENTS | SERVES 4 | 45 MINUTES

1 cup Arborio rice

4½ cups water, divided

1 tablespoon grapeseed oil

Juice from ½ large lemon

1 clove garlic, finely chopped

1 teaspoon salt

½ teaspoon freshly ground black pepper

Zest from 1 lemon

¼ cup fresh parsley

1 tablespoon pine nuts, toasted

1 tablespoon grated Parmesan cheese

Arborio Rice

Arborio rice cooks much differently than other varieties of rice. Arborio rice is typically used in risotto dishes, which require a creamier texture. By slowly adding the water and continuously stirring, the rice releases starches, which make the texture much more creamy.

1. In a large saucepan, combine the rice with 1½ cups of the water over high heat and bring to a boil. Reduce heat to medium, stirring continuously until the water is absorbed.

2. In ¼-cup increments, add remaining 3 cups water to the saucepan. Continue to stir constantly while adding the water and until all 3 cups of water have been absorbed.

3. In a small bowl, mix the oil and lemon juice.

4. Transfer the rice to a medium-sized serving bowl. Add garlic and lemon juice mixture, and season with salt and pepper.

5. Add the lemon zest, parsley, and pine nuts, and toss. Top with Parmesan cheese.

PER SERVING Calories: 230 | Fat: 5g | Protein: 4g | Sodium: 600mg | Fiber: 2g | Carbohydrates: 40g | Sugar: 0g

Scalloped Potatoes with Bacon SC

Scalloped potatoes are an ideal dish for the slow cooker. Potatoes cooked slowly over low heat are extremely tender and delicious.

INGREDIENTS | SERVES 8

2 tablespoons cornstarch

1 teaspoon salt

½ teaspoon ground black pepper

2 cups whole milk

4 cups thinly sliced potatoes (about 6–8 medium potatoes)

½ pound bacon, cooked and crumbled

3 tablespoons butter, cut in small pieces

½ cup shredded Cheddar cheese

½ cup sliced scallions

Make It Dairy-Free

For a recipe like this you can easily make it dairy-free by using coconut oil or olive oil in place of the butter, coconut milk or almond milk in place of the dairy milk, and Daiya (soy-free, gluten-free, and dairy-free cheese product) in place of the dairy cheese.

1. Grease a 4–6-quart slow cooker with gluten-free nonstick cooking spray.

2. In a small bowl mix together the cornstarch, salt, pepper, and milk.

3. Place ¼ of the potatoes in the bottom of the slow cooker. Pour ⅓ of the milk mixture over the potatoes. Sprinkle ⅓ of the bacon over the milk. Continue to layer ingredients, finishing with potato slices.

4. Dot butter over potatoes. Cover slow cooker and cook on low for 6–8 hours until potatoes are tender.

5. Thirty minutes prior to serving sprinkle cheese and scallions on top of potatoes. Allow cheese to melt and then serve.

PER SERVING Calories: 290 | Fat: 21g | Protein: 8g | Sodium: 600mg | Fiber: 2g | Carbohydrates: 17g | Sugar: 4g

Sweet Potato Gratin with Leeks and Onions SC

The combination of sweet and savory makes this a fascinating, unique, and delicious dish.

INGREDIENTS | SERVES 6

2 medium leeks, white part only, rinsed and chopped

2 large sweet onions, peeled and finely chopped

2 stalks celery with tops, finely chopped

4 tablespoons olive oil

4 medium sweet potatoes, peeled and sliced thinly

1 teaspoon dried thyme

1 teaspoon salt

½ teaspoon ground black pepper

3 cups 1% milk

1½ cups gluten-free cornbread crumbs

2 tablespoons butter or margarine, cut in small pieces

Instead of . . .

Instead of gluten-free cornbread, you can also use crushed corn tortillas as a topping. Several brands such as Utz and Food Should Taste Good actually have "This is a gluten-free food" listed on some of their products. If you have any questions about a product, make sure to call the company to ask about their gluten cross-contamination prevention policies.

1. In a medium skillet over medium heat add the leeks, onions, celery, and olive oil and sauté for 3–5 minutes, until softened.

2. Grease a 4–6-quart slow cooker with gluten-free nonstick cooking spray.

3. Layer the sweet potato slices in the slow cooker with the sautéed vegetables. Sprinkle thyme, salt, and pepper on each layer as you go along. Finish with a layer of potatoes.

4. Add the milk until it meets the top layer of potatoes. Then add the cornbread crumbs. Dot with butter or margarine.

5. Cover and cook on high for 4 hours or on low for 8 hours, until the potatoes are fork-tender. In the last hour of cooking, vent the lid of the slow cooker with a chopstick or wooden spoon handle to allow excess condensation to escape.

PER SERVING Calories: 390 | Fat: 21g | Protein: 8g | Sodium: 700mg | Fiber: 6g | Carbohydrates: 43g | Sugar: 15g

Slow-Cooked Collard Greens **SC**

This is a Southern side dish staple that goes perfectly with barbecue chicken or ribs and cornbread.

INGREDIENTS | SERVES 8

1 meaty smoked ham hock, rinsed

1 large carrot, peeled and chopped

1 large onion, peeled and chopped

1 (1-pound) package fresh chopped collard greens, with tough stems removed

1 teaspoon minced garlic

½ teaspoon crushed red pepper

¼ teaspoon ground black pepper

6 cups gluten-free chicken broth

1 cup water

1. Place ham hock, carrot, and onion in a 6-quart slow cooker.

2. Add collard greens. Sprinkle greens with garlic, crushed red pepper, and black pepper.

3. Pour broth and water over collard greens.

4. Cover and cook on low for 8 hours. To serve, remove greens to a serving bowl. Remove meat from ham bone and discard fat and bones. Chop meat and add to greens. Ladle 1–2 cups broth over greens.

PER SERVING Calories: 100 | Fat: 3g | Protein: 5g | Sodium: 800mg | Fiber: 3g | Carbohydrates: 15g | Sugar: 1g

Baked Mexican Rice Casserole

This casserole is a quick and easy side dish you can get into the oven in just a few minutes.

INGREDIENTS | SERVES 4 | 30 MINUTES

1 (15-ounce) can black beans, drained and rinsed

¾ cup salsa

2 teaspoons chili powder

1 teaspoon cumin

½ cup corn kernels

2 cups cooked rice

½ cup grated Cheddar cheese

⅓ cup sliced black olives

1. Preheat oven to 350°F.

2. In a large pot over low heat, combine the beans, salsa, chili powder, and cumin and partially mash beans with a large fork.

3. Remove from heat and stir in corn and rice. Transfer to a casserole dish.

4. Top with cheese and sliced olives and bake for 20 minutes.

PER SERVING Calories: 315 | Fat: 7g | Protein: 13g | Sodium: 800mg | Fiber: 8g | Carbohydrates: 51g | Sugar: 4g

Fried Rice

*Fried rice doesn't have to contain egg! If you add some chicken
or ham to this easy recipe, you've created a main dish.*

INGREDIENTS | SERVES 6 | 20 MINUTES

¼ cup gluten-free vegetable broth

1 tablespoon gluten-free soy sauce

1 tablespoon minced fresh gingerroot

⅛ teaspoon ground black pepper

2 tablespoons olive oil

½ cup chopped onion

3 cloves garlic, minced

½ cup shredded carrot

½ cup chopped scallions

4 cups long-grain rice, cooked and cooled

Try a Rice Cooker

If you have trouble cooking rice, get a rice cooker. This inexpensive appliance cooks rice to fluffy perfection every time. Another option is to cook rice like you cook pasta—in a large pot of boiling water. Keep tasting the rice; when it's tender, thoroughly drain and use in a recipe or serve.

1. In small bowl, combine broth, soy sauce, gingerroot, and pepper. Mix well and set aside.

2. In wok or large skillet, heat olive oil over medium-high heat. Add onion and garlic and stir-fry for 3 minutes. Add carrot and scallion and stir-fry for 2–3 minutes longer.

3. Add rice and stir-fry until rice is hot and grains are separate, about 4–5 minutes. Stir broth mixture and then add to wok. Stir-fry until the mixture bubbles, about 3–4 minutes. Serve immediately.

PER SERVING Calories: 500 | Fat: 5g | Protein: 10g | Sodium: 200mg | Fiber: 2g | Carbohydrates: 102g | Sugar: 2g

Fluffy Buttermilk Biscuits

These fluffy, light biscuits are perfect topped with jam and a slice of cheese.
Or dip them in your favorite soup.

INGREDIENTS | SERVES 9 | 30 MINUTES

1 cup brown rice flour, plus more for rolling out the dough

½ cup arrowroot starch

1 teaspoon xanthan gum

2 teaspoons baking powder

1 teaspoon baking soda

½ teaspoon salt

1 teaspoon sugar

½ cup cold butter, cut into chunks

2 large eggs

⅓ cup buttermilk

2 tablespoons whole milk

1 teaspoon coarse salt

Make Savory Biscuits

To make these biscuits savory, add ½ teaspoon of garlic powder or Italian seasoning (or even both) to the dry ingredients. Or, try a tablespoon of chopped fresh chives.

1. Preheat oven to 425°F. Line a baking sheet with parchment paper, and sprinkle with some brown rice flour. Set aside.

2. In the bowl of a food processor, combine all the dry ingredients and pulse to combine. (If you don't have a food processor, combine all dry ingredients in a medium-sized mixing bowl.)

3. Add the butter and pulse until the butter is the size of a lentil/pea. (Or, use a pastry blender to cut the butter into the dry ingredients. Work quickly, because you want the butter to stay cold.)

4. Add the eggs and buttermilk, and run the food processor until the dough comes together in a ball. (Alternately, you can use a wooden spoon and stir until the dough comes together.)

5. Turn dough out onto baking sheet, and flour your hands with more brown rice flour. Working quickly, pat the dough down into a square shape, approximately 10" × 10" and ¾" thick. Using a sharp knife, cut the dough into 9 biscuits.

6. Gently rearrange the biscuits so they are not touching and have room to expand while baking. Brush the tops of the biscuits with milk and sprinkle with coarse salt.

7. Bake for 14–16 minutes, or until golden brown. Allow to cool for 5 minutes on a cooling rack before serving. You can store any remaining biscuits in an airtight container on the counter for 2–3 days.

PER SERVING Calories: 200 | Fat: 12g | Protein: 3g | Sodium: 600mg | Fiber: 1g | Carbohydrates: 22g | Sugar: 1g

Confetti Corn with Bacon

*This dish has absolutely everything you could want in a corn side dish
(like bacon and cream), without the annoying kernels in your teeth.*

INGREDIENTS | SERVES 6 | 25 MINUTES

4 slices low-sodium bacon

1 medium onion, peeled and chopped

4 cloves garlic, chopped

1 medium orange bell pepper, seeded and chopped

4 cups sweet corn kernels (about 6–8 ears)

½ cup canned gluten-free creamed corn

4 ounces Neufchâtel cheese

3 ounces soft goat cheese

¼ teaspoon salt

⅛ teaspoon ground black pepper

¼ teaspoon dried oregano

1 tablespoon water

⅓ cup light cream

1. Cook bacon in a medium skillet over medium-high heat until crispy. Remove bacon from skillet, chop into small pieces, and set aside. Remove all but 1 tablespoon of bacon fat from the skillet.

2. Add onion to the bacon fat and cook until just fragrant, about 2 minutes. Stir in garlic, bell pepper, and corn and cook until corn is soft, about 6 more minutes.

3. Add creamed corn, Neufchâtel cheese, goat cheese, salt, pepper, oregano, water, and cream. Reduce heat to medium and cook until cheeses have melted and mixture is thick and creamy, about 6 more minutes.

4. Garnish mixture with chopped bacon and serve immediately.

PER SERVING Calories: 365 | Fat: 21g | Protein: 15g | Sodium: 440mg | Fiber: 4g | Carbohydrates: 33g | Sugar: 6g

Roasted Red Potatoes with Garlic

Simple, classic, and oh-so-easy to make, these roasted red potatoes with garlic are a great go-to for any busy weeknight or a last-minute potluck party.

INGREDIENTS | SERVES 4 | 45 MINUTES

1½ pounds red potatoes, quartered
2½ tablespoons olive oil
4 garlic cloves, minced
1 teaspoon salt
1 teaspoon ground black pepper
⅔ cup chopped parsley leaves
3 tablespoons grated Parmesan cheese

1. Preheat oven to 400°F. Spray a 9" × 13" baking dish with gluten-free nonstick cooking spray.

2. Arrange potatoes in a single layer in the baking dish. Mix oil, garlic, salt, and pepper and pour over the potatoes. Toss to coat.

3. Bake for about 35–40 minutes or until edges are golden brown and crispy. Toss with parsley and Parmesan cheese before serving.

PER SERVING Calories: 220 | Fat: 10g | Protein: 5g | Sodium: 650mg | Fiber: 3g | Carbohydrates: 29g | Sugar: 2g

Simple Zucchini-Parmesan Sticks

This is an easy, delicious side dish that complements any entrée. These are also perfect for a light, healthy snack.

INGREDIENTS | SERVES 4 | 10 MINUTES

1 large zucchini, sliced into 2–3" sticks
Misto sprayer filled with extra-virgin olive oil
1 tablespoon shaved Parmesan cheese
1 teaspoon salt
1 teaspoon ground black pepper

1. Preheat oven to broil. Line baking sheet with aluminum foil and spray with gluten-free nonstick cooking spray.

2. Place sliced zucchini sticks on aluminum foil and spray lightly with olive oil sprayer.

3. Sprinkle Parmesan cheese on top. Season with salt and pepper.

4. Broil until cheese melts and turns light brown, about 2 minutes.

PER SERVING Calories: 32 | Fat: 2g | Protein: 1g | Sodium: 600mg | Fiber: 1g | Carbohydrates: 3g | Sugar: 2g

Quinoa Fried "Rice"

Forget regular fried rice, this quinoa fried "rice" is the new thing in town.
Not only is it quick to whip up; it's completely gluten-free. Serve it with the zesty
Orange Chicken in Chapter 8 or those fabulous Crispy Egg Rolls in Chapter 7.

INGREDIENTS | SERVES 8 | 35 MINUTES

1¾ cups gluten-free chicken broth

½ cup regular quinoa

½ cup red quinoa

1 tablespoon sesame or peanut oil

½ cup chopped onion

2 large carrots, peeled and chopped

½ medium green bell pepper, seeded and chopped

3 chives, chopped

4 garlic cloves, minced

1 cup chopped sugar snap peas

2 tablespoons gluten-free teriyaki sauce

3 tablespoons gluten-free soy sauce

1 tablespoon fish sauce

1 teaspoon salt

½ teaspoon ground black pepper

2 large eggs, beaten

Chopped fresh parsley, for garnish, optional

1. Bring the broth to a boil in a large saucepan over high heat. Stir in regular quinoa and red quinoa and reduce heat to medium-low. Cook until softened, about 12–15 minutes. Fluff with a fork and transfer to a large bowl.

2. Heat the oil in a large skillet over medium heat. Add the onion, carrots, bell pepper, chives, garlic, and sugar snap peas. Cook until softened, about 6–7 minutes. Stir in the quinoa.

3. In a small bowl, whisk together the teriyaki sauce, soy sauce, fish sauce, salt, and pepper. Pour the sauce over the quinoa mixture.

4. Pour in the eggs and stir-fry 3–4 minutes, or until set. Serve immediately. Garnish with parsley if desired.

PER SERVING Calories: 160 | Fat: 5g | Protein: 7g | Sodium: 1,200mg | Fiber: 3g | Carbohydrates: 22g | Sugar: 3g

Mexican-Seasoned Baked Avocado Fries

Avocado is typically served chilled in soups, salads, or guacamoles, but not often warm. These soft, spicy, baked avocado fries almost melt in your mouth when they're done. Dip them into some buttermilk ranch dressing or a spicy mayo.

INGREDIENTS | SERVES 4 | 30 MINUTES

1 cup light cream

1 cup gluten-free all-purpose flour

½ cup almond meal or flour

½ cup gluten-free panko bread crumbs

1 tablespoon gluten-free taco seasoning

½ teaspoon chili powder

1 teaspoon salt

1 teaspoon ground black pepper

4 medium ripe avocados, peeled, pitted, and sliced

1. Preheat oven to 425°F. Line 2 baking sheets with parchment paper and lightly spray with gluten-free cooking spray.

2. Pour cream into a shallow bowl. In a medium bowl, whisk flour, almond meal, and bread crumbs. Stir in taco seasoning, chili powder, salt, and pepper. Stir to combine.

3. Dip each avocado slice into the cream and then dredge in the bread crumb/almond meal mixture. Place the avocado slices on the baking sheets in a single layer.

4. Bake for about 10 minutes on each side. Serve hot.

PER SERVING Calories: 690 | Fat: 49g | Protein: 14g | Sodium: 780mg | Fiber: 17g | Carbohydrates: 57g | Sugar: 3g

Asian-Spiced Kale Chips

Salty, crunchy, and low-fat, these Asian-Spiced Kale Chips are guilt-free and irresistible!

INGREDIENTS | SERVES 6 | 25 MINUTES

1 large bunch fresh kale

2 tablespoons sesame oil

2 tablespoons gluten-free soy sauce

½ tablespoon lemon juice

½ teaspoon garlic powder

¼ teaspoon ground ginger

1½ teaspoons salt, divided

1 teaspoon ground black pepper, divided

½ cup mayonnaise

¼ cup gluten-free ketchup

1 tablespoon sriracha sauce

½ teaspoon onion powder

Watch Those Chips!

The key to perfectly crispy kale chips is the timing. A too-short baking time will leave them limp and sad, but if you leave them in too long, they'll burn quickly. Cooking times can vary from 10–20 minutes. So it's a good idea to keep an eye on them while they're baking.

1. Preheat oven to 350°F. Line a baking sheet with parchment paper and set aside.

2. Wash and rinse kale. Remove ribs and cut leaves into large chips.

3. In a large mixing bowl, add sesame oil, soy sauce, lemon juice, garlic powder, ginger, 1 teaspoon salt, and ½ teaspoon pepper. Add the kale chips and mix to coat.

4. Place the chips on the parchment paper in a single layer. Bake for about 10–15 minutes, or until crispy.

5. In a small bowl, mix mayonnaise, ketchup, sriracha sauce, onion powder, and remaining salt and pepper. Serve the chips with the sauce.

PER SERVING Calories: 215 | Fat: 20g | Protein: 3g | Sodium: 1,000mg | Fiber: 1g | Carbohydrates: 10g | Sugar: 2g

CHAPTER 12

Grains and Pasta

Classic Italian Risotto SC

Risotto should be very creamy on the outside, with just a bit of toothsome resistance on the inside of each grain of rice.

INGREDIENTS | SERVES 4

2 tablespoons butter

2 tablespoons olive oil

½ cup finely chopped sweet onion

2 stalks celery, finely chopped

¼ cup celery leaves, chopped

1½ cups Arborio rice

1 teaspoon salt

5 cups gluten-free chicken or vegetable broth

¼ cup chopped parsley

½ teaspoon freshly ground black pepper

⅔ cup freshly grated Parmesan cheese

1. Place the butter and oil in a heavy-bottomed pot, melt butter, and add the onion, celery, and celery leaves. Cook for 3–5 minutes, until vegetables are softened.

2. Add the rice and stir to coat with butter and oil. Stir in salt. Add rice and softened vegetables to a greased 4–6-quart slow cooker.

3. Add remaining ingredients, except cheese, to the slow cooker. Cover and cook on high for 3 hours or on low for 6 hours.

4. Twenty minutes before serving, stir in Parmesan cheese.

PER SERVING Calories: 600 | Fat: 23g | Protein: 19g | Sodium: 2,000mg | Fiber: 3g | Carbohydrates: 77g | Sugar: 1.5g

Retro Tuna Pasta Casserole SC

The popular tuna casserole can now be made gluten-free! In this recipe the pasta is cooked separately, so it doesn't become overcooked in the casserole.

INGREDIENTS | SERVES 4

2 cans water-packed white tuna, drained and flaked

1 cup heavy cream

¾ cup mayonnaise

4 large hard-cooked eggs, chopped

1 cup finely diced celery

½ cup finely minced onion

1 cup frozen garden peas

¼ teaspoon ground black pepper

1½ cups crushed potato chips, divided

2 cups gluten-free pasta, cooked

1. In a large bowl combine tuna, cream, mayonnaise, eggs, celery, onion, peas, ground pepper, and ¾ cup crushed potato chips.

2. Pour tuna mixture into a greased 4–6-quart slow cooker. Top with remaining potato chips. Cover and cook on low for 3 hours or on high for 1½ hours.

3. To serve: place tuna casserole on top of ½ cup of pasta per person.

PER SERVING Calories: 1,020 | Fat: 75g | Protein: 41g | Sodium: 705mg | Fiber: 5g | Carbohydrates: 47g | Sugar: 5g

Chicken Alfredo Pasta SC

Quartered artichokes add a tangy flavor to this easy pasta casserole.

INGREDIENTS | SERVES 4

1 pound boneless, skinless chicken thighs, cut into ¾" pieces

1 (14-ounce) can quartered artichokes, drained

1 (16-ounce) jar gluten-free Alfredo sauce

1 cup water

½ cup sun-dried tomatoes, drained and chopped

8 ounces gluten-free pasta, uncooked

2 tablespoons shredded Parmesan cheese

1. In a greased 4–6-quart slow cooker, mix chicken, artichokes, Alfredo sauce, and water. Cover and cook on high for 3 hours or on low for 6 hours.

2. Forty-five minutes before serving, stir tomatoes and uncooked pasta into chicken mixture.

3. Cover lid and continue to cook until pasta is al dente. Sprinkle Parmesan cheese over individual servings.

PER SERVING Calories: 1,010 | Fat: 47g | Protein: 51g | Sodium: 2,700mg | Fiber: 10g | Carbohydrates: 97g | Sugar: 11g

Quinoa Angel Hair with Bolognese Sauce

*Quinoa pasta has become popular for its added protein and wonderful texture.
Many grocery stores and specialty markets carry quinoa pasta. If you can't find it,
feel free to substitute with another wheat-free pasta or rice.*

INGREDIENTS | SERVES 6 | 40 MINUTES

1 tablespoon extra-virgin olive oil

2 cloves garlic, chopped

½ medium onion, peeled and chopped

1 pound lean ground beef, turkey, or chicken

2 ounces diced pancetta

½ cup ground pork

½ cup chopped mushrooms

½ cup chopped carrots

1 recipe Spicy Marinara Sauce (see recipe in Chapter 3)

1 (8-ounce) package quinoa pasta

2 tablespoons grated Parmesan cheese

1. In a large skillet over medium heat, heat the oil. Sauté garlic and onion for 3–4 minutes, until onions are translucent and tender.

2. Add the ground beef, pancetta, and ground pork and brown over medium heat until no longer pink, about 5–8 minutes.

3. Once the meat is cooked, add mushrooms and carrots and cook for 3–4 minutes, until they soften.

4. Add Spicy Marinara Sauce and simmer over low heat for 20 minutes, stirring occasionally.

5. Meanwhile, cook quinoa pasta according to package instructions. Drain pasta and transfer to a serving dish. Top with sauce and Parmesan cheese.

PER SERVING Calories: 490 | Fat: 22g | Protein: 27g | Sodium: 890mg | Fiber: 7g | Carbohydrates: 42g | Sugar: 9g

Pasta Primavera with Summer Vegetables

*This dish can be served over brown rice pasta, quinoa pasta, rice, or even quinoa.
Feel free to add some shrimp or chicken to it if you'd like.*

INGREDIENTS | SERVES 6 | 30 MINUTES

16 ounces gluten-free pasta

3 tablespoons extra-virgin olive oil

½ scallion, chopped

2 garlic cloves, minced

1 large carrot, peeled and diced

1 large zucchini, peeled and diced

1 summer squash, peeled and diced

½ medium green bell pepper, seeded and diced

½ medium red bell pepper, seeded and diced

½ cup chopped green beans

½ small eggplant, peeled and cut into ¼" slices

½ cup sliced plum tomatoes

½ cup Spicy Marinara Sauce (see recipe in Chapter 3)

2 tablespoons grated Parmesan cheese

1 teaspoon salt

½ teaspoon freshly ground black pepper

1. Cook pasta according to package instructions. Rinse with cool water and set aside.

2. In a large skillet over medium heat, heat oil, sauté scallion and garlic for 2–3 minutes, until scallion and garlic become tender.

3. Add carrot, zucchini, summer squash, bell peppers, green beans, eggplant, and tomatoes. Cook vegetables about 10 minutes, until they soften. Remove from heat.

4. Add the marinara sauce to the vegetables and stir to combine. Add pasta and stir once again. Top with Parmesan cheese, salt, and pepper.

PER SERVING Calories: 400 | Fat: 9g | Protein: 13g | Sodium: 475mg | Fiber: 6g | Carbohydrates: 66g | Sugar: 8g

Baked Mushroom and Fontina Risotto

You can add so many other ingredients—cut-up cooked chicken or turkey, chopped pears or apples, and your favorite herbs.

INGREDIENTS | SERVES 8 | 45 MINUTES

3 tablespoons butter, divided

3 tablespoons olive oil

1 small onion, peeled and minced

2 garlic cloves, minced

1 teaspoon salt

½ teaspoon freshly ground black pepper

6 large leaves fresh sage, ripped or cut up, or 2 teaspoons dried sage, crumbled

1 cup long-grain rice

2½ cups gluten-free chicken broth

½ cup white vermouth

8 ounces mixed mushrooms (shiitakes, porcinis, morels, chanterelles)

⅓ cup grated fontina cheese

A Misunderstood Italian Staple

Most cooks think that risotto is simply rice that has been boiled with broth and herbs. But it's so much more—the technique is simple but demanding. The secret is the rice and how it's slow cooked, adding a bit of liquid until it's absorbed and then adding a bit more. It's been said that the rice will tell you when to add liquid—it hisses and sizzles, asking for the broth!

1. Preheat the oven to 350°F.

2. Heat 1 tablespoon butter and the olive oil in an ovenproof casserole. Sauté the onion and garlic over a low flame until softened, about 3–4 minutes.

3. Add the salt, pepper, sage, and rice and stir to coat. Add the broth and vermouth. Cover the rice and place in the oven.

4. After the rice has cooked for 20 minutes, sauté the mushrooms in the remaining 2 tablespoons butter and stir into the rice. Re-cover the casserole and continue to cook for 15 minutes.

5. Just before serving, stir in the fontina cheese.

PER SERVING Calories: 250 | Fat: 12g | Protein: 5g | Sodium: 660mg | Fiber: 1g | Carbohydrates: 26g | Sugar: 1g

Hawaiian-Style Rice with Pineapple, Mango, and Macadamia Nuts

This is perfect with grilled or roasted ham, pork chops, or pork tenderloin. Fruit blends well with the rice and is a fine side dish. You can also add crumbled, crisp bacon as an interesting garnish.

INGREDIENTS | SERVES 6 | 35 MINUTES

1 cup water

1½ cups orange juice

1½ cups short-grain rice

Minced zest of 1 medium orange

1 teaspoon salt

½ teaspoon hot pepper sauce

½ cup chopped pineapple

1 ripe mango, diced

2 tablespoons butter

½ cup toasted macadamia nuts

1. In a large saucepan, bring the water and juice to a boil. Stir in the rice and return to a boil. Cover and simmer for about 30 minutes, or until the rice is tender.

2. Reduce heat to medium, add the rest of the ingredients except the butter and nuts, and heat everything through. Serve hot with butter and nuts arranged over the top.

PER SERVING Calories: 350 | Fat: 13g | Protein: 5g | Sodium: 400mg | Fiber: 3g | Carbohydrates: 55g | Sugar: 12g

Spanish-Style Rice MA

This is an excellent side with a great steak. It can be made in advance and then reheated just before serving time.

INGREDIENTS | SERVES 4 | 30 MINUTES

3 cups water

2 teaspoons salt

1 cup white rice

½ cup olive oil

1 large onion, peeled and chopped

1 clove garlic

2 jalapeño or poblano peppers, cored, seeded, and chopped

1 roasted red pepper, from a jar or your own, chopped

4 medium plum tomatoes, cored and chopped

1 teaspoon lemon zest

10 black olives, pitted and sliced

½ teaspoon freshly ground black pepper

1. Bring the water to a boil and add the salt and the rice. Reduce the heat to a simmer, cover, and cook until tender, about 25 minutes.

2. While the rice is cooking, heat the oil in a large frying pan. Add the onion, garlic, and hot peppers. Sauté over low heat for 8–10 minutes. Stir in roasted pepper, tomatoes, lemon zest, olives, and black pepper and simmer for 10 minutes.

3. Add vegetable mixture to the hot rice and serve.

PER SERVING Calories: 465 | Fat: 28g | Protein: 5g | Sodium: 1,250mg | Fiber: 3g | Carbohydrates: 48g | Sugar: 5g

Ground Pepper

You can get pink, white, and black peppercorns. Some cooks like to mix them. Some say there is a taste difference among the three. Other cooks use white pepper in white food so you won't see the black specks. Try a coarsely ground pepper in recipes like this Spanish-Style Rice. To coarse-grind, place 6–8 peppercorns between two pieces of waxed paper. Use a heavy frying pan to press down on the corns until they are cracked and in coarse pieces.

Shrimp Fra Diavolo

This dish is spicy, but you can easily adjust the amount of crushed red pepper according to your taste.

INGREDIENTS | SERVES 6 | 40 MINUTES

2 tablespoons extra-virgin olive oil

6 cloves garlic, chopped

½ medium onion, peeled and minced

4 medium tornatoes, chopped

1 tablespoon ground basil

1 tablespoon ground oregano

½ cup dry white wine

1 teaspoon salt

½ teaspoon crushed red pepper flakes

16 ounces small shrimp, peeled and deveined

8 ounces gluten-free pasta, cooked according to package instructions

1 tablespoon chopped fresh parsley

1. Heat oil in a large skillet over medium heat. Sauté garlic and onion for 3–4 minutes, until tender and aromatic.

2. Add the tomatoes, basil, oregano, white wine, salt, and red pepper flakes. Reduce heat to low and simmer 25 minutes, stirring occasionally.

3. Add shrimp to tomato mixture and cook 5–8 minutes, until cooked through.

4. Pour shrimp sauce over cooked pasta. Top with chopped parsley.

PER SERVING Calories: 300 | Fat: 6g | Protein: 21g | Sodium: 500mg | Fiber: 2.5g | Carbohydrates: 34g | Sugar: 4g

Fra Diavolo

"Fra Diavolo" means "brother devil" in Italian, named for its spicy taste. If you like it even spicier, increase the red pepper flakes to 1 teaspoon. You can also use any type of shellfish in this dish for variety.

Confetti and Rice Pasta with Chicken

This is fun to eat and pretty to look at. The "confetti" is minced vegetables.
Lots of Parmesan cheese completes the dish.

INGREDIENTS | SERVES 4 | 25 MINUTES

½ cup extra-virgin olive oil

½ cup finely chopped red bell pepper

½ cup finely chopped yellow summer squash

½ cup finely chopped zucchini squash

1 bunch scallions, finely chopped

2 cloves garlic, finely chopped

½ cup rice or corn flour

1 teaspoon salt

½ teaspoon ground black pepper

½ teaspoon dried thyme

¾ pound boneless, skinless chicken breast, cut into bite-sized pieces

½ cup gluten-free chicken broth

8 medium plum (Roma) tomatoes, chopped, or 1½ cups canned tomatoes

1 teaspoon dried oregano

1 teaspoon dried basil

1 tablespoon red pepper flakes

1 pound rice pasta, cooked

1 cup freshly grated Parmesan cheese

1. In a large skillet over medium heat, heat the olive oil and add the pepper, squash, scallions, and garlic. Sauté, stirring frequently, for 3–4 minutes.

2. While the vegetables are sautéing, mix the flour, salt, pepper, and thyme on a piece of waxed paper.

3. Dredge the chicken in the flour mixture and add to the pan along with the vegetables.

4. Add the broth, tomatoes, oregano, basil, and red pepper flakes. Cook, uncovered, for 10 minutes to make sure the chicken is done.

5. Add the rice pasta to the pan of sauce and mix. Sprinkle with Parmesan cheese and serve.

PER SERVING Calories: 710 | Fat: 30g | Protein: 40g | Sodium: 1,200mg | Fiber: 8g | Carbohydrates: 70g | Sugar: 12g

Rice Pasta

Rice pasta is available online and at Asian markets. Many supermarkets also carry it. Soba—Japanese noodles—have both buckwheat flour and wheat flour in them, and sometimes the contents are listed in Japanese characters.

Corn Pasta in Rich Cream Sauce with Prosciutto, Gorgonzola, and Walnuts

Feel free to lighten this up using half-and-half instead of the cream (but the cream really adds to the flavor).

INGREDIENTS | SERVES 4 | 25 MINUTES

1 (10-ounce) package corn pasta

3 tablespoons unsalted butter

3 tablespoons corn flour

2 cups medium cream, warmed

2 tablespoons minced prosciutto

½ cup crumbled Gorgonzola or blue cheese

¼ teaspoon ground nutmeg

½ cup walnut pieces, toasted

½ teaspoon salt

½ teaspoon freshly ground black pepper

1. Cook corn pasta according to instructions on the package.

2. Melt the butter in a large skillet over medium-low heat and stir in the flour. Sauté, stirring for 4–5 minutes. Add the warm cream, whisking constantly until thickened to desired consistency (about 5 minutes more).

3. Remove from the heat and stir in the prosciutto, cheese, nutmeg, walnuts, and salt and pepper. Toss with pasta. Serve immediately.

PER SERVING Calories: 865 | Fat: 61g | Protein: 19g | Sodium: 640mg | Fiber: 3g | Carbohydrates: 63g | Sugar: 2g

Rich Cream Sauces Are Versatile

You can add herbs, stock, or even bacon to a rich cream sauce. You can add cheese such as mascarpone or some prosciutto. Mushrooms add body and flavor, too! You can adapt a cream sauce to loads of fish, meat, and vegetable dishes and benefit from the lush flavors.

Spaghetti with Mushroom Cream Sauce

This simple, creamy pasta is one of the easiest dishes in the book, and certainly one of the most flavorful. The caramelized onions and soft mushrooms make the perfect topping for any gluten-free spaghetti noodles.

INGREDIENTS | SERVES 4 | 35 MINUTES

8 ounces gluten-free spaghetti

2 tablespoons unsalted butter

1 medium yellow onion, peeled and chopped

½ pound baby bella mushrooms

½ pound shiitake mushrooms

½ cup gluten-free low-sodium chicken stock

½ cup dry white wine

½ teaspoon salt

½ teaspoon ground black pepper

1 cup heavy cream

1 tablespoon chopped chives

½ tablespoon chopped fresh rosemary

¾ cup grated Parmesan cheese

1. Bring a large pot of salted water to a rapid boil. Add spaghetti and cook until al dente, about 6–8 minutes. Drain and set aside.

2. In a large skillet, melt butter over medium-high heat. Add onion and mushrooms and cook until softened, about 6–8 minutes.

3. Stir in stock, wine, salt, and pepper. Bring to a boil, reduce heat to low, and simmer until liquid is almost evaporated, about 6 minutes.

4. Add cream and stir to combine. Simmer another 4–6 minutes, or until thickened. Stir in chives, rosemary, and cheese.

5. Pour the sauce over the spaghetti and serve warm.

PER SERVING Calories: 620 | Fat: 35g | Protein: 20g | Sodium: 400mg | Fiber: 4g | Carbohydrates: 54g | Sugar: 4g

Four-Cheese Baked Penne with Prosciutto

This is like macaroni and cheese, but so much better. The rich, creamy cheese sauce and crispy prosciutto take this baked pasta to the next level. Serve with a dash of cayenne or crushed red pepper for more spice.

INGREDIENTS | SERVES 4 | 45 MINUTES

8 ounces gluten-free penne pasta

2 teaspoons salt, divided

3 tablespoons unsalted butter

¼ cup gluten-free all-purpose flour

1½ cups whole milk

1 cup heavy cream

1 teaspoon ground black pepper

½ teaspoon gluten-free Cajun seasoning

1½ cups shredded Cheddar cheese

¾ cup shredded mozzarella cheese

¼ cup shredded fontina cheese

½ cup shredded Parmesan cheese

4 ounces prosciutto, chopped into bite-sized pieces

1. Bring a large pot of water to a boil over high heat. Add pasta and 1 teaspoon salt and cook until al dente, about 8 minutes. Drain and set aside.

2. Preheat oven to 375°F. Spray a 9" × 12" baking dish with gluten-free nonstick cooking spray and set aside.

3. In a Dutch oven, melt butter over medium-high heat. Whisk in flour and stir until a thick paste forms, about 2 minutes. Whisk in the milk, cream, remaining salt, pepper, and Cajun seasoning.

4. Heat another 4 minutes, or until the mixture coats the back of a spoon. Immediately remove from heat and stir in Cheddar, mozzarella, and fontina. Mix until cheese is melted and sauce is smooth. Stir pasta into the cheese sauce.

5. Pour pasta mixture into baking dish and top with Parmesan cheese and prosciutto.

6. Bake for about 15 minutes, or until prosciutto is crispy and cheese is bubbly.

PER SERVING Calories: 940 | Fat: 62g | Protein: 40g | Sodium: 2,000mg | Fiber: 2g | Carbohydrates: 55g | Sugar: 7g

Spicy Thai Chicken and Peanut Noodles

This pasta has everything you could want in a dish: spice, creaminess, incredible flavor, and crunch.

INGREDIENTS | SERVES 8 | 30 MINUTES

10 ounces thin Thai rice noodles

2½ tablespoons sesame oil

½ cup chopped onion

¾ cup shredded carrot

¼ cup chopped leek

1¼ pounds boneless, skinless chicken breasts, cut into thin slices

¼ cup gluten-free low-sodium soy sauce

¼ cup crunchy peanut butter

¼ cup honey

1 tablespoon lime juice

1 tablespoon Thai chili paste

½ tablespoon crushed red pepper

1½ tablespoons rice vinegar

1 teaspoon salt

1 teaspoon ground black pepper

½ cup chopped cilantro

¼ cup chopped unsalted peanuts

1. Bring a large pot of water to a boil. Remove from heat and stir in rice noodles. Let sit for about 4–5 minutes, then drain and set aside.

2. Heat sesame oil in a large skillet or wok over medium heat. Add onion and cook until just softened, about 2 minutes. Stir in carrot and leek and cook another 2–3 minutes. Add chicken and cook until browned on all sides, about 6–8 minutes. Mix in the noodles.

3. In a small bowl, whisk the soy sauce, peanut butter, honey, lime juice, chili paste, crushed red pepper, vinegar, salt, and pepper together. Pour the sauce over the chicken and noodles and stir to combine.

4. Remove from heat and garnish with cilantro and peanuts.

PER SERVING Calories: 340 | Fat: 13g | Protein: 22g | Sodium: 850mg | Fiber: 2g | Carbohydrates: 35g | Sugar: 11g

Buckwheat with Tomatoes, Feta, and Mint

Fresh mint, tomatoes, and feta instantly add pizzazz to buckwheat, which can be bland if not properly seasoned. Serve this as a side dish or even a main dish with some chicken or fish.

INGREDIENTS | SERVES 4 | 25 MINUTES

1 teaspoon salt

1 cup buckwheat groats

1 cup crumbled feta cheese

2 shallots, peeled and minced

1 cup chopped fresh mint

1 medium cucumber, peeled and chopped

1 cup halved cherry tomatoes

2½ tablespoons lemon juice

2½ tablespoons extra-virgin olive oil

1. Bring a large pot of water to a boil and add salt. In a large skillet, toast the buckwheat groats over medium-high heat, shaking the pan often, for about 4–5 minutes, or until lightly browned. Transfer buckwheat to the pot of boiling water. Reduce heat to low and simmer until just tender, about 5–6 minutes. Drain buckwheat and transfer to a large bowl.

2. Stir in feta, shallots, mint, cucumber, and tomatoes.

3. In a small bowl, whisk the lemon juice and oil together. Pour the dressing over the buckwheat mixture and serve immediately.

PER SERVING Calories: 350 | Fat: 17g | Protein: 12g | Sodium: 900mg | Fiber: 7g | Carbohydrates: 40g | Sugar: 4g

Spinach and Artichoke Casserole

This spinach and artichoke casserole turns a popular creamy appetizer into a luscious side dish. Topped with bubbly cheese, it's a great accompaniment for holiday meals as well as everyday dinners.

INGREDIENTS | SERVES 4 | 45 MINUTES

2 cups water

1½ cups gluten-free wild rice

½ teaspoon salt

2 tablespoons unsalted butter, divided

1 (14-ounce) can artichoke hearts, drained and chopped

10 ounces fresh spinach, stems removed

4 large eggs, beaten

1 cup whole milk

2 tablespoons heavy cream

⅓ cup sour cream

¼ cup lemon juice

¼ cup grated Parmesan cheese

¼ cup shredded mozzarella cheese

¼ cup toasted pine nuts

1. Preheat oven to 350°F. Grease an 8" × 8" baking dish with gluten-free nonstick cooking spray.

2. Bring 2 cups of water to a rapid boil in a large saucepan over high heat. Add rice and salt. Reduce heat to medium-low and simmer 15 minutes. Remove from heat and stir in 1 tablespoon butter.

3. While rice cooks, heat remaining butter over medium heat in a large skillet. Add artichokes and spinach and cook until spinach starts to wilt, about 4 minutes.

4. Stir in eggs, milk, heavy cream, sour cream, and lemon juice. Bring to a boil and then reduce heat to low. Cook about 2 minutes and stir in the rice.

5. Pour the mixture into the prepared baking dish. Top with cheeses and pine nuts.

6. Bake for about 8 minutes, or until cheese is melted.

PER SERVING Calories: 600 | Fat: 28g | Protein: 27g | Sodium: 650mg | Fiber: 14g | Carbohydrates: 66g | Sugar: 7g

CHAPTER 13

Vegetarian

Homemade Bean and Vegetable Burgers

Homemade bean burgers are much better than their frozen, store-bought counterparts, and you know these don't contain any extra fillers.

INGREDIENTS | SERVES 4 | 15 MINUTES

1 (15-ounce) can dark red kidney beans, drained

1 large Yukon gold potato, cooked and cooled

⅓ cup cornmeal

⅓ cup fresh or defrosted frozen peas

2 tablespoons minced onion

¼ teaspoon ground chipotle

¼ teaspoon paprika

¼ teaspoon freshly ground black pepper

¼ teaspoon sea salt

2 tablespoons apple cider vinegar

2 tablespoons oil

1. In a medium bowl, mash the beans and potato together using a potato masher. Add the remaining ingredients, except the oil. Mix and form into 4 patties.

2. Heat the oil on medium-high in a medium skillet. Cook the burgers, flipping once, until cooked through and browned on both sides, about 5 minutes per side.

PER SERVING Calories: 105 | Fat: 7g | Protein: 1g | Sodium: 145mg | Fiber: 1g | Carbohydrates: 10g | Sugar: 0g

Spicy Beans and Rice Casserole sc

Using salsa instead of tomatoes and added spices makes this casserole super easy to put together. It's delicious topped with a dollop of sour cream.

INGREDIENTS | SERVES 8

1 (15-ounce) can whole kernel corn, drained

1 (15-ounce) can black beans, rinsed and drained

1 (10-ounce) can diced tomatoes with green chilies

1 cup brown rice, uncooked

2¼ cups gluten-free vegetable broth, or water

1 cup salsa

1 cup shredded Cheddar cheese

¼ cup chopped fresh cilantro

1. Grease a 4–6-quart slow cooker. Add corn, beans, tomatoes, rice, vegetable broth or water, and salsa. Cover and cook on high for 3 hours or on low for 6 hours.

2. Once rice has absorbed water and is fully cooked, stir in Cheddar cheese. Cook an additional 20 minutes on high to melt cheese and serve. Garnish with cilantro.

PER SERVING Calories: 255 | Fat: 6g | Protein: 11g | Sodium: 650mg | Fiber: 6g | Carbohydrates: 43g | Sugar: 5g

Cottage Pie with Carrots, Parsnips, and Celery ▪SC

*Cottage pie is typically made with ground beef. This version uses
lots of vegetables and vegetarian sausage.*

INGREDIENTS | SERVES 6

1 large onion, peeled and diced

3 cloves garlic, minced

1 large carrot, peeled and diced

1 large parsnip, peeled and diced

1 stalk celery, diced

1 pound gluten-free vegetarian sausage, diced

1½ cups gluten-free vegetable stock

½ teaspoon hot paprika

½ teaspoon crushed rosemary

1 tablespoon gluten-free vegetarian Worcestershire sauce

½ teaspoon dried savory

⅛ teaspoon salt

¼ teaspoon freshly ground black pepper

1 tablespoon cornstarch and 1 tablespoon water, mixed (if necessary)

¼ cup minced fresh parsley

2¾ cups plain mashed potatoes

1. In a large nonstick skillet, sauté the onion, garlic, carrot, parsnip, celery, and vegetarian sausage until the sausage is browned, about 5–6 minutes. Transfer the mixture to a greased 4–6-quart slow cooker.

2. Add the stock, paprika, rosemary, Worcestershire sauce, savory, salt, and pepper to the slow cooker. Stir.

3. Cook on low for 6–8 hours. If the mixture still looks very thin, create a slurry by mixing together 1 tablespoon cornstarch and 1 tablespoon water. Stir this into the meat mixture.

4. In a medium bowl, mash the parsley and potatoes using a potato masher. Spread on top of the sausage mixture in the slow cooker. Cover and cook on high for 30–60 minutes or until the potatoes are warmed through.

PER SERVING Calories: 265 | Fat: 8g | Protein: 16g | Sodium: 975mg | Fiber: 3g | Carbohydrates: 35g | Sugar: 4g

Save Time in the Morning

Take a few minutes the night before cooking to cut up any vegetables you need for a recipe. Place them in an airtight container or plastic bag and refrigerate until morning. Measure any dried spices and place them in a small container on the counter until needed.

Lasagna with Spinach SC

There is no need to precook the gluten-free noodles in this recipe. All you need to do is assemble this super easy lasagna in the morning, and you'll have a hearty, family-pleasing meal waiting for you when you get home.

INGREDIENTS | SERVES 10

28 ounces low-fat ricotta cheese

1 cup defrosted and drained frozen cut spinach

1 large egg

½ cup part-skim shredded mozzarella cheese

8 cups (about 2 jars) marinara sauce

½ pound uncooked gluten-free lasagna noodles

1. In a medium bowl, stir together the ricotta, spinach, egg, and mozzarella.

2. Ladle a quarter of the marinara sauce along the bottom of a greased 6-quart slow cooker. The bottom should be thoroughly covered in sauce. Add a single layer of lasagna noodles on top of the sauce, breaking noodles if needed to fit in the sides.

3. Ladle an additional quarter of sauce over the noodles, covering all of the noodles. Top with half of the cheese mixture, pressing firmly with the back of a spoon to smooth. Add a single layer of lasagna noodles on top of the cheese, breaking noodles if needed to fit in the sides.

4. Ladle another quarter of the sauce on top of the noodles, and top with the remaining cheese. Press another layer of noodles onto the cheese and top with the remaining sauce. Take care that the noodles are entirely covered in sauce.

5. Cover and cook on low heat for 4–6 hours until cooked through.

PER SERVING Calories: 390 | Fat: 11g | Protein: 18g | Sodium: 950mg | Fiber: 6g | Carbohydrates: 49g | Sugar: 18g

Easy Italian Spaghetti SC

It doesn't get any easier than this. Because this meal cooks so quickly,
you can put it together as soon as you get home from work.

INGREDIENTS | SERVES 4

1 pound Morningstar Veggie Crumbles
(vegetarian ground beef substitute)

1 (16-ounce) jar marinara sauce

1 cup water

8 ounces gluten-free pasta, uncooked

½ cup grated Parmesan cheese

1. Add Veggie Crumbles, marinara sauce, and water to a greased 4–6-quart slow cooker. Cook on high for 2 hours or on low for 4 hours.

2. Forty-five minutes prior to serving, stir dry gluten-free pasta into meat sauce. The pasta will cook in the sauce. Serve with Parmesan cheese sprinkled on top of each serving.

PER SERVING Calories: 530 | Fat: 12g | Protein: 36g | Sodium: 1,100mg | Fiber: 12g | Carbohydrates: 66g | Sugar: 11g

Zucchini Pasta with Parmesan and Spicy Marinara Sauce

This is such a fun substitution for regular noodles or pasta.
This dish is also a perfect way to get more vegetables into your diet.

INGREDIENTS | SERVES 4 | 15 MINUTES

4 large zucchini

1 tablespoon grapeseed oil

3 cloves garlic, minced

1 teaspoon salt

½ teaspoon freshly ground black pepper

3 tablespoons grated Parmesan cheese

1 recipe Spicy Marinara Sauce (see recipe in Chapter 3)

1. Cut the zucchini into thin, noodle-like strips using a peeler or mandoline.

2. Heat the oil in a large skillet over medium-high heat. Add zucchini and garlic; cook and stir until just tender, about 5 minutes. Season with salt and pepper.

3. Sprinkle with Parmesan cheese. Top with Spicy Marinara Sauce.

PER SERVING Calories: 300 | Fat: 16g | Protein: 9g | Sodium: 1,800mg | Fiber: 8g | Carbohydrates: 30g | Sugar: 17g

Tofu and Vegetables in Asian Citrus Sauce

The tastes and textures come together beautifully in this Asian-inspired dish. Serve over rice.

INGREDIENTS | SERVES 4 | 15 MINUTES

1 tablespoon sesame seed oil

3 tablespoons peanut or other vegetable oil

1 bunch scallions, chopped

1 clove garlic, minced

1" piece gingerroot, peeled and minced

⅔ pound sugar snap peas, ends trimmed

2 cups mung bean sprouts

2 cups shredded Chinese cabbage

½ teaspoon brown sugar

½ orange, juice and rind, pulsed in the food processor

1 teaspoon Asian five-spice powder

1 teaspoon Chinese mustard or Japanese wasabi

¼ cup sake

¼ cup light gluten-free soy sauce

1 pound satin tofu, cubed

1. Heat the oils in a wok. Add the scallions, garlic, and gingerroot. Lightly mix in sugar snap peas, bean sprouts, and cabbage and toss in the oil for 3–4 minutes. Place the cooked vegetables in a large, warm serving bowl.

2. In a small bowl, mix together the brown sugar, orange juice and rind, five-spice powder, mustard or wasabi, sake, and soy sauce.

3. Stir into the wok until blended. Add the tofu cubes and vegetables, and mix to coat. Serve hot.

PER SERVING Calories: 240 | Fat: 10g | Protein: 17g | Sodium: 950mg | Fiber: 4g | Carbohydrates: 18g | Sugar: 7g

A Source of Protein for Vegetarians

Tofu, long used in Asia because meat and milk were both scarce and expensive, has become an important part of the vegetarian diet. It can be flavored to taste like many kinds of meat. Or it can be sweetened and prepared with fruit for desserts. It's delicious in soups and with vegetables.

Spinach, Kale, and Mushroom Pizza

This pizza goes beyond the typical red sauce and mozzarella cheese.
Goat cheese makes a wonderful addition to this sauceless pizza.

INGREDIENTS | SERVES 4 | 15 MINUTES

1 tablespoon grapeseed oil
½ medium onion, peeled and chopped
2 cloves garlic, chopped
2 cups kale
2 cups spinach
1 cup sliced mushrooms
1 Cauliflower Pizza Crust (see recipe in this chapter)
½ cup goat cheese, crumbled
Handful of fresh basil, torn

Pizza Is a Family Affair

Making pizzas can be a fun and easy family activity. Let the kids sprinkle the cheese, add the vegetables, or tear the basil. Doing simple prep work is an easy way to expose "future chefs" to the joy of cooking.

1. Preheat broiler.

2. Heat oil in a large skillet over medium-high heat. Sauté onion and garlic for 4–5 minutes. Add kale, spinach, and mushrooms and sauté for 3–4 minutes more, until mushrooms soften and the greens wilt.

3. Place the vegetables on top of pizza crust. Top with goat cheese and basil.

4. Place under the broiler for 2 minutes until cheese is melted. Serve hot.

PER SERVING Calories: 270 | Fat: 18g | Protein: 18g | Sodium: 370mg | Fiber: 2g | Carbohydrates: 9g | Sugar: 2g

Cauliflower Pizza Crust

Being on a wheat-free diet doesn't mean you can't have pizza!
This makes a 1"-thick crust, but it can be doubled for a larger pizza.

INGREDIENTS | SERVES 4 | 25 MINUTES

1 cup raw cauliflower, grated (or finely chopped in food processor)
1 large egg
½ cup Parmesan cheese
1 teaspoon oregano
2 teaspoons parsley
Handful of fresh basil
1 garlic clove, finely diced

Cauliflower Pizza Crust Tips

Approximately 2¼ cups of cauliflower, chopped into 1" pieces, will grate into 1 cup of grated cauliflower.

1. Preheat oven to 425°F. Spray a cookie sheet with gluten-free nonstick spray or use parchment paper.

2. Combine all ingredients in a large bowl. Mix well with your hands.

3. Press mixture evenly on baking pan or pizza stone. Bake for 15–20 minutes, until the edges start to brown. You may turn over once if desired.

4. Remove the pan from the oven. Use immediately for pizza or refrigerate up to one week.

PER SERVING Calories: 80 | Fat: 5g | Protein: 7g | Sodium: 245mg | Fiber: 1g | Carbohydrates: 2g | Sugar: 1g

Indian Vegetable Cakes

This is a great way to get kids to eat their veggies! A nonstick pan helps prevent sticking.
Sour cream makes a very good garnish.

INGREDIENTS | SERVES 6 | 20 MINUTES

1 tablespoon extra-virgin olive oil
1 (10-ounce) package frozen chopped spinach, thawed and squeezed of excess moisture
5 ounces frozen baby peas, thawed
½ bunch scallions, chopped
1 teaspoon curry powder
½ teaspoon turmeric
½ teaspoon ground black pepper
1 teaspoon salt
¼ teaspoon hot pepper sauce
¼ cup cornmeal
5 extra-large eggs, well beaten
½ cup grated Parmesan cheese

1. Heat olive oil in a large nonstick skillet over medium heat.

2. In a large bowl, mix together all the ingredients except the Parmesan cheese. Form into patties.

3. Drop patties, 3 or 4 at a time, into the pan and fry until delicately browned, 3–4 minutes per side. Turn and sprinkle with cheese before serving.

PER SERVING Calories: 170 | Fat: 9g | Protein: 12g | Sodium: 600mg | Fiber: 3g | Carbohydrates: 11g | Sugar: 2.5g

Potato Frittata with Cheese and Herbs

Use both gluten-free nonstick spray and butter in this recipe, or the starch in the potatoes will stick. Spinach would make a lovely addition to this.

INGREDIENTS | SERVES 4 | 30 MINUTES

1 large Yukon gold potato, peeled

4 teaspoons butter

1 teaspoon salt

½ teaspoon ground black pepper

6 large eggs

½ cup grated Parmesan cheese

½ small green onion, finely minced

1 teaspoon dried parsley

6 sage leaves, minced

Striking Yukon Gold

Yukon gold potatoes were developed in the 1970s at the University of Guelph, Ontario, Canada. They were initially slow to capture the market but are now widely popular, and particularly suited for baking, and in salads and soup.

1. Using a mandoline, slice the potato as thinly as possible. Prepare a heavy 12" pan, first with gluten-free nonstick spray, then with butter.

2. Add the potatoes, making a thin layer, and season with salt and pepper. Cook over medium heat for 10 minutes—this will be the crust.

3. In a large bowl, beat the eggs well. Add the cheese, onion, parsley, and minced sage. Pour over the potatoes and turn down heat to the lowest possible setting. Cook for 10 minutes.

4. When the eggs have set, run the frittata under the broiler until golden brown on top. Cut into wedges and serve at once or at room temperature.

PER SERVING Calories: 230 | Fat: 15g | Protein: 15g | Sodium: 875mg | Fiber: 1g | Carbohydrates: 10g | Sugar: 1g

Quinoa "Mac and Cheese" in Tomato Bowls

These broiled tomatoes make edible bowls for this tasty quinoa dish. The juices of the tomato will combine with the quinoa mixture and taste delicious.

INGREDIENTS | SERVES 4 | 30 MINUTES

¼ cup uncooked quinoa, rinsed and drained

1 tablespoon grapeseed oil

2 tablespoons pine nuts

2 cloves garlic, minced

1 cup chopped spinach leaves

Juice of ½ large lemon

¼ cup grated cheese of your choice

4 large beefsteak tomatoes, top 1" sliced off, pulp and seeds scooped out

Quinoa's Superpowers

Quinoa is so versatile and can be used in so many different ways. Quinoa is actually a seed that is loaded with magnesium, iron, and calcium. Quinoa is just like a grain, but it is the only one to have all nine essential amino acids, which also makes it the only one to be a complete protein. It is low calorie, has a lot of fiber, and is also wheat- and gluten-free.

1. Bring a pot of lightly salted water to a boil over high heat. Add the quinoa and cook until the quinoa is tender, about 15 minutes. Drain in a mesh strainer and rinse until cold; set aside.

2. Heat oil in a large skillet over medium heat. Stir in pine nuts and cook until lightly toasted, about 2 minutes.

3. Stir in the garlic and cook until the garlic softens, about 2 minutes. Stir in the quinoa and spinach; cook and stir until the quinoa is hot and the spinach has wilted, about 3–4 minutes. Stir in the lemon juice and the cheese.

4. Meanwhile, place tomatoes in a baking dish and place sliced top back on top of the tomato. Place under preheated broiler for 5 minutes until they soften slightly but still remain intact.

5. Take tomatoes out and place the quinoa mixture inside the tomatoes, using them like bowls.

PER SERVING Calories: 165 | Fat: 10g | Protein: 6g | Sodium: 120mg | Fiber: 3g | Carbohydrates: 14g | Sugar: 3g

Black Bean–Quinoa Chili

This comforting dish could also be made in a slow cooker or on the stove in a Dutch oven. Plus, it freezes well so it can be made a few days ahead of time for easy enjoyment.

INGREDIENTS | SERVES 10 | 35 MINUTES

1 cup uncooked red quinoa, rinsed and drained

2 cups gluten-free vegetable broth

1 tablespoon canola oil

1 scallion, chopped

5 cloves garlic, chopped

1 tablespoon chili powder

1 tablespoon cumin

1 teaspoon coriander

2 cups plum tomatoes, diced

2 (14.5-ounce) cans black beans, rinsed and drained

1 medium green bell pepper, seeded and chopped

1 jalapeño pepper, seeded and chopped

1 tablespoon dried chipotle pepper

1 zucchini, chopped

1 teaspoon dried oregano

½ teaspoon dried cinnamon

1 teaspoon salt

½ teaspoon freshly ground black pepper

1 cup frozen corn

1 cup chopped portobello mushrooms

¼ cup chopped fresh cilantro

1 medium avocado, pitted and sliced

1 cup plain low-fat Greek yogurt

1 cup shredded Cheddar cheese

1. Place quinoa and broth in a medium saucepan over high heat and bring to a boil. Cover, reduce heat to medium-low, and let simmer for 15 minutes, until all the broth is absorbed. Set aside.

2. While quinoa is cooking, heat oil in a large skillet over medium-high heat. Add the scallion and garlic, and sauté for 3–4 minutes, until soft. Add the chili powder, cumin, and coriander. Stir to combine.

3. Add the tomatoes, beans, peppers, zucchini, oregano, and cinnamon. Mix well and season with salt and black pepper. Bring to a boil over high heat, reduce to low heat, cover, and simmer for 20 minutes.

4. Add the quinoa, corn, and mushrooms, and cook for an additional 5 minutes to soften corn and mushrooms. Remove from heat.

5. Top with cilantro, avocado slices, a dollop of yogurt, and shredded cheese.

PER SERVING Calories: 275 | Fat: 10g | Protein: 16g | Sodium: 675mg | Fiber: 9g | Carbohydrates: 35g | Sugar: 6g

Slow Cook It!

This dish can be made easily in the slow cooker. Sauté onion and garlic in a skillet for 3–4 minutes, until soft. Add chili powder, cumin, and coriander and mix thoroughly. Add all the other ingredients except the corn and mushrooms. Cook on low for 5–6 hours. Add corn and mushrooms in the last hour and garnish with toppings.

Vegetarian Quinoa–Black Bean Cakes

*These vegetarian patties are light, crispy, and super delicious. Serve them with
a green salad for an entrée or alone as an appetizer.*

INGREDIENTS | SERVES 8 | 30 MINUTES

3 tablespoons grapeseed oil (or extra-virgin olive oil), divided

½ cup finely chopped green bell pepper

3 cloves garlic, chopped

1 medium onion, peeled and finely chopped

½ cup finely chopped plum tomatoes

1 (15-ounce) can organic black beans, thoroughly rinsed and drained

2 cups quinoa, cooked in gluten-free vegetable broth

1 tablespoon fresh cilantro leaves

½ teaspoon cumin

½ teaspoon red pepper flakes

1 teaspoon salt

½ teaspoon freshly ground black pepper

1 large egg white, beaten

1 cup wheat-free bread crumbs

¼ cup chopped fresh cilantro

½ cup diced plum tomatoes

1. Heat 2 tablespoons oil in a large skillet over medium-high heat. Add the green pepper and sauté until soft, about 3 minutes. Add the garlic, onion, and tomatoes, and continue to sauté until soft, about 3–4 minutes.

2. Remove from heat and combine with black beans, quinoa, cilantro, cumin, and red pepper flakes. Allow to cool for a few minutes. Add salt and pepper. Place in food processor and pulse until chunky but not completely smooth.

3. Transfer mixture to a large bowl. Add the beaten egg white and mix well.

4. Place bread crumbs in a shallow dish. Heat remaining 1 tablespoon oil in the skillet over medium-high heat.

5. Form bean mixture into patties, dredge in bread crumbs, and place in heated skillet. Sauté 5 minutes on each side. Garnish patties with cilantro and diced tomatoes.

PER SERVING Calories: 315 | Fat: 9g | Protein: 12g |
Sodium: 550mg | Fiber: 7g | Carbohydrates: 48g | Sugar: 3g

Stuffed Artichokes with Lemon and Olives

Artichokes have a way of making everything around them taste incredible. They can be eaten with just a little butter, mayonnaise, or lemon juice. They're even better with a buttery olive sauce.

INGREDIENTS | SERVES 4 | 40 MINUTES

4 large artichokes, trimmed and split lengthwise

4 quarts water

½ medium lemon, sliced

1 cup cooked rice

10 green olives, chopped

10 kalamata olives, chopped

2 tablespoons minced parsley

3 tablespoons butter or margarine, melted

1 teaspoon garlic salt

½ teaspoon freshly ground black pepper

1 large egg

1. Boil the artichokes in 4 quarts of water with lemon for 20 minutes. Remove artichokes from water with a slotted spoon and lay on a baking sheet, cut-side up.

2. Preheat the oven to 350°F. Mix the remaining ingredients together in a large bowl.

3. Spoon the filling over the artichokes, pressing between the leaves. Bake for 15 minutes, until hot.

PER SERVING Calories: 260 | Fat: 11g | Protein: 8g | Sodium: 850mg | Fiber: 10g | Carbohydrates: 36g | Sugar: 2g

Corn Pockets Stuffed with Spinach, Cheese, and Artichokes

*This is one of the creative and exciting vegetarian and gluten-free dishes
you can make with the Corn Crepes in Chapter 10.*

INGREDIENTS | SERVES 8 | 30 MINUTES

1 (10-ounce) box frozen artichoke hearts,
cooked according to package directions

1 (10-ounce) box frozen spinach, thawed,
moisture squeezed out

1 cup ricotta cheese

4 ounces cream cheese

¼ cup minced chives

¼ teaspoon freshly ground nutmeg

1 teaspoon salt

½ teaspoon freshly ground black pepper

2 large eggs, divided

8 large (8–9" in diameter) Corn Crepes
(see recipe in Chapter 10)

1. Place cooked, drained artichokes in a food processor
   with spinach and process, slowly adding the cheeses,
   chives, seasonings, and 1 egg.

2. Preheat oven to 350°F. Lay out the crepes on a
   nonstick baking sheet or one covered with a sheet of
   aluminum foil. Lightly beat the remaining egg.

3. Divide the filling among the crepes, spooning onto one
   half and leaving the other half plain.

4. Wet the rims of the crepes with beaten egg. Fold over
   and press lightly to seal, and then bake for 20 minutes
   or until well browned and filling is bubbling out.

PER SERVING Calories: 265 | Fat: 17g | Protein: 11g |
Sodium: 650mg | Fiber: 4g | Carbohydrates: 19g | Sugar: 3g

Fried Potato Balls

*You can hide savory surprises inside these treats, such as olives,
halved cherry tomatoes, or cubes of gooey cheese.*

INGREDIENTS | SERVES 6 | 20 MINUTES

3 large eggs separated, whites whisked
stiff

1¾ cups finely grated Parmesan cheese,
divided

¼ cup potato flour, more if the mixture
is loose or wet

1 teaspoon salt

½ teaspoon ground black pepper

1½ cups boiled and riced potatoes

2 cups oil for frying

1. Beat the egg yolks and place in a large bowl with 1
   cup of the Parmesan cheese, flour, salt, and pepper.
   Add potatoes and mix well. Fold in the whisked egg
   whites.

2. Form into balls about the size of large marbles. Roll in
   the remaining Parmesan cheese. If too soft, place on a
   cookie sheet in the freezer for a few minutes.

3. Bring oil to 375°F. Carefully add the balls and fry until
   well browned, about 3–4 minutes.

4. Drain on paper towels and serve hot.

PER SERVING Calories: 250 | Fat: 15g | Protein: 16g |
Sodium: 950mg | Fiber: 1g | Carbohydrates: 13g | Sugar: 1g

Tofu Steaks with Creamy Red Pepper Sauce

These hefty, hearty tofu steaks stand up to regular meats and take on the flavor of anything you add to them. The creamy red pepper sauce gives the tofu a kick of spice.

INGREDIENTS | SERVES 6 | 35 MINUTES

1 (12-ounce) package extra-firm tofu, pressed

2 tablespoons olive oil

1 teaspoon salt

1 teaspoon ground black pepper

1 tablespoon butter

2 medium red bell peppers, seeded and chopped

3 cloves garlic, chopped

1 teaspoon cayenne pepper

1 cup sour cream

¾ cup low-sodium gluten-free vegetable broth

¾ cup grated Parmesan cheese

2 tablespoons chopped parsley

1. Slice tofu into 6 slices, about ½" thick. Rub slices with oil and sprinkle with salt and pepper.

2. Preheat a gas or charcoal grill to medium-high. Spray the grill with gluten-free nonstick cooking spray.

3. Cook the tofu slices on the grill for about 8 minutes on each side, or until firm with grill marks. Remove from heat.

4. Meanwhile, melt butter in a large saucepan over medium heat. Add bell peppers and garlic and cook until softened, about 6 minutes. Stir in the cayenne pepper.

5. Quickly stir in the sour cream and broth. Reduce heat to low and simmer for 5–7 minutes, or until thickened. Stir in cheese.

6. Top the steaks with parsley and a drizzle of sauce.

PER SERVING Calories: 230 | Fat: 19g | Protein: 10g | Sodium: 720mg | Fiber: 1g | Carbohydrates: 6g | Sugar: 4g

Black Bean Cakes with Avocado and Cilantro Cream

What makes these cakes so good is the addition of cayenne pepper, Mexican oregano, and cilantro. Plus, you can't go wrong with an avocado cream sauce!

INGREDIENTS | SERVES 8 | 25 MINUTES

4 tablespoons extra-virgin olive oil, divided

2 small yellow onions, peeled and diced

3 garlic cloves, minced

4 (15-ounce) cans black beans, drained and rinsed

3 cups gluten-free panko bread crumbs

4 large eggs, divided

1 teaspoon cayenne pepper

⅓ cup almond meal

⅓ cup gluten-free all-purpose flour

1 tablespoon Mexican oregano

1 tablespoon crushed red pepper

½ teaspoon salt

1 large ripe avocado, peeled, pitted, and halved

1 ounce heavy cream

3 ounces sour cream

2 tablespoons lemon juice

¼ cup chopped cilantro

1 teaspoon salt

1 teaspoon ground black pepper

1. Heat 1 tablespoon oil in a large skillet over medium-high heat. Add onions and garlic and cook until softened and translucent, about 5 minutes. Remove from heat and put into a food processor.

2. Add beans, bread crumbs, 2 eggs, cayenne pepper, almond meal, and 1 tablespoon oil to onion mixture. Pulse until the mixture is smooth.

3. Whisk the remaining eggs in a shallow bowl. Combine flour, oregano, and crushed red pepper into another shallow bowl.

4. Form the bean mixture into 8 patties. Dip each into the eggs and then dredge in the flour mixture.

5. Heat the remaining 2 tablespoons of olive oil in a large skillet over medium-high heat. Add the patties and cook until browned on each side, about 6 minutes total.

6. In a food processor, purée avocado, heavy cream, sour cream, lemon juice, and cilantro. Add salt and pepper.

7. Garnish each black bean cake with avocado cream and serve.

PER SERVING Calories: 560 | Fat: 22g | Protein: 22g | Sodium: 1,400mg | Fiber: 16g | Carbohydrates: 70g | Sugar: 8g

CHAPTER 14

Kids' Favorites

Cheesiest Macaroni and Cheese

Giving up gluten also means giving up the macaroni and cheese from a box. This homemade version makes a comforting meal that tastes way better than the box stuff anyway.

INGREDIENTS | SERVES 4 | 45 MINUTES

1 cup uncooked gluten-free elbow macaroni

2 tablespoons butter or margarine

1 tablespoon cornstarch

¼ teaspoon salt

¼ teaspoon ground black pepper

¼ teaspoon gluten-free dry mustard

¼ teaspoon gluten-free Worcestershire sauce

1 cup milk

1½ cups cubed or shredded sharp Cheddar cheese

2 tablespoons crushed gluten-free corn flakes

1. Preheat the oven to 275°F.

2. Cook macaroni noodles in a large pot of water according to package directions. Drain in a colander.

3. While the macaroni cooks, melt the butter in a large saucepan over medium heat. Reduce the heat to low. Add the cornstarch, salt, pepper, mustard, and Worcestershire sauce. Stir until smooth.

4. Add the milk and cheese. Continue stirring until the cheese melts and the sauce is creamy and smooth, about 5–8 minutes.

5. Stir the macaroni noodles into the cheese sauce.

6. Pour the mixture into a 2-quart casserole dish. Top with the crushed corn flakes.

7. Bake 30 minutes, or until the casserole is heated through and lightly browned. Let the casserole dish sit about 5 minutes before serving so the cheesy, creamy sauce has a chance to thicken.

PER SERVING Calories: 365 | Fat: 22g | Protein: 16g | Sodium: 450mg | Fiber: 1g | Carbohydrates: 26g | Sugar: 4g

No-Bake Honey Balls

Let the kids get their hands dirty. These sweet and chewy no-bake cookies are a good choice for beginning cooks.

INGREDIENTS | SERVES 15 | 15 MINUTES

½ cup honey

½ cup golden raisins

½ cup dry milk powder

2 cups gluten-free crushed crisp rice cereal, divided

¼ cup confectioners' sugar

1 cup finely chopped dates

1. In a food processor, combine honey and raisins; process until smooth.

2. Scrape mixture into a small bowl and add milk powder, 1 cup crushed cereal, confectioners' sugar, and dates, and mix well. You may need to add more powdered sugar or honey for desired consistency.

3. Form mixture into ¾" balls and roll in remaining crushed cereal. Store in airtight container at room temperature.

PER SERVING Calories: 140 | Fat: 1g | Protein: 2g | Sodium: 80mg | Fiber: 1g | Carbohydrates: 32g | Sugar: 24g

Grilled Cheese and Tomato Sandwich

What's better than a warm and crispy grilled cheese sandwich? Here's a slightly different spin on the old favorite that makes it more nutritious, too.

INGREDIENTS | SERVES 1 | 10 MINUTES

2 slices gluten-free bread

2 teaspoons butter

1 slice Cheddar cheese

1 or 2 thin slices of tomato

1. Spread the butter on one side of each slice of bread. Make a sandwich with the cheese and tomato between the two slices of bread, with the butter on the outside of the sandwich.

2. Place the sandwich in a small skillet over medium heat and cook it for about 2 minutes on each side, until the cheese is melted and the bread becomes slightly browned and crispy.

PER SERVING Calories: 370 | Fat: 18g | Protein: 15g | Sodium: 575mg | Fiber: 2g | Carbohydrates: 38g | Sugar: 3g

Never-Enough Nachos

For a quick vegetarian version, try making this without the beef. You can enjoy it as a snack with friends or even as an appetizer before a family meal.

INGREDIENTS | SERVES 8 | 40 MINUTES

1 pound lean ground beef
1 cup prepared salsa
2 cups gluten-free tortilla chips
½ cup sour cream
1 medium tomato, chopped
4 scallions, chopped
½ cup chopped lettuce
1 cup shredded Cheddar cheese

1. Preheat the oven to 350°F.

2. In a large skillet, cook the ground beef for 8–10 minutes, until it is cooked throughout. Drain the ground beef, and then place it in a large bowl.

3. Add the salsa and mix well.

4. In a 2-quart casserole, layer the ingredients in the following order starting at the bottom:

   - Gluten-free tortilla chips

   - Ground beef/salsa mixture

   - Sour cream

   - Tomatoes

   - Scallions

   - Lettuce

   - Shredded cheese

5. Bake nachos in the preheated oven for 20–30 minutes, or until the cheese is completely melted.

PER SERVING Calories: 260 | Fat: 15g | Protein: 18g | Sodium: 400mg | Fiber: 2g | Carbohydrates: 14g | Sugar: 3g

Chewy Granola Bars MA

These granola bars are perfect to grab on the way out the door. Make up a batch and you will never be stuck without something to snack on.

INGREDIENTS | SERVES 26

2 cups certified gluten-free quick-cooking oats
¾ cup rice bran
¼ cup ground flaxseed
¼ cup slivered almonds
¼ cup uncooked quinoa
¼ cup shelled sunflower seeds
¼ cup sesame seeds

¼ cup flaked coconut
⅔ cup brown sugar
½ cup honey
4 tablespoons butter
½ teaspoon ground cinnamon
½ teaspoon salt
2 teaspoons gluten-free vanilla extract
1 cup chopped dried fruit (cherries, cranberries, blueberries, apricots, etc.)

1. Preheat oven to 400°F. Line a large rimmed baking sheet with foil.

2. Mix together oats, rice bran, flaxseeds, almonds, quinoa, sunflower seeds, sesame seeds, and coconut on the baking sheet. Place in the oven and toast for 10–12 minutes, stirring every few minutes to prevent them from burning. As soon as the ingredients are toasted, remove the pan from the oven.

3. While the dry ingredients are toasting, line a 9" × 13" pan with parchment paper and spray lightly with gluten-free cooking oil.

4. Place a small saucepan over medium-high heat and add the brown sugar, honey, butter, cinnamon, and salt. Bring the mixture to a strong boil for 2 minutes, stirring constantly. Turn off the heat and stir in vanilla.

5. Place the toasted ingredients in a large bowl, and stir in the dried fruit. Pour the hot liquids into the bowl and stir aggressively until all the ingredients are moist and well combined.

6. Using a wooden spoon, scrape the mixture onto the prepared baking sheet, pressing down to evenly spread out the mixture. Using a wet rubber spatula helps to keep the granola from sticking, allowing you to press the mixture down enough. Set the baking sheet aside and let the mixture cool for 2–3 hours until it is hardened.

7. Once the mixture is hard, remove it from the pan and turn the granola out onto a cutting board. Remove the parchment paper. Cut the granola into bars by pressing straight down with a long knife (don't saw or they will crumble). Cut approximately 26 bars, 1" × 5½".

8. Wrap the bars individually in plastic wrap, and store in an airtight container at room temperature for up to 1 week.

PER SERVING Calories: 140 | Fat: 6g | Protein: 3g | Sodium: 45mg | Fiber: 2.5g | Carbohydrates: 23g | Sugar: 14g

Tex-Mex Pork SC

Many kids enjoy the flavors of Mexican spices as long as you don't make a dish too hot. Feel free to add more or less of the spices depending on your family's spiciness preference.

INGREDIENTS | SERVES 6

3 pounds boneless pork roast

1 packet gluten-free taco seasoning mix, such as McCormick's Taco Seasoning

1 teaspoon garlic powder

1 teaspoon cumin

½ teaspoon cayenne pepper

2 tablespoons lime juice

2 tablespoons chopped green chilies with juice

¾ cup water

1. Place pork roast into a greased 4–6-quart slow cooker.

2. In a small bowl mix together taco seasoning, garlic powder, cumin, cayenne pepper, lime juice, chilies, and water. Pour seasoning mixture over pork roast.

3. Cook on high for 4 hours or cook on low for 8 hours until pork is very tender.

PER SERVING Calories: 305 | Fat: 8g | Protein: 50g | Sodium: 850mg | Fiber: 2g | Carbohydrates: 6g | Sugar: 2g

Easy Pizza Sauce

This delicious sauce will enhance the flavor of any type of pizza you make. This also makes a wonderful dipping sauce for quesadillas, chicken tenders, or even French fries.

INGREDIENTS | MAKES 2¾ CUPS | 15 MINUTES

1 teaspoon extra-virgin olive oil

1 or 2 cloves garlic, finely chopped

½ medium onion, peeled and finely chopped

1 (15-ounce) can tomato sauce

1 (6-ounce) can tomato paste

1 tablespoon ground oregano

1 teaspoon ground basil

½ teaspoon turbinado sugar

½ teaspoon salt

1. In a medium skillet over medium heat, heat oil. Sauté garlic and onions until they soften, about 3–4 minutes.

2. In a medium bowl, mix together tomato sauce and tomato paste until smooth. Stir in oregano, basil, sugar, and salt. Add the cooked garlic and onions.

3. Use immediately or refrigerate for up to one week. Makes sauce for about 4 (10") pizzas.

PER SERVING (¼ CUP) | Calories: 30 | Fat: 0.5g | Protein: 1g | Sodium: 420mg | Fiber: 1g | Carbohydrates: 6g | Sugar: 4g

French Fry Casserole SC

Here's a kid favorite that the whole family will love. Frozen French fries, ground beef, and a simple gluten-free cream sauce make a tasty weeknight meal. Serve with a salad or steamed green beans.

INGREDIENTS | SERVES 4

1 pound ground beef

1 tablespoon butter

½ small onion, peeled and finely diced

1 cup mushrooms, sliced

½ small green bell pepper, seeded and diced

2 tablespoons cornstarch

1⅓ cups whole milk

½ teaspoon salt

½ teaspoon ground black pepper

3 cups frozen gluten-free shoestring-cut French fries

¾ cup shredded Cheddar cheese

Gluten-Free Shortcuts

You can make several batches of gluten-free cream sauce at the beginning of the week to make meals even easier to put together. Simply make a batch, pour in a glass jar with an airtight lid, and store in the refrigerator for up to 1 week.

1. Brown ground beef in a medium skillet on medium heat for approximately 3–5 minutes. Drain cooked ground beef and then place into a greased 2.5-quart or larger slow cooker.

2. In a medium-sized saucepan, melt butter. Add onion, mushrooms, and green pepper. Cook for 3–5 minutes until softened.

3. In a small bowl, mix cornstarch with milk and then slowly add to cooked vegetables. Whisk together for 5–10 minutes over medium heat until thickened.

4. Pour cream sauce over ground beef in slow cooker. Sprinkle with salt and black pepper. Top casserole with French fries. Vent the lid of the slow cooker with a chopstick to prevent extra condensation on the fries. Cook on high for 3–4 hours or on low for 4–6 hours.

5. One hour prior to serving sprinkle cheese on casserole. Cook an additional 45–60 minutes until cheese is melted.

PER SERVING Calories: 640 | Fat: 32g | Protein: 35g | Sodium: 1,100mg | Fiber: 4g | Carbohydrates: 53g | Sugar: 6g

One-Pot Spaghetti and Meatballs SC

Spaghetti and meatballs is a classic comfort food for the whole family. It takes a little extra work to make the homemade gluten-free meatballs, but your family will agree it's well worth the effort when they taste this fabulous one-pot meal.

INGREDIENTS | SERVES 4

1 slice gluten-free bread, torn in very small pieces

¼ cup 2% milk

1 pound ground beef

½ teaspoon salt

½ teaspoon ground black pepper

1½ teaspoons dried onion

1 large egg

1 tablespoon olive oil

1½ cups Spicy Marinara Sauce (see recipe in Chapter 3)

⅓ cup water

4 ounces gluten-free spaghetti, uncooked and broken into small pieces

1. In a large bowl mix together bread and milk. Set aside for 5 minutes. Add ground beef, salt, pepper, dried onion, and egg. Mix well and roll into small meatballs.

2. In a large skillet over medium heat, cook the meatballs in small batches in the olive oil until they are browned, approximately 5–6 minutes. Add meatballs to a greased 4–6-quart slow cooker.

3. Add spaghetti sauce and water to the slow cooker. Cook on high for 4 hours or on low for 8 hours.

4. An hour before serving add in the spaghetti pieces and stir into the sauce. Cook spaghetti for 1 hour. Try not to overcook the pasta, as it will become mushy.

PER SERVING Calories: 455 | Fat: 19g | Protein: 30g | Sodium: 775mg | Fiber: 3g | Carbohydrates: 38g | Sugar: 9g

Honey Mustard Chicken Fingers SC

This recipe uses a "foil rack" technique in your slow cooker to create chicken fingers that stay relatively crunchy with the added kick of a sweet honey mustard sauce. Plus, it can be made while you're out all day!

INGREDIENTS | SERVES 6

4 large boneless, skinless chicken breasts, patted dry and cut into strips
1 large egg, beaten
1½ cups gluten-free bread crumbs or 1½ cups blanched almond flour
⅓ cup honey
⅓ cup gluten-free Dijon mustard
1 teaspoon dried basil
1 teaspoon paprika
½ teaspoon salt
½ teaspoon ground black pepper
½ teaspoon dried parsley

1. Dip chicken strips into the egg and dredge through the gluten-free bread crumbs or blanched almond flour.

2. Using gluten-free nonstick spray or olive oil, brown chicken strips in a medium skillet in small batches just until they are golden brown, approximately 1 minute per side.

3. Make a 2–3" foil rack in the bottom of a 4–6-quart slow cooker by placing rolled strips of aluminum foil in the bottom of the greased insert. Make a grill pattern with the strips. This will allow the chicken to cook above the juices while sitting on the rack.

4. In a small bowl mix together the honey, mustard, basil, paprika, salt, pepper, and parsley.

5. Place browned chicken fingers on the rack in the slow cooker. Drizzle half of the honey mustard sauce evenly over the chicken. Cook on high for 3 hours or on low for 6 hours. Serve the chicken tenders with remaining honey mustard sauce.

PER SERVING Calories: 365 | Fat: 7g | Protein: 39g | Sodium: 740mg | Fiber: 2g | Carbohydrates: 36g | Sugar: 17g

Parmesan-Flax-Crusted Chicken Tenders

These tenders are so tasty, the whole family will love them.
Kids love to dip, so experiment with different dipping sauces, too.

INGREDIENTS | SERVES 4 | 45 MINUTES

2 egg whites and 1 whole egg, beaten

1 cup ground flaxseed

1 teaspoon dried basil

1 teaspoon dried oregano

1½ teaspoons red pepper flakes

2 cloves garlic, minced

½ teaspoon salt

½ teaspoon ground black pepper

⅓ cup grated Parmesan cheese

1 pound chicken tenderloins

Homemade Is Better

Chicken tenders you find in the grocery store can have a lot of preservatives and ingredients in them that you may not expect. This recipe is a perfect example of how easy they are to make at home.

1. Preheat the oven to 350°F. Spray 9" × 13" casserole dish with gluten-free cooking spray.

2. Place egg whites and egg in a large bowl.

3. In a separate large bowl, place ground flaxseed, basil, oregano, red pepper flakes, garlic, salt, pepper, and cheese. Stir until mixed.

4. Start by placing each chicken tender in egg mixture, then coat with flax mixture; make sure it is thoroughly coated on both sides. Place in prepared casserole dish.

5. Place casserole dish in the oven and cook for 35 minutes, making sure to turn tenders over halfway through cooking time. Serve with your favorite dipping sauce!

PER SERVING Calories: 340 | Fat: 18g | Protein: 38g | Sodium: 550mg | Fiber: 10g | Carbohydrates: 11g | Sugar: 0g

Pepperoni Pizza Quesadillas

What happens when pizza meets a wheat-free tortilla? You get pizza quesadillas that everyone in your family will devour. Try adding other toppings, like sliced mushrooms, peppers, or onions to appease anyone's taste buds.

INGREDIENTS | SERVES 4 | 15 MINUTES

8 corn or brown rice flour tortillas

2 cups Easy Pizza Sauce (see recipe in this chapter), plus extra for dipping

8 ounces shredded mozzarella cheese

⅓ pound pepperoni, sliced

1. Brush each tortilla with a thin layer of pizza sauce (so thin that if you turned it over, none would drip).

2. Sprinkle cheese on top of 4 tortillas. Top with pepperoni. Sprinkle with another layer of cheese and place another tortilla on top (sauce-side in).

3. Lay out tortilla and place it on a griddle or in a pan sprayed with gluten-free cooking spray and cook for 3–5 minutes on each side, until cheese is melted and tortillas are crispy.

4. Slice into quarters and serve with a little bowl of pizza dipping sauce.

PER SERVING Calories: 545 | Fat: 33g | Protein: 27g | Sodium: 2,000mg | Fiber: 7g | Carbohydrates: 39g | Sugar: 12g

Fettuccine Alfredo with Chicken

When dining out, ordering Italian food can be difficult when eating a gluten-free diet. Here is a restaurant-quality recipe you can make at home. Add a tossed salad and a slice of gluten-free garlic toast, and your dinner is complete.

INGREDIENTS | SERVES 4 | 25 MINUTES

8 ounces uncooked gluten-free fettuccine noodles

2 tablespoons olive oil

2 (5-ounce) boneless, skinless chicken breasts, pounded to ¾" thickness

2 teaspoons salt, divided

1½ teaspoons freshly ground black pepper, divided

½ cup butter

2 cloves garlic, minced

1 cup heavy cream

1 cup grated Parmesan cheese

1 tablespoon chopped fresh parsley

1. Prepare gluten-free fettuccine according to package directions. Drain and set aside.

2. While pasta is cooking, heat olive oil in a medium skillet over medium-high heat. Sprinkle chicken breasts with 1 teaspoon salt and ½ teaspoon pepper. Add chicken to the skillet and sauté chicken breasts until done, about 6 minutes per side.

3. Add butter and minced garlic to the chicken in the skillet. Once the butter has melted, add the heavy cream. Heat until the cream is starting to boil, about 5 minutes, and add the Parmesan cheese.

4. Reduce the heat to low and cook 2 minutes more, until the cheese is blended and the mixture begins to thicken. Remove from heat.

5. Stir in the fettuccine and remaining salt and pepper. Add parsley before serving.

PER SERVING Calories: 870 | Fat: 62g | Protein: 33g | Sodium: 1,600mg | Fiber: 2g | Carbohydrates: 46g | Sugar: 2g

Mexican Lasagna

Although this dish goes together quickly enough for a weeknight meal, you can also make the lasagna ahead of time and keep it covered in the refrigerator. This will require you to increase the baking time by 20–30 minutes. Since it also freezes well, it's a perfect gift for new moms!

INGREDIENTS | SERVES 12 | 45 MINUTES

1¼ pounds lean ground beef

½ cup diced onion

½ cup diced red bell pepper

1½ cups frozen corn

1 (19-ounce) can kidney beans

2 tablespoons gluten-free taco seasoning

1½ cups salsa

1 cup sour cream

15 (4") corn tortillas

3 cups shredded Cheddar cheese

¼ cup chopped cilantro

Make Your Own Taco Seasoning

Mix together 2 tablespoons chili powder, 2 teaspoons ground cumin, 1 teaspoon each paprika and salt, and ½ teaspoon each garlic powder, onion powder, dried oregano, and ground black pepper. Store in an airtight container, and use in any recipes that call for taco seasoning.

1. Grease a 9" × 13" baking pan, and preheat the oven to 375°F.

2. In a large skillet, cook the ground beef until nearly cooked, about 5 minutes. Add the onion, red pepper, and corn. Fry for 5–7 minutes, stirring occasionally, until the onion is transparent and the corn is defrosted.

3. Stir in kidney beans, taco seasoning, and salsa. Cook 8 minutes more, then remove from heat. Stir in the sour cream and set aside.

4. Cut 9 of the corn tortillas in half. Line the bottom of the baking pan with 5 corn tortillas (6 halves and 2 whole), with the straight side of the halves facing the outside.

5. Top with half of the ground beef mixture. Sprinkle on half of the cheese followed by another layer of corn tortillas. Spread the remaining ground beef mixture over the lasagna. Top with the third layer of corn tortillas and sprinkle with the remaining cheese.

6. Cover with foil and bake for 30 minutes. Allow to sit for 5 minutes before slicing and serving. Sprinkle with chopped cilantro before serving.

PER SERVING Calories: 375 | Fat: 18g | Protein: 23g | Sodium: 750mg | Fiber: 5g | Carbohydrates: 31g | Sugar: 4g

Parmesan Rosemary Popcorn

You don't need butter to top your popcorn. This healthier snack is perfect for movie night!

INGREDIENTS | SERVES 4 | 10 MINUTES

3 tablespoons olive oil

⅓ cup popcorn kernels

⅓ cup grated Parmesan cheese

½ teaspoon minced rosemary

½ teaspoon minced tarragon

½ teaspoon chopped parsley

1 teaspoon salt

½ teaspoon ground black pepper

Who Needs Microwavable Popcorn?

It's easy to make your own popcorn from scratch with seasoned kernels. To keep your popcorn from burning or undercooking, add the kernels to an even layer of oil in a large saucepan. This will make sure all kernels pop at the same time.

1. Place the olive oil in a deep (at least 3 quarts) saucepan over high heat. Toss in 1 or 2 popcorn kernels. When they pop, the oil is hot enough.

2. Add the rest of the kernels into the pan in an even layer. Cover with a lid, remove from heat, and then wait about 30 seconds. Return the pan to the stove and shake gently. The popcorn will start vigorously popping. To keep the popcorn crisp, leave the lid slightly ajar.

3. Once the popping starts to stop, remove from heat and pour into a bowl. Immediately top with cheese, rosemary, tarragon, parsley, salt, and pepper. Toss to coat.

PER SERVING Calories: 140 | Fat: 13g | Protein: 4g | Sodium: 710mg | Fiber: 1g | Carbohydrates: 3g | Sugar: 0g

Buffalo Chicken Nuggets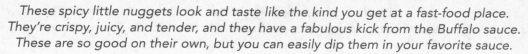

These spicy little nuggets look and taste like the kind you get at a fast-food place. They're crispy, juicy, and tender, and they have a fabulous kick from the Buffalo sauce. These are so good on their own, but you can easily dip them in your favorite sauce.

INGREDIENTS | SERVES 4

2 (5-ounce) boneless, skinless chicken breasts, cut into 1½" pieces

⅔ cup Buffalo-style hot sauce (such as Frank's Red Hot)

1 cup gluten-free panko bread crumbs

1½ tablespoons crushed red pepper

1 teaspoon salt

½ teaspoon ground black pepper

1. Place chicken in a large bowl. Toss with hot sauce, cover, and refrigerate at least 4 hours or overnight.

2. Preheat oven to 500°F. Grease a baking sheet with gluten-free cooking spray. Set aside.

3. Mix bread crumbs, crushed red pepper, salt, and black pepper in a shallow bowl.

4. Dip each nugget into the bread crumbs and cover liberally. Place on cookie sheet. Repeat until all chicken is covered. Bake for 10–12 minutes or until chicken is crispy.

PER SERVING Calories: 195 | Fat: 4g | Protein: 19g | Sodium: 1,800mg | Fiber: 2g | Carbohydrates: 21g | Sugar: 2g

Sneaky Kiwi-Pineapple Smoothie

This smoothie is a terrific way to get some spinach into your kids' diet! If they are suspicious of the bright green color, tell them that it's the kiwi that turned the smoothie green.

INGREDIENTS | SERVES 2 | 10 MINUTES

1 cup pineapple chunks, fresh or frozen

2 medium kiwis, peeled and chopped

½ large banana

6 ounces plain low-fat Greek yogurt

½ cup pineapple juice

½–1 cup ice (you can use less if you use frozen pineapple)

2 tablespoons chia seed or flaxseed

1 cup spinach

Place all the ingredients in a blender. Blend until smooth. Serve immediately.

PER SERVING Calories: 240 | Fat: 6g | Protein: 7g | Sodium: 50mg | Fiber: 7g | Carbohydrates: 45g | Sugar: 22g

Fresh Corn and Sweet Pepper Muffins

If you can't get your kids to eat their vegetables, why not sneak them into muffins? These fluffy corn muffins are filled with fresh vegetables, but your kids won't know as they're gobbling them down.

INGREDIENTS | SERVES 12 | 35 MINUTES

1¼ cups gluten-free all-purpose flour

½ cup cornmeal

¼ cup almond meal

⅓ cup brown sugar

1 tablespoon baking powder

1 teaspoon baking soda

½ teaspoon salt

1 cup low-fat plain Greek yogurt

¼ cup heavy cream

2 tablespoons olive oil

2 tablespoons unsweetened applesauce

2 large eggs

1 cup fresh corn kernels

3 medium orange bell peppers, seeded and chopped

1. Preheat oven to 375°F. Grease a muffin tin or use with paper liners.

2. In a large bowl, whisk the flour, cornmeal, almond meal, sugar, baking powder, baking soda, and salt.

3. Make a well in the center of the flour mixture and stir in the yogurt, cream, oil, applesauce, and eggs. Mix until combined. Fold in the corn kernels and sweet peppers.

4. Pour batter into prepared muffin tin. Bake for about 22–26 minutes, or until golden brown.

PER SERVING Calories: 185 | Fat: 7g | Protein: 5g | Sodium: 350mg | Fiber: 2g | Carbohydrates: 28g | Sugar: 9g

CHAPTER 15

Gluten- and Dairy-Free Meals

Honey-Glazed Chicken Drumsticks SC

It can be a challenge to eat at Chinese restaurants when you are avoiding gluten. But this Asian-inspired chicken is a great substitute for take-out! Serve with white rice, a salad, and egg drop soup.

INGREDIENTS | SERVES 4

2 pounds chicken drumsticks
1 tablespoon melted vegan butter
¼ cup lemon juice
¾ cup honey
1 teaspoon sesame oil
3 cloves garlic, crushed
½ teaspoon ground ginger
½ teaspoon salt

1. Place chicken drumsticks in a greased 4–6-quart slow cooker.

2. In a small bowl or glass measuring cup whisk together the vegan butter, lemon juice, honey, sesame oil, garlic, ginger, and salt.

3. Pour the honey sauce over the drumsticks. Cook on high for 3–4 hours or on low for 6–8 hours.

PER SERVING Calories: 595 | Fat: 24g | Protein: 44g | Sodium: 480mg | Fiber: 0g | Carbohydrates: 54g | Sugar: 53g

Sesame Oil

Sesame oil is a highly flavored oil made from pressing either toasted or plain sesame seeds. It provides a unique nutty and earthy flavor to savory dishes. A little goes a long way, and it's not very expensive.

Almond Chicken SC

The dried minced onion (sometimes sold as dried onion flakes) will absorb some of the chicken broth during the cooking process and naturally thicken the sauce. For a more subtle flavor, use freeze-dried shallots instead.

INGREDIENTS | SERVES 4

1 (14-ounce) can gluten-free chicken broth
4 strips bacon, cooked
2 pounds boneless, skinless chicken breasts
¼ cup dried minced onion
1 (4-ounce) can sliced mushrooms, drained
2 tablespoons gluten-free soy sauce
1½ cups sliced celery
2 cups cooked white rice
1 cup toasted slivered almonds

1. Add the chicken broth to a greased 4-quart slow cooker.

2. Cut the bacon and chicken into bite-sized pieces; add to the slow cooker along with the onion, mushrooms, soy sauce, and celery. Stir to combine.

3. Cover and cook on low for 6 hours.

4. Serve over rice and top with almonds.

PER SERVING Calories: 640 | Fat: 28g | Protein: 59g | Sodium: 1,250mg | Fiber: 5g | Carbohydrates: 37g | Sugar: 4g

Sloppy Joes

*Sloppy Joes are perfect for nights when everyone is eating at different times,
as the meat can be kept in a slow cooker on low heat for hours before serving.
Just be sure to add more water if it seems to be getting too dry.*

INGREDIENTS | SERVES 8

2 pounds lean ground beef

1½ teaspoons onion powder

½ teaspoon garlic powder

1 tablespoon gluten-free Worcestershire sauce

½ cup gluten-free ketchup

1 teaspoon chili powder

¼ cup brown sugar

¾ cup water

2 tablespoons white vinegar

1 tablespoon gluten-free prepared yellow mustard

1 teaspoon salt

½ teaspoon ground black pepper

8 Gluten-Free Buns (see recipe in this chapter)

1. In a large frying pan, cook the ground beef over medium heat until completely browned. To eliminate a lot of the fat, you can spoon the beef into a colander, and rinse under running hot water before returning it to the frying pan.

2. Add the rest of the ingredients. Bring to a boil, and then turn heat down to low and simmer for 20–30 minutes, stirring occasionally.

3. Serve on Gluten-Free Buns with your favorite toppings.

PER SERVING Calories: 338 | Fat: 11g | Protein: 28g | Sodium: 750mg | Fiber: 3g | Carbohydrates: 31g | Sugar: 11g

Great for Even the Pickiest Eaters

By using dried garlic and onion powder, this recipe is full of great flavor and perfect for those picky eaters who don't like to see chopped onions in their food. If you wish, you can use ½ cup diced onion and 1 clove minced garlic in place of the dried powders.

Gluten-Free Buns MA

Being able to eat food on a bun is definitely taken for granted while eating a regular diet. Bake a batch of these buns and you can eat your Sloppy Joes, burgers, and sandwiches on a bun again!

INGREDIENTS | SERVES 6

½ cup warm water

1 teaspoon rapid-rise yeast

1 teaspoon granulated sugar or honey

¼ cup plus 2 tablespoons brown rice flour

¼ cup sorghum flour

¼ cup potato starch

¼ cup ground flaxseed

2 tablespoons tapioca starch

1½ teaspoons xanthan gum

½ teaspoon salt

1 teaspoon apple cider vinegar

1 large egg

1 large egg white

2 tablespoons oil

Thinking Outside the Pan

When it comes to gluten-free baking, sometimes you have to think of things a little differently. Since gluten-free buns need more support than wheat-based buns, you can't just form them on a baking sheet like you would regular buns. Repurposing 4" potpie tins for baking buns works great, giving you a nice-sized bun for a burger. You can also use English muffin rings, jumbo muffin tins, or tins from canned tuna that have been washed really well.

1. In a small bowl, combine the warm water, yeast, and sugar. Allow to sit for 10 minutes, or until it's bubbly.

2. In the bowl of a stand mixer, mix together the brown rice flour, sorghum flour, potato starch, ground flaxseed, tapioca starch, xanthan gum, and salt.

3. Add the apple cider vinegar, egg, egg white, and oil to the yeast mixture. Whisk to combine.

4. With the mixer on low speed, pour the wet ingredients into the dry ingredients. Increase speed to medium-high and mix for 3 minutes, scraping down the bowl.

5. Lightly grease 6 (4") potpie tins and place them on a baking sheet. Divide the dough between the 6 tins, with each tin having about ¼ cup dough. Using a spoon dipped in water, smooth the dough into an even layer across the bottom of the tin.

6. Let dough rise in a warm, draft-free place for 20–30 minutes, or until the dough has nearly doubled in size.

7. While the dough is rising, preheat the oven to 350°F. Once the buns have risen, place baking sheet with the tins on it into preheated oven. Bake for 25–30 minutes. Remove from oven and leave in the tins for 5 minutes before removing buns to a wire cooling rack. Let cool before serving. Once they are cooled they can be stored in an airtight container.

8. Buns can be wrapped in plastic wrap and stored in a resealable bag in the freezer. That way you can remove the buns from the freezer as you need them.

PER SERVING Calories: 180 | Fat: 7g | Protein: 5g | Sodium: 225mg | Fiber: 3.5g | Carbohydrates: 25g | Sugar: 1g

Cabbage and Beef Casserole SC

This low-carbohydrate dish is a savory and satisfying weeknight dinner.

INGREDIENTS | SERVES 6

2 pounds ground beef

1 small onion, peeled and chopped

1 head cabbage, shredded

1 (16-ounce) can tomatoes

½ teaspoon garlic salt

¼ teaspoon ground thyme

¼ teaspoon red pepper flakes

½ teaspoon oregano

1 (8-ounce) can tomato sauce

1. In a large skillet over medium heat, brown the ground beef for about 5–6 minutes. Remove ground beef to a bowl and set aside. In same skillet sauté onion until softened, about 3–5 minutes.

2. In a greased 4–6-quart slow cooker, layer cabbage, onion, tomatoes, garlic salt, thyme, pepper flakes, oregano, and beef. Repeat layers, ending with beef. Pour tomato sauce over casserole.

3. Cook on low for 8 hours or on high for 4 hours.

PER SERVING Calories: 325 | Fat: 15g | Protein: 33g | Sodium: 625mg | Fiber: 5g | Carbohydrates: 15g | Sugar: 9g

Asian-Style Soup with Rice Noodles

This can be served in small bowls as a first course or in large bowls as lunch. The contrast between soft and crunchy, spicy and sweet, makes this interesting and delicious.

INGREDIENTS | SERVES 4 | 20 MINUTES

1 quart gluten-free chicken broth

2 cloves garlic, minced

1" piece fresh gingerroot, peeled and minced

1 bunch scallions, thinly sliced

12 canned water chestnuts

1 cup bean sprouts, well rinsed

½ cup dry sherry

½ cup wheat-free soy sauce

½ pound satin tofu

2 cups rice noodles, cooked

12 snow peas, sliced on the diagonal

1. In a Dutch oven over high heat, bring the chicken broth to a boil and add all but the tofu, noodles, and snow peas. Reduce heat to medium-low, cover, and simmer for 10 minutes.

2. Add the tofu. Stir gently and add the cooked noodles. Garnish with the snow peas and serve.

PER SERVING Calories: 245 | Fat: 2g | Protein: 10g | Sodium: 2,200mg | Fiber: 2g | Carbohydrates: 40g | Sugar: 8g

Sausage and Shrimp Jambalaya SC

This version of a "red" jambalaya originated in the French Quarter of New Orleans when saffron wasn't readily available. This Creole-type jambalaya contains tomatoes, whereas a rural Cajun jambalaya (also known as "brown jambalaya") does not.

INGREDIENTS | SERVES 8

2 tablespoons olive oil

1 large onion, peeled and chopped

2 medium celery stalks, chopped

1 medium green bell pepper, seeded and chopped

3 garlic cloves, minced

1 (28-ounce) can diced tomatoes, undrained

2 cups fully cooked gluten-free smoked sausage, sliced into 1" pieces

1 tablespoon parsley flakes

½ teaspoon dried thyme leaves

½ teaspoon salt

¼ teaspoon ground black pepper

¼ teaspoon red pepper sauce

2 teaspoons gluten-free Creole seasoning

¾ pound uncooked, peeled, deveined medium shrimp, thawed if frozen

4 cups hot cooked rice

¼ cup fresh parsley, chopped

1. In a large skillet, heat oil. Sauté onions, celery, and bell pepper until softened, about 3–5 minutes. Add garlic and cook 1 minute more.

2. Grease a 4–6-quart slow cooker and add sautéed vegetables and all remaining ingredients except shrimp, rice, and parsley.

3. Cover and cook on low for 6 hours or on high for 3 hours.

4. Add shrimp and continue to cook on low for 45 minutes to 1 hour until shrimp are bright pink. Serve jambalaya over a bed of rice and garnished with chopped fresh parsley.

PER SERVING Calories: 395 | Fat: 19g | Protein: 20g | Sodium: 720mg | Fiber: 2g | Carbohydrates: 34g | Sugar: 4g

Instead of Shrimp

Use your favorite type of seafood instead of shrimp. Scallops, cod, or diced tilapia fillets would also work well in this dish.

Chicken Pesto Polenta SC

This recipe uses precooked polenta that is cut and layered in a casserole lasagna-style. Most prepared polenta comes in tube form and is naturally gluten-free. Make sure to read the ingredients and call the manufacturer if you have any questions.

INGREDIENTS | SERVES 6

4 boneless, skinless chicken breasts, cut into bite-sized pieces

1 cup prepared pesto, divided

1 medium onion, peeled and finely diced

4 cloves garlic, minced

1½ teaspoons dried Italian seasoning

1 (16-ounce) tube prepared polenta, cut into ½" slices

2 cups chopped fresh spinach

1 (14.5-ounce) can diced tomatoes

1 (8-ounce) bag shredded vegan cheese

Make Your Own Pesto

Instead of using prepared pesto you can easily make your own: In a high-powered blender or food processor add 2 cups fresh basil leaves, ½ cup extra-virgin olive oil, ½ cup vegan cheese, ½ cup pine nuts, 3 garlic cloves, and salt and pepper to taste. Blend on high for a few minutes until mixture is creamy.

1. In a large bowl, combine chicken pieces with ½ cup pesto, onion, garlic, and Italian seasoning.

2. In a greased 4–6-quart slow cooker, layer half of chicken mixture, half the polenta, half the spinach, and half the tomatoes. Continue to layer, ending with tomatoes. Cover and cook on low for 4–6 hours or on high for 2–3 hours.

3. An hour before serving drizzle remaining pesto over casserole and top with shredded cheese. Cover and continue to cook for 45–60 minutes until cheese has melted.

PER SERVING Calories: 605 | Fat: 35g | Protein: 46g | Sodium: 875mg | Fiber: 3g | Carbohydrates: 27g | Sugar: 3g

Caribbean Chicken Curry SC

Traditional Jamaican curries are cooked for long periods of time on the stovetop, making them a logical fit for the slow cooker. The spices meld together, and the chicken is very tender.

INGREDIENTS | SERVES 8

1 tablespoon gluten-free Madras curry powder

1 teaspoon allspice

½ teaspoon ground cloves

½ teaspoon ground nutmeg

1 teaspoon ground ginger

2 pounds boneless, skinless chicken thighs, cubed

1 teaspoon canola oil

1 medium onion, peeled and chopped

2 cloves garlic, chopped

2 medium jalapeños, chopped, seeds removed

½ pound red skin potatoes, cubed

⅓ cup light coconut milk

1. In a medium bowl, whisk together the curry powder, allspice, cloves, nutmeg, and ginger. Add the chicken and toss to coat each piece evenly.

2. Place the chicken in a nonstick skillet and quickly sauté until the chicken starts to brown. Add to a 4–6-quart slow cooker along with the remaining spice mixture.

3. Heat the oil in a nonstick skillet and sauté the onion, garlic, and jalapeños until fragrant, about 3–5 minutes. Add to the slow cooker.

4. Add the potatoes and coconut milk to the slow cooker. Stir. Cook 7–8 hours on low.

PER SERVING Calories: 190 | Fat: 7g | Protein: 23g | Sodium: 100mg | Fiber: 1g | Carbohydrates: 8g | Sugar: 1g

Pork Steaks in Apple and Prune Sauce SC

Serve this dish over mashed potatoes (available ready-made in most supermarket refrigerator or freezer cases; double-check ingredients to make sure they are gluten-free) and alongside easy "steam-in-the-bag" green beans.

INGREDIENTS | SERVES 6

12 pitted prunes (dried plums)

3 pounds boneless pork steaks, trimmed of fat

2 Granny Smith apples, peeled, cored, and sliced

¾ cup dry white wine

¾ cup almond milk

1 teaspoon salt

½ teaspoon freshly ground pepper

1 tablespoon red currant jelly

1 tablespoon soy butter (like Earth Balance)

1. Add the prunes, pork steak, apple slices, wine, and almond milk to a 4–6-quart slow cooker. Sprinkle with salt and pepper. Cover and cook on low for 6 hours.

2. Remove the pork from the slow cooker and keep warm. Skim the fat from the liquid in the slow cooker, and use an immersion blender to blend the fruit into the creamy broth.

3. Cook uncovered on high for 30 minutes or until the pan juices begin to bubble around the edges. Reduce the setting to low or simmer, and cook for 15 more minutes or until the mixture is reduced by half and thickened.

4. Whisk in the red currant jelly and butter. Ladle the sauce over the meat or pour it into a heated gravy boat.

PER SERVING Calories: 390 | Fat: 10g | Protein: 51g | Sodium: 500mg | Fiber: 2g | Carbohydrates: 16g | Sugar: 10g

Slow Cooker Stuffing SC

The key to a really good gluten-free stuffing is to find or make a gluten-free bread that is very dry and somewhat dense.

INGREDIENTS | SERVES 6

6 cups toasted, cubed, and very dry gluten-free bread

½ cup vegan butter

1 cup diced onion

1 cup diced celery

1½ teaspoons salt

1 teaspoon ground black pepper

2 tablespoons poultry seasoning

1 pound gluten-free mild pork sausage

2½ cups gluten-free chicken broth

Gluten-Free Bread—Worth the Expense?

Store-bought gluten-free bread is expensive. It's less expensive to buy gluten-free baking ingredients, but either way you're spending more money than you would have for wheat bread. If you plan on keeping gluten-free bread in your diet (and sometimes that sandwich is just worth it!), make sure to save leftovers in a zip-top bag in your freezer for recipes like this.

1. Place bread cubes in a very large bowl and set aside. Melt butter in a large sauté pan over medium-high heat. When warm and sizzling, add onion and celery. Sauté until onion is translucent, about 3–5 minutes. Add salt, pepper, and poultry seasoning. Pour onion and butter mixture over bread cubes in bowl.

2. Add sausage to the sauté pan, breaking it up into small pieces. Brown sausage until completely cooked through. Pour sausage into stuffing mixture in bowl. Stir together thoroughly.

3. Pour stuffing into a greased 4–6-quart slow cooker. Slowly add chicken broth. If you prefer a moister dressing, add additional chicken broth until desired consistency is reached.

4. Cook stuffing on high for 3–4 hours or on low for 6–8 hours. During the last hour and a half of cooking vent the lid of the slow cooker with a chopstick to let excess moisture escape.

PER SERVING Calories: 470 | Fat: 35g | Protein: 16g | Sodium: 1,500mg | Fiber: 2g | Carbohydrates: 23g | Sugar: 3g

White Chicken Chili

This is the perfect comfort food any time of the year.
Wheat-free cornbread would go perfectly with this dish.

INGREDIENTS | SERVES 6 | 30 MINUTES

1 tablespoon grapeseed oil

1 medium onion, peeled and chopped

4 cloves garlic, chopped

1 cup chopped mushrooms

1½ cups frozen corn

½ cup chopped green bell pepper

1 (4-ounce) can chopped green chili peppers

1½ teaspoons ground cumin

¼ teaspoon ground cayenne pepper

½ teaspoon chili powder

1 teaspoon oregano

3 (15-ounce) cans navy white beans, rinsed and drained

2 (14.5-ounce) cans gluten-free chicken broth

1½ pounds cooked skinless, boneless chicken breast, chopped

1 tablespoon chopped cilantro

2 tablespoons chopped scallions

Spice It Up

Do you like your chili a little spicier? Just add a fresh jalapeño (seeded and diced), or increase the cayenne pepper and chili powder. This dish can be made to suit your taste.

1. Heat oil in a large pot or Dutch oven over medium-low heat, and add onion and garlic. Cook for 3–4 minutes, until onions become translucent.

2. Add mushrooms, corn, and bell pepper, and cook until they soften a bit, about 2–3 minutes.

3. Add chili peppers, cumin, cayenne pepper, chili powder, and oregano. Stir to combine.

4. Take 1 can of white beans and place in a blender or food processor until completely blended. You might need to add a bit of water if it becomes too thick.

5. Pour blended bean mixture into pot along with chicken broth, remaining 2 cans of beans, cooked chicken, and cilantro, and stir. Reduce heat to low and continue to simmer about 10–15 minutes, stirring occasionally.

6. Top with chopped scallions.

PER SERVING Calories: 510 | Fat: 7g | Protein: 53g | Sodium: 415mg | Fiber: 12g | Carbohydrates: 60g | Sugar: 4g

Curried Lamb Grilled on Skewers

Serve these delicious grilled morsels with your favorite dipping sauce.

INGREDIENTS | SERVES 4

½ cup peanut oil

1 teaspoon curry powder

2 tablespoons lemon juice

4 cloves garlic, minced

½ teaspoon ground coriander

2 teaspoons hot sauce

1 pound bite-sized lamb chunks, from the leg or shoulder

1. Soak 8–10 wooden skewers in water for at least 40 minutes.

2. In a medium bowl, mix together the peanut oil, curry, lemon juice, garlic, coriander, and hot sauce.

3. Add the lamb and turn to coat with the marinade. Cover and refrigerate for at least 2 hours.

4. String the lamb on the skewers and grill over hot coals for 4 minutes per side. Serve hot.

PER SERVING Calories: 320 | Fat: 48g | Protein: 19g | Sodium: 135mg | Fiber: 0g | Carbohydrates: 2g | Sugar: 0g

Stuffed Peppers with Veggie-Burger Filling and Spices

Veggie burgers are typically well seasoned and quite delicious. They can be a great alternative to regular meats, although this recipe can also be prepared using ground beef, chicken, or turkey.

INGREDIENTS | SERVES 4 | 35 MINUTES

¼ cup extra-virgin olive oil

1 tablespoon Asian sesame oil

4 large garlic cloves, minced

1 large onion, peeled and minced

1 pound wheat-free veggie burgers

½ teaspoon salt

¼ teaspoon freshly ground black pepper

4 large green or red bell peppers

Dry Veggie Burgers?

You can do several things to keep veggie burgers moist. Mixing a bit of chopped fresh tomato into the mix is one option. Another is to add olive oil, milk, or cream (if you can consume dairy) before grilling. A bit of cooked, mashed potatoes also adds bulk and moisture. Add about 1 tablespoon of tomato, oil, milk, or mashed potato per burger.

1. In a medium skillet over medium heat, heat olive and sesame oils. Sauté the garlic and onion until soft, about 3–4 minutes.

2. Add the veggie burgers, break them up into pieces with a wooden spoon, and stir. Add salt and pepper and cook until heated through, about 5–6 minutes.

3. Preheat oven to 350°F. Prepare a baking sheet with gluten-free nonstick spray.

4. Cut the peppers in half lengthwise and scoop out seeds and cores. Fill with the burger mixture. Place on the baking sheet.

5. Bake for 25 minutes. Serve hot.

PER SERVING Calories: 370 | Fat: 22g | Protein: 24g | Sodium: 800mg | Fiber: 11g | Carbohydrates: 21g | Sugar: 6g

Homemade Baked Chicken Nuggets

Every kid's favorite, these easy baked chicken nuggets are coated either with gluten-free bread crumbs or blanched almond flour. Both options make crispy, dippable nuggets!

INGREDIENTS | SERVES 4 | 40 MINUTES

1½ cups gluten-free bread crumbs or 1½ cups blanched almond flour

1 teaspoon dried basil

1 teaspoon paprika

½ teaspoon salt

½ teaspoon ground black pepper

½ teaspoon dried parsley

1½ pounds boneless, skinless chicken breasts, cut into small strips

3 large eggs, beaten

1. Preheat oven to 350°F. Line a baking sheet with foil and grease foil with gluten-free nonstick cooking spray or olive oil.

2. In a medium bowl whisk together bread crumbs or almond flour, basil, paprika, salt, pepper, and parsley. Dip chicken strips into the beaten eggs and dredge through the bread-crumb mixture.

3. Place dredged chicken strips onto baking sheet.

4. Bake for 25–30 minutes until strips are crispy and chicken is cooked through. (Pierce several chicken nuggets with a sharp knife, and the juices should run clear. If they are red or pink, the chicken is not done cooking.) Serve nuggets with a tray of dipping sauces and steamed carrots or broccoli.

PER SERVING Calories: 405 | Fat: 10g | Protein: 46g | Sodium: 820mg | Fiber: 2g | Carbohydrates: 30g | Sugar: 3g

Golden Corn Fritters

Fritters are really fun to make and to eat. They can be as plain or as interesting as you want. The idea is to make them really creamy on the inside and golden on the outside.

INGREDIENTS | SERVES 8 | 20 MINUTES

1 large egg

1½ cups gluten-free beer

1½ cups almond milk

⅔ cup cornstarch or corn flour

1½ teaspoons baking powder

½ teaspoon salt

½ teaspoon red pepper flakes

⅛ teaspoon freshly grated nutmeg

1 cup fresh corn, cut off the cob or frozen

2 cups peanut, canola, or other cooking oil (not olive oil)

Frittering Away

Fritters are a great side dish with chicken or steak, especially if the entrée includes a sauce or gravy. You can also use them as hors d'oeuvres to dip in salsa. Also, you can vary the flavor by using chopped clams instead of corn.

1. Starting with the egg, beer, and milk, place everything but the corn and oil in a food processor and blend until smooth.

2. Scrape the mixture into a large bowl and fold in the corn.

3. Heat oil to 350°F in a deep pot over high heat.

4. Drop the fritters by the tablespoonful into the hot oil. Fry until golden, about 5–7 minutes. Drain on paper towels and serve hot.

PER SERVING Calories: 150 | Fat: 6g | Protein: 3g | Sodium: 270mg | Fiber: 1g | Carbohydrates: 19g | Sugar: 3g

Vegetarian Coconut Curry

Looking for an easy one-pot dinner? Try this slow cooker coconut curry. It's filled with incredible Indian flavors and spices, like coconut milk and curry powder.

INGREDIENTS | SERVES 6

1 cup chopped parsnips

1 small onion, peeled and diced

1 pound butternut squash, chopped (about 2 cups)

½ pound chopped sweet potato (about 1 cup)

1 cup quartered Brussels sprouts

½ cup uncooked rice

1¼ cups gluten-free vegetable broth

½ cup coconut milk

1 teaspoon brown sugar

1 garlic clove, minced

1 teaspoon curry powder

½ teaspoon turmeric

1 teaspoon salt

1 teaspoon ground black pepper

1. Place parsnips, onion, squash, sweet potato, and Brussels sprouts in a 4–6-quart slow cooker. Add rice, broth, coconut milk, brown sugar, garlic, curry powder, turmeric, salt, and pepper. Stir the mixture to combine.

2. Cook on low for 4–5 hours or until rice is fully cooked and vegetables are soft. For the best results, stir the mixture halfway through the cooking so the rice cooks evenly.

PER SERVING Calories: 170 | Fat: 4g | Protein: 3g | Sodium: 520mg | Fiber: 4g | Carbohydrates: 32g | Sugar: 5g

Cioppino

Cioppino is a fish stew that is quite popular in San Francisco. It's a blend of Italian and American flavors, and is the perfect one-pot summer meal. Every fish lover in your house will gobble this up!

INGREDIENTS | SERVES 4 | 35 MINUTES

1 tablespoon rosemary-infused olive oil

1½ large leeks, chopped

2 large shallots, peeled and chopped

3 garlic cloves, minced

½ cup dry white wine

4 ounces fish sauce

1 tablespoon chopped fresh rosemary

1 teaspoon salt

½ teaspoon ground black pepper

½ pound ahi tuna, cut into bite-size pieces

1 pound littleneck clams

1 (14.5-ounce) can Italian diced tomatoes, undrained

8 ounces large shrimp, deveined

8 ounces bay scallops

2 tablespoons chopped cilantro

1. Heat the oil in a large Dutch oven over medium heat. Add leeks, shallots, and garlic. Cook until softened, about 6 minutes. Stir in wine, fish sauce, rosemary, salt, and pepper. Reduce heat to low and simmer 8 minutes.

2. Stir in tuna and cook another 3 minutes. Add clams, tomatoes, shrimp, and scallops. Cover with a lid and cook another 5 minutes, or until the clams have opened.

3. Discard any unopened shells and garnish with cilantro.

PER SERVING Calories: 380 | Fat: 9g | Protein: 51g | Sodium: 2,500mg | Fiber: 2g | Carbohydrates: 18g | Sugar: 5g

Vegan Gluten-Free Fettuccine Alfredo

Alfredo pasta is one of those dishes that vegans and people with gluten allergies typically shy away from. But this ultra-creamy, decadent pasta is completely vegan (no dairy, cheese, or butter) and gluten-free! Now you can have your favorite pasta without guilt.

INGREDIENTS | SERVES 6 | 20 MINUTES

16 ounces gluten-free fettuccine

1½ pounds extra-firm tofu, drained

½ cup soy milk

2 tablespoons chopped basil

½ cup soy Parmesan

4 tablespoons vegan butter (such as Earth Balance)

1 teaspoon salt

1 teaspoon ground black pepper

1¼ cups peas

1. Bring a large pot of salted water to a boil. Add the pasta and boil for about 6–8 minutes, or until al dente. Drain and set aside.

2. While the pasta cooks, combine the tofu, soy milk, basil, soy Parmesan, vegan butter, salt, and pepper in a blender. Blend until thick and creamy.

3. Mix the sauce with the pasta and stir in peas.

PER SERVING Calories: 450 | Fat: 11g | Protein: 24g | Sodium: 625mg | Fiber: 4g | Carbohydrates: 64g | Sugar: 6g

CHAPTER 16

Desserts

Apple Cobbler with Cheddar Biscuit Crust

This cobbler is very easy to prepare in advance—bake it just before serving.

INGREDIENTS | SERVES 8

1 cup brown rice flour

1 cup arrowroot starch or tapioca starch

½ teaspoon xanthan gum

½ teaspoon salt

4 teaspoons baking powder

½ teaspoon cayenne pepper

¼ cup butter, softened

¾ cup buttermilk

¾ cup grated sharp Cheddar cheese

8 large tart apples such as Granny Smiths, peeled, cored, and sliced

⅓ cup lemon juice

2 teaspoons cinnamon

¼ teaspoon nutmeg

1½ tablespoons cornstarch

¼ cup dark brown sugar

¼ cup sugar

Pinch salt

4 tablespoons butter

1. Preheat the oven to 325°F.

2. In a large bowl, mix the brown rice flour, arrowroot starch or tapioca starch, xanthan gum, salt, baking powder, and cayenne pepper. Cut in the butter with a fork until it looks like oatmeal. Add the buttermilk and stir. Stir in the cheese and set aside.

3. Place the apples in a 9" × 13" baking dish or a 2-quart casserole. Sprinkle them with lemon juice.

4. In a small bowl, mix together cinnamon, nutmeg, cornstarch, sugars, and salt. Pour over the apples and toss together. Dot with butter. Drop the cheese mixture by the tablespoonful over the top.

5. Bake for 50 minutes, or until crust is browned and the apples are bubbling. Serve with extra slices of cheese or vanilla ice cream.

PER SERVING Calories: 420 | Fat: 16g | Protein: 5g | Sodium: 475mg | Fiber: 4g | Carbohydrates: 68g | Sugar: 31g

Old-Fashioned Chocolate Cobbler

This rich and delicious gluten-free chocolate dessert creates its own chocolate sauce underneath the cake. Don't be alarmed if it doesn't look like a normal cake. It's meant to be served with ice cream or whipped cream on top.

INGREDIENTS | SERVES 8

4 tablespoons butter
1 cup brown rice flour
½ teaspoon baking powder
¼ teaspoon salt
½ cup plus ⅓ cup sugar, divided
2 tablespoons plus ¼ cup cocoa powder, divided
1 teaspoon gluten-free vanilla
¾ cup milk
1 large egg
1¼ cups boiling water

1. Preheat oven to 350°F. Place the butter into a 2–3-quart casserole dish and place in the hot oven to melt.

2. In a small bowl whisk together the brown rice flour, baking powder, salt, ½ cup sugar, and 2 tablespoons cocoa powder. Stir in the vanilla, milk, and egg. Using potholders, remove the dish from the oven. Pour the batter into the dish and spread it evenly over the butter. It's okay if the butter comes up around the batter. Sprinkle the additional ⅓ cup of sugar and ¼ cup cocoa powder over the cake batter. Then pour the boiling water over the entire cake.

3. Bake for 35 minutes until the topping is deep brown and chocolate sauce is bubbling around the edges of the pan. The actual "cake" part of the cobbler will *not* be pretty—it may seem too dark and it may not crisp up. That's okay. Allow cobbler to cool for at least 40 minutes before serving. This is crucial to allow the chocolate sauce to set up underneath the cobbler top.

4. Serve warm with vanilla ice cream or whipped cream.

PER SERVING Calories: 235 | Fat: 8g | Protein: 4g | Sodium: 120mg | Fiber: 2g | Carbohydrates: 40g | Sugar: 22g

Cherry Oat Crisp

This crisp is special because it has a rich bottom crust, so it's almost like a pie with a crispy topping.

INGREDIENTS | SERVES 8 | 45 MINUTES

Crust

1 cup brown rice flour

¼ teaspoon sea salt

¼ cup packed brown sugar

½ cup softened butter or Spectrum Organic Shortening

Filling

¾ cup sugar

¼ cup cornstarch

1 cup cherry juice blend or apple juice

4 cups pitted dark-red plain cherries, not cherry pie filling (frozen or canned; if canned, drain before using)

Crisp Topping

1½ cups gluten-free rolled oats

¼ cup packed brown sugar

¼ cup brown rice flour

5 tablespoons butter, softened

1. Preheat oven to 350°F. Grease a 2-quart baking dish, pie pan, or casserole dish and set aside.

2. In a medium bowl mix together 1 cup brown rice flour, salt, and ¼ cup brown sugar. Cut in ½ cup butter with a pastry blender, until mixture is crumbly. Press crust mixture into the bottom of the baking dish. Bake for 15 minutes and remove from oven.

3. While the crust is baking, make the filling: In a small saucepan add sugar, cornstarch, and juice. Mix or whisk together and cook over high heat, stirring constantly until boiling. Allow to boil for 1 minute. The cornstarch/juice mixture will turn translucent and thicken. Remove from heat and add cherries. Pour cherry filling over the baked crust.

4. In another small bowl whisk together oats, ¼ cup brown sugar, and ¼ cup brown rice flour. Cut in 5 tablespoons of butter with a pastry blender, until the mixture is crumbly. Sprinkle the topping evenly over the cherry filling.

5. Place crisp on a cookie sheet to prevent spills in the oven while baking. Bake for 25 minutes until crispy topping is golden brown and cherry filling is bubbling around the edges. Serve plain or with ice cream.

PER SERVING Calories: 510 | Fat: 20g | Protein: 5g | Sodium: 82mg | Fiber: 4g | Carbohydrates: 82g | Sugar: 45g

Easy Peanut Butter Cookies

Here's a quick-to-make cookie made from three easy ingredients—it doesn't get any better than that! These cookies are a great project to make with kids—their tiny hands can easily roll the dough into balls.

INGREDIENTS | MAKES 2 DOZEN COOKIES | 20 MINUTES

1 cup peanut butter
1 cup sugar
1 large egg

Make "Other" Butter Cookies

People with peanut allergies can make these cookies with almond, cashew, walnut, or pecan butters, or even a seed butter like SunButter, made from sunflower seeds. These "other" butters are often available at specialty grocery stores, health-food stores, and online.

1. Preheat oven to 350°F. Line a cookie sheet with parchment paper and set aside.

2. In a large bowl cream together the peanut butter and sugar. Once thoroughly mixed, stir in the egg.

3. The batter will be very thick and sticky. For small cookies, use a spoon to scoop out about 1 tablespoon of batter, roll it into a ball, and place on the cookie sheet about 1" apart. For large cookies, scoop out about 2 tablespoons of dough, roll into a larger ball, and place on the cookie sheet about 2" apart.

4. Using a fork, flatten cookies and make a crisscross pattern on them. Place in oven and bake for 8–10 minutes until golden brown. Allow cookies to cool on baking sheet for about 10 minutes before placing them on a cooling rack.

5. Store cookies in an airtight container on the counter for 2–3 days. Cookies and cookie dough can also be frozen for up to 1 month.

PER SERVING (2 COOKIES) | Calories: 200 | Fat: 11g | Protein: 6g | Sodium: 100mg | Fiber: 1g | Carbohydrates: 21g | Sugar: 19g

Stovetop Oatmeal Fudge Cookies

You may know these cookies as "Stovetop Cookies," "Oatmeal Fudgies," or "No-Bake Cookies." If you need cookies fast, these are the way to go!

INGREDIENTS | MAKES 2 DOZEN COOKIES | 20 MINUTES

½ cup butter

2 cups sugar

½ cup milk

½ cup baking cocoa

1 teaspoon gluten-free vanilla extract

½ cup peanut butter

2 cups gluten-free quick-cooking oats

Make Them Dairy-Free

You can make these cookies dairy-free by using ⅓ cup coconut oil or ⅓ cup Spectrum Organic Shortening in place of the butter (you use less because butter contains some milk/liquid) and your favorite nondairy milk such as almond or cashew milk.

1. Line 2 or 3 cookie sheets with parchment paper and set aside. Melt butter in a medium-sized saucepan over medium heat until fully melted. Add sugar, milk, and cocoa to the butter and whisk to remove any lumps.

2. Continue to cook over medium-high heat until mixture is simmering. Cook for an additional 6–7 minutes, stirring constantly to prevent the mixture from burning. Remove from heat.

3. Add vanilla extract and peanut butter and stir until peanut butter has dissolved into the hot mixture. Quickly stir in the oats.

4. Working quickly (as the mixture will harden as it sets), drop cookie mixture 1 tablespoon at a time onto the parchment paper. You should have enough batter to make 24–30 cookies.

5. Allow cookies to cool completely before serving or moving to a storage container. Cookies should be somewhat soft, but will harden enough so that they can be picked up and held. Store cookies at room temperature in an airtight container between sheets of parchment paper or plastic wrap. The cookies will stick to each other and be hard to pull apart if placed in a container without being separated.

PER SERVING (2 COOKIES) | Calories: 325 | Fat: 15g | Protein: 6g | Sodium: 55mg | Fiber: 3g | Carbohydrates: 47g | Sugar: 35g

Classic Blondies MA

As with basic cocoa brownies, you can mix in different ingredients just before baking to create your own signature blondie. Stir in ½ cup chocolate chips, butterscotch morsels, chopped nuts, or a combination of all three.

INGREDIENTS | SERVES 24

1½ cups butter, softened, or 1 cup Spectrum Organic Shortening

1⅔ cups sugar

1 cup brown sugar

4 large eggs

2 tablespoons gluten-free vanilla extract

1½ cups brown rice flour

1½ cups arrowroot starch

1 teaspoon xanthan gum

2 teaspoons baking powder

½ teaspoon sea salt

1. Preheat oven to 350°F. Line a 9" × 13" baking dish with parchment paper and set aside.

2. In a large bowl cream butter and sugars until light and fluffy. Stir in eggs and vanilla until well incorporated.

3. In a medium bowl whisk together brown rice flour, arrowroot starch, xanthan gum, baking powder, and salt. Stir the flour mixture into sugar mixture, until fully incorporated.

4. Pour batter into baking dish. Bake for 40–45 minutes until golden brown. Allow to cool completely before cutting. Store in an airtight container in the refrigerator for up to 5 days.

PER SERVING Calories: 270 | Fat: 12g | Protein: 2g | Sodium: 100mg | Fiber: 1g | Carbohydrates: 38g | Sugar: 23g

Spiced Winter Fruit Compote SC

This warm compote is spiced with ginger, cardamom, and nutmeg. It would be perfect spooned over toasted gluten-free pound cake, your favorite vanilla bean custard, or ice cream.

INGREDIENTS | SERVES 8

3 medium pears, cored and cubed

1 (15.5-ounce) can pineapple chunks, undrained

1 cup dried apricots, quartered

½ cup dried cranberries

3 tablespoons frozen orange juice concentrate

2 tablespoons packed brown sugar

3 tablespoons tapioca starch

½ teaspoon ground ginger

¼ teaspoon cardamom

½ teaspoon freshly grated nutmeg

2 cups frozen unsweetened pitted dark sweet cherries

½ cup toasted flaked coconut

½ cup toasted pecans

1. In a greased 4–6-quart slow cooker combine pears, pineapple, apricots, and cranberries.

2. In a small bowl whisk together orange juice concentrate, brown sugar, tapioca starch, ginger, cardamom, and nutmeg. Pour orange juice mixture over fruit.

3. Cover and cook on low for 6–8 hours or on high for 3–4 hours. Stir in cherries 1 hour prior to serving.

4. To serve, spoon warm compote into dessert dishes. Top with coconut and nuts.

PER SERVING Calories: 280 | Fat: 10g | Protein: 3g | Sodium: 7mg | Fiber: 7g | Carbohydrates: 51g | Sugar: 38g

Hummingbird Cake with Cream Cheese Icing

This old-fashioned fruit-filled cake is perfect for birthdays. It's delicious topped with luscious cream cheese frosting, and it's impossible to have just one piece! For an easy weeknight dessert, make the cake one day and frost it the next.

INGREDIENTS | SERVES 10

Cake

1 cup plus 2 tablespoons brown rice flour, plus more for dusting pan

1 cup arrowroot starch or tapioca starch

1 cup sugar

2 teaspoons baking powder

1 teaspoon baking soda

1 teaspoon xanthan gum

1 teaspoon ground cinnamon

½ teaspoon sea salt

1 (8-ounce) can crushed pineapple in juice, undrained

1 cup mashed bananas (2 or 3 very ripe bananas)

½ cup water

½ cup light-tasting olive oil

3 large eggs

1 teaspoon gluten-free vanilla extract

Cream Cheese Frosting

1½ cups butter, softened

8 ounces cream cheese, softened

3 cups confectioners' sugar

1 teaspoon gluten-free vanilla extract

1. Preheat oven to 350°F. Line 2 (9") round baking pans with parchment paper and then grease with oil or gluten-free nonstick cooking spray. Dust pans lightly with brown rice flour.

2. In a medium-sized bowl, whisk together brown rice flour, arrowroot starch or tapioca starch, sugar, baking powder, baking soda, xanthan gum, ground cinnamon, and salt.

3. In a smaller bowl whisk together crushed pineapple in juice, mashed bananas, water, oil, eggs, and vanilla until fully combined.

4. Slowly add the wet ingredients into the dry ingredients and stir until fully incorporated. Pour into baking pans.

5. Bake cakes for 30–35 minutes until a toothpick inserted in the middle comes out clean, they are golden brown, and the top springs back when touched lightly.

6. Cool cakes for 5 minutes in their pans and then transfer to a wire rack to cool completely before icing with the cream cheese frosting.

7. In a large bowl, using a hand mixer, cream together the butter and cream cheese. Stir in confectioners' sugar and vanilla extract. Mix until the frosting is thick enough to spread and very creamy. Use to fill the middle layer of the cake and to frost outside of cake.

PER SERVING Calories: 670 | Fat: 48g | Protein: 5g | Sodium: 440mg | Fiber: 2g | Carbohydrates: 57g | Sugar: 28g

Strawberry-Blueberry Coulis

This is wonderful on ice cream or over your favorite pound cake. You can also mix it into rice pudding for a different take on an old-fashioned dessert.

INGREDIENTS | MAKES 1½ CUPS
10 MINUTES

½ pint blueberries, rinsed

½ pint strawberries, rinsed

¼ cup water

¼ cup sugar

1" × ½" strip orange rind

Place all of the ingredients in a medium saucepan and bring to a boil. Remove from the heat and cool. Whisk until smooth. Serve warm or cool.

PER SERVING (¼ CUP) | Calories: 55 | Fat: 0g | Protein: 0g | Sodium: 1mg | Fiber: 1g | Carbohydrates: 13g | Sugar: 13g

Mango Coconut Ice Cream MA

This rich, creamy, and sweet ice cream is made with fresh mangos and two kinds of coconut, giving it a dreamy tropical flavor. For an even more decadent dessert, substitute full-fat coconut milk for the light version.

INGREDIENTS | SERVES 8

1 large mango

1 cup 2% milk

3 tablespoons light brown sugar

1 (13.5-ounce) can light coconut milk

¾ cup light cream

½ cup sweetened coconut

1. Cut mango in half and remove the skin from the flesh. Scoop out the flesh and place into a blender. Blend until thick and smooth. Add milk, brown sugar, coconut milk, and cream. Blend until mixture is thick and creamy. Cover with the top of the blender and chill for about 2 hours.

2. Pour the mixture into the frozen canister of an ice cream maker. Turn on the ice cream maker and blend until thick and creamy, about 15 minutes. Serve with coconut on top.

PER SERVING Calories: 210 | Fat: 17g | Protein: 3g | Sodium: 30mg | Fiber: 1g | Carbohydrates: 14g | Sugar: 11g

Chocolate Raspberry Cupcakes with
Fluffy Raspberry Frosting

These cupcakes are lighter than air, but they are heavy on chocolate flavor.

INGREDIENTS | SERVES 24 | 45 MINUTES

Cupcakes

1½ cups sugar

¾ cup sorghum flour

¾ cup arrowroot starch or tapioca starch

¾ cup unsweetened cocoa powder

1 teaspoon xanthan gum

2 teaspoons baking soda

2 teaspoons baking powder

½ teaspoon salt

1 cup whole milk

2 large eggs

½ cup oil

2 teaspoons gluten-free raspberry extract

1 cup boiling water

Frosting

1 cup unsalted butter, softened

½ teaspoon salt

4 tablespoons raspberry purée

2 teaspoons gluten-free raspberry extract

4 cups confectioners' sugar

2 tablespoons heavy cream

24 fresh, plump raspberries

No Seeds, Please

To make the frosting free of seeds, push the mashed berries through a mesh strainer with the back of a spoon. This will leave you with seedless raspberry purée.

1. Preheat oven to 350°F. Line muffin tins with paper liners. In a large bowl, whisk together the sugar, sorghum flour, arrowroot starch or tapioca starch, cocoa powder, xanthan gum, baking soda, baking powder, and ½ teaspoon salt until evenly blended.

2. In a small bowl, whisk together the milk, eggs, oil, and 2 teaspoons raspberry extract. Pour the wet ingredients into the dry ingredients, and beat for 1 minute. Add the boiling water, and using a wooden spoon, stir until it is completely mixed into the batter. The batter will be thin.

3. Fill the muffin tins ⅔ full with the batter. Bake on the center rack for 20–22 minutes. Test to see if cupcakes are completely baked by inserting a toothpick into the middle. If the toothpick comes out clean, the cupcakes are done. If there is still batter on the toothpick, bake for another 2 minutes and test again.

4. Remove from oven and let sit for 5 minutes before removing cupcakes to wire rack to cool completely.

5. Make the frosting: In a stand mixer fitted with a paddle attachment, beat the butter until lightly colored. Add salt, raspberry purée, and raspberry extract. Beat until completely mixed. Add the confectioners' sugar and run the mixer until it all comes together. Scrape down the sides and mix again. Add the cream, 1 tablespoon at a time, until you get the frosting the consistency you want.

6. Spread the frosting on with a knife, or pipe it on with a piping bag with a large tip. Top each cupcake with a fresh raspberry. Store the cupcakes in an airtight container. They are best in the first 2 days.

PER SERVING Calories: 215 | Fat: 14g | Protein: 2g | Sodium: 250mg | Fiber: 2g | Carbohydrates: 24g | Sugar: 13g

Cream Puffs (Choux Paste)

This dough, called choux paste, can be used to make both cream puffs and éclairs. To make éclairs, pipe the dough into 4" logs, about 1½" wide, and bake according to these directions.

INGREDIENTS | SERVES 12 | 45 MINUTES

⅔ cup white rice flour
⅓ cup sweet rice flour
½ teaspoon xanthan gum
Pinch salt

1 teaspoon baking powder
1 cup water
½ cup unsalted butter
4 large eggs, room temperature

1. Preheat the oven to 400°F. Line a baking sheet with parchment paper and set aside.

2. In a mixing bowl, whisk together the white rice flour, sweet rice flour, xanthan gum, salt, and baking powder. Set aside.

3. In a medium saucepan, bring the water and butter to a boil. Once they have reached a boil, pour all of the dry ingredients in at once, and stir with a wooden spoon until the dry ingredients are completely incorporated and the mixture looks similar to play dough.

4. Place hot dough into a large mixing bowl or bowl of a stand mixer fitted with a paddle attachment. Beat on medium-high speed for 1–2 minutes to cool the dough down a bit. With the mixer on medium speed, add eggs, one at a time. Beat dough until the egg is completely incorporated before adding the next one. Repeat until all 4 eggs have been added.

5. Mix on medium-high speed for 1 minute, until the dough is smooth.

6. Spoon the dough (about ¼ cup per cream puff) onto prepared baking sheet, leaving about 2" between cream puffs.

7. Bake in preheated oven for 30 minutes. Turn off the oven, open the door, and pierce each cream puff with a sharp knife. This will help any steam trapped inside them to escape, giving a nice, crisp cream puff. Leave the cream puffs in the oven, with the door open a few inches, until the oven has cooled completely.

8. Once cream puffs have completely cooled, fill them with a sweet or savory filling. They are best served the same day, but can be stored in an airtight container. To crisp unfilled cream puffs again, place in a 400°F oven for 10 minutes.

PER SERVING Calories: 140 | Fat: 9g | Protein: 3g | Sodium: 90mg | Fiber: 0g | Carbohydrates: 11g | Sugar: 0g

Chestnut Cookies

These are festive and delicious. They're easy enough for an everyday dessert, but they also make great party fare.

INGREDIENTS | MAKES ABOUT 48 COOKIES | 30 MINUTES

1 (2-ounce) can roasted peeled chestnuts, packed in water

1½ cups chestnut flour

½ cup milk

2 egg yolks

1 teaspoon gluten-free vanilla

1 teaspoon salt

2 teaspoons baking powder

½ cup granulated sugar

½ cup unsalted butter, melted

3 egg whites, beaten stiff

1. Drain the chestnuts and chop in the food processor. Place in the bowl of an electric mixer. With the motor on low, add the chestnut flour, milk, egg yolks, vanilla, salt, baking powder, sugar, and melted butter.

2. Preheat the oven to 350°F. Fold the egg whites into the chestnut mixture. Drop by the teaspoonful on cookie sheets lined with parchment paper.

3. Bake for 12–15 minutes. Cool and place on platters for immediate use, or store in tins for later use.

PER SERVING (2 COOKIES) | Calories: 110 | Fat: 9g | Protein: 2g | Sodium: 150mg | Fiber: 1g | Carbohydrates: 7g | Sugar: 5g

Blackberry-Yogurt Pops

These ice pops are attractive and nutritious. Blackberries are an excellent source of fiber, vitamin C, vitamin K, and folic acid. Mix the pops early in the day and toss them in the freezer if you don't have one of those quick pop makers.

INGREDIENTS | SERVES 6

2 cups plain yogurt

½ cup sugar

½ cup puréed blackberries

Crack the Ice Pop Code

The secret to a good ice pop is simple: sugar. Sugar lowers the freezing point of the pop so it stays soft and smooth, not brittle like an ice cube. So resist the urge to fully eliminate sugar from ice pop recipes that call for it.

1. In a medium bowl, whisk together the yogurt and sugar until the sugar dissolves.

2. Divide half of the yogurt mixture between 6 ice pop molds. Evenly divide all of the blackberry purée between the six ice pop molds. Top with remaining yogurt mixture.

3. Insert pop sticks and freeze until solid.

PER SERVING Calories: 120 | Fat: 3g | Protein: 3g | Sodium: 35mg | Fiber: 1g | Carbohydrates: 22g | Sugar: 21g

Baked Chocolate Doughnuts

One of the things you might miss most when on a gluten-free diet is doughnuts.
These quick doughnuts are baked, making them a (slightly) healthier option.
Make these mini by baking them in a mini doughnut pan for cute treats kids will love!

INGREDIENTS | SERVES 6 | 40 MINUTES

Doughnuts

½ cup brown rice flour

¼ cup sorghum flour

2 tablespoons potato starch

1 tablespoon tapioca starch

½ teaspoon xanthan gum

2 tablespoons dry gluten-free instant chocolate pudding mix (or dry milk powder)

3 tablespoons cocoa powder

½ cup granulated sugar

1 teaspoon baking powder

¼ teaspoon salt

2 large eggs

¼ cup oil

¼ cup milk

½ teaspoon apple cider vinegar

Frosting

1 cup confectioners' sugar

2 tablespoons cocoa powder

2 tablespoons butter, softened

1–2 tablespoons milk

1. Preheat your oven to 375°F. Lightly grease a doughnut pan.

2. In a large bowl, whisk together all the dry doughnut ingredients.

3. In a smaller bowl, whisk together all the wet doughnut ingredients.

4. Pour the wet ingredients into the dry ingredients and stir until fully combined.

5. Spoon mixture into prepared doughnut pan. Bake in preheated oven for 10–12 minutes, or until a toothpick inserted into the thickest part of the doughnut comes out clean.

6. Let doughnuts sit for 5 minutes before turning them out onto a cooling rack. Allow to cool completely before frosting.

7. For the frosting: Stir together the confectioners' sugar, 2 tablespoons cocoa powder, butter, and enough milk to make the glaze the consistency you want. Dip your cooled doughnuts into the glaze, and top with sprinkles, chopped nuts, or shredded coconut, if you prefer.

PER SERVING Calories: 335 | Fat: 17g | Protein: 6g | Sodium: 230mg | Fiber: 3g | Carbohydrates: 45g | Sugar: 18g

Blueberry Cobbler SC

An old-fashioned cobbler with sweetened fruit on the bottom and a crunchy,
biscuity topping, this dessert can be served plain or with ice cream.

INGREDIENTS | SERVES 6

¾ cup water

⅔ cup plus 2 tablespoons sugar, divided

2 tablespoons cornstarch

3 cups fresh or frozen blueberries

½ cup brown rice flour

½ cup arrowroot starch

1 teaspoon baking powder

¼ teaspoon xanthan gum

⅓ cup 2% milk

1 tablespoon melted butter

½ teaspoon cinnamon mixed with 2 teaspoons sugar

2 tablespoons cold butter, cut into small pieces

Make It Easier

If you don't want to go to the trouble of making your own fruit filling, use a can of cherry pie filling, apple pie filling, or even a can of whole cranberry jelly. Make the cobbler even easier by replacing the brown rice flour, arrowroot starch, baking powder, and xanthan gum with 1 cup of Gluten-Free Bisquick.

1. Grease a 4–6-quart slow cooker.

2. In a small saucepan add water, ⅔ cup sugar, and cornstarch. Whisk together and cook over high heat, stirring constantly until boiling. Allow to boil for 1 minute. The mixture will turn translucent and thicken. Remove from heat and add blueberries. Pour blueberry filling into the greased slow cooker.

3. In a small bowl whisk together flour, arrowroot starch, baking powder, 2 tablespoons sugar, and xanthan gum. Make a well in the center of the dry ingredients and add milk and melted butter. Mix until you have a thick batter.

4. Drop batter by tablespoons on top of the blueberry filling and use a fork to spread evenly over the casserole.

5. Sprinkle cinnamon and sugar mixture over the top of the casserole. Dot with butter.

6. Cover and vent slow cooker lid with a chopstick or the end of a wooden spoon. Cook on high for 2½–3 hours or until fruit filling is bubbling on the sides of the topping and the biscuit topping is cooked through.

PER SERVING Calories: 305 | Fat: 6g | Protein: 2g | Sodium: 90mg | Fiber: 3g | Carbohydrates: 62g | Sugar: 36g

Vanilla Poached Pears SC

Slow poaching makes these pears meltingly tender and infuses them with a rich vanilla flavor.

INGREDIENTS | SERVES 4

4 Bosc pears, peeled
1 vanilla bean, split
2 tablespoons gluten-free vanilla extract
2 cups water or apple juice

In a Pinch . . .

If you need an easy dessert, but don't have fresh fruit, use a large can of sliced or halved pears. Drain and rinse them thoroughly. Make the recipe as written, except use only ½ cup of water or apple juice.

1. Stand the pears up in a 4–6-quart slow cooker. Add the remaining ingredients.

2. Cook on low for 2 hours or until the pears are tender. Discard all cooking liquid prior to serving.

PER SERVING Calories: 115 | Fat: 0g | Protein: 0g | Sodium: 2mg | Fiber: 5g | Carbohydrates: 26g | Sugar: 17g

Green Tea–Kiwi Popsicles MA

These are healthy and refreshing. If you are making these for children, you can easily use decaffeinated green tea matcha powder.

INGREDIENTS | SERVES 4

1½ teaspoons green tea matcha powder
1 tablespoon boiling water
2 kiwis, peeled and diced
12 ounces vanilla Greek yogurt
1 teaspoon fresh lemon juice
3 tablespoons honey

1. \In a small bowl, combine matcha powder and boiling water. Stir to combine to create a smooth paste. Set aside.

2. In a large bowl, mix the diced kiwis, Greek yogurt, lemon juice, and honey. Stir in matcha paste, and make sure it is thoroughly combined.

3. Spoon mixture into Popsicle molds, making sure to only fill ¾ of the way. Place in the freezer until frozen.

PER SERVING Calories: 140 | Fat: 1g | Protein: 4g | Sodium: 55mg | Fiber: 1g | Carbohydrates: 30g | Sugar: 25g

Quinoa Pumpkin Chocolate Chip Squares

Quinoa adds a wonderful texture, protein, antioxidants, and fiber to these squares.
You won't feel guilty having your second!

INGREDIENTS | SERVES 20 | 45 MINUTES

2 cups wheat-free all-purpose flour
½ cup ground flaxseed
1 teaspoon pumpkin pie spice
1½ teaspoons cinnamon
1 teaspoon baking soda
½ teaspoon salt
½ cup butter, at room temperature
2 tablespoons turbinado sugar
3 tablespoons pure maple syrup
1 large egg
1 cup cooked quinoa, cooled
1½ teaspoons wheat-free vanilla extract
1½ cups pumpkin purée
¾ cup dark chocolate chips

1. Preheat oven to 350°F. Spray a 9" × 9" or 9" × 13" baking dish with gluten-free nonstick cooking spray.

2. Mix flour, flaxseed, pumpkin pie spice, cinnamon, baking soda, and salt in a medium-sized bowl. Set the bowl aside.

3. In a large bowl, mix the butter, sugar, and maple syrup until thoroughly combined. Add egg, quinoa, and vanilla and mix again.

4. Slowly add in pumpkin purée and continue to mix well. Once completely mixed, slowly add flour mixture. Feel free to add small amounts of water in increments of 1 teaspoon if batter seems too thick.

5. Once the flour mixture is thoroughly mixed, add chocolate chips and mix well. Pour into prepared baking dish.

6. Place in oven and bake for 40 minutes or until you place a toothpick in the center and it comes out clean. Allow to cool before cutting into squares.

PER SERVING Calories: 165 | Fat: 8g | Protein: 3g | Sodium: 125mg | Fiber: 2g | Carbohydrates: 21g | Sugar: 7g

Chocolate Chip Peanut Butter Sandwich Cookies

The only thing better than soft-baked chocolate chip cookies are soft-baked chocolate chip cookie sandwiches filled with fluffy peanut butter mousse. These cookies are so soft, they'll melt in your mouth!

INGREDIENTS | SERVES 8

1 cup unsalted butter, softened, divided
¾ cup brown sugar
¼ cup granulated sugar
1 large egg
1 teaspoon gluten-free vanilla extract
½ teaspoon baking soda
¼ teaspoon salt
1¼ cups gluten-free all-purpose flour
1 cup gluten-free oat flour
¾ cup chocolate morsels
3 tablespoons chia seeds
1 cup creamy peanut butter
3 tablespoons heavy cream
2 cups powdered sugar
½ cup chopped peanuts

1. In a large mixing bowl, beat ½ cup butter, brown sugar, granulated sugar, egg, and vanilla together. Beat until smooth.

2. In another bowl, whisk baking soda, salt, and flours. Fold the dry ingredients into the wet ingredients. Gently stir in the chocolate morsels and chia seeds. Cover the dough with plastic wrap and chill for at least 3 hours.

3. Preheat oven to 350°F. Line a baking sheet with parchment paper.

4. Place spoonfuls of dough onto the baking sheet, about 1" apart. Bake for about 12 minutes, or until golden brown.

5. Move the cookies to a wire cooling rack and cool completely.

6. Beat remaining butter, peanut butter, cream, powdered sugar, and peanuts together in a small bowl.

7. Top half of the cookies with a spoonful of frosting and top with remaining cookies.

PER SERVING Calories: 920 | Fat: 53g | Protein: 16g | Sodium: 300mg | Fiber: 6g | Carbohydrates: 100g | Sugar: 70g

Fresh Berry Pie MA

This pie is made with two kinds of fresh berries and freshly whipped cream.
The crust is to die for—you won't even miss the flour!

1. Preheat oven to 400°F.

2. Whisk the flour and salt together in a large bowl. Using a pastry blender, cut in the butter or shortening until the mixture resembles coarse sand. Add the water, 1 tablespoon at a time, until the mixture just comes together.

3. On a floured surface, gently knead the dough until it's softened and pliable. Roll the dough into a circle about ¼" thick.

4. Grease a pie plate with gluten-free nonstick cooking spray. Carefully place the dough into the pie plate and press into the plate.

5. Bake crust for about 15 minutes, or until golden brown.

6. Meanwhile, mash raspberries and 2 cups strawberries together in a medium saucepan. Add the lemon juice, vanilla, and cornstarch.

7. Heat for about 5 minutes over medium heat, or until filling has thickened.

8. Pour the filling into the piecrust. Arrange blueberries and remaining strawberries over the top of the filling. Chill for at least 4 hours, or until set. Garnish with whipped cream.

PER SERVING Calories: 420 | Fat: 31g | Protein: 5g | Sodium: 98mg | Fiber: 3g | Carbohydrates: 33g | Sugar: 6g

APPENDIX A:

Additional Resources

AMAZON.COM
A variety of gluten-free products and ingredients can be purchased from Amazon.com.
www.amazon.com

ARROWHEAD MILLS
Arrowhead Mills offers a wide variety of baking mixes, flours, beans, grains, and nut butters.
www.arrowheadmills.com

BETTY CROCKER
Betty Crocker has a line of gluten-free products. Included are cake, brownie, and cookie mixes, as well as gluten-free Bisquick.
www.bettycrocker.com/products

BOB'S RED MILL
Bob's Red Mill carries a variety of gluten-free flours, oats, baking mixes, and other ingredients.
www.bobsredmill.com

CELIAC.COM
Celiac.com is a resource for the latest information on celiac disease and gluten sensitivity. The website includes a popular forum, blogs, and advice for people newly diagnosed with celiac disease.
www.celiac.com

CELIAC CENTRAL
Celiac Central is the website for the National Foundation for Celiac Awareness, a not-for-profit organization that supports raising awareness for celiac disease and gluten sensitivity.
www.celiaccentral.org

CELIAC DISEASE FOUNDATION (CDF)
CDF provides information about celiac disease, treatment, research, and living gluten-free.
www.celiac.org

CELIAC SUPPORT ASSOCIATION (CSA)
This is a great resource for finding local gluten-free support groups, along with basic information on starting the gluten-free diet.
www.csaceliacs.org

COOKING GLUTEN-FREE!
Cooking Gluten-Free! provides gluten-free recipes and resources.
www.cookingglutenfree.com

ENJOY LIFE FOODS
Enjoy Life Foods products are gluten-free and free of the eight most common allergens (wheat, dairy, peanuts, tree nuts, egg, soy, fish, and shellfish).
www.enjoylifefoods.com

THE GEORGE MATELJAN FOUNDATION FOR THE WORLD'S HEALTHIEST FOODS
The George Mateljan Foundation for the World's Healthiest Foods was established to discover, develop, and share scientifically proven information about the benefits of healthy eating.
www.whfoods.com

GF HARVEST
GF Harvest sells a variety of certified gluten-free oat products, including flour, rolled oat, groats, and granola. Products are also available to purchase in bulk.
www.glutenfreeoats.com

GLUTENFREEDA FOODS
The Glutenfreeda program was created to help people with celiac disease learn to prepare all the foods they love, gluten-free.
www.glutenfreeda.com

THE GLUTEN-FREE MALL
The Gluten-Free Mall offers high-quality gluten-free products.
www.celiac.com/glutenfreemall

THE GLUTEN INTOLERANCE GROUP
The Gluten Intolerance Group's mission is "to support persons with gluten intolerances, celiac disease, dermatitis herpetiformis, and other gluten sensitivities, through consumer and industry services and programs that positively promote healthy lives."
www.gluten.net

GLUTEN SOLUTIONS
Gluten Solutions is an online store for gluten-free foods and products.
www.glutensolutions.com

GLUTINO
Glutino produces a wide variety of gluten-free products. The site also features recipes, advice, blogs, and information on celiac disease.
www.glutino.com

KING ARTHUR FLOUR
Whether you are looking for gluten-free mixes for bread, pancakes, or cake, King Arthur Flour carries them all.
www.kingarthurflour.com/glutenfree

KINNIKINNICK FOODS
Although a lot of Kinnikinnick Foods products are available in stores, you can save a few dollars by ordering online. Kinnikinnick Foods carries baking mixes, breads, cookies, and snacks that are free from gluten, soy, eggs, and sesame seeds.
http://consumer.kinnikinnick.com

LE VENEZIANE
Le Veneziane produces gluten-free corn pasta in very unique shapes.
www.leveneziane.it/en/gluten-free-pasta

LIVING WITHOUT
Living Without is a lifestyle guide for people with allergies and food sensitivities. It discusses a wide variety of health issues, including allergies, food sensitivities and intolerance, chronic diseases, and diets that heal.
www.livingwithout.com

NAMASTE FOODS
Namaste Foods carries a variety of baking and cooking mixes, ranging from cakes and cookies to pasta salad and macaroni and dairy-free "cheese." All of their mixes are free from wheat, gluten, corn, soy, potato, dairy, casein, tree nuts, and peanuts.
www.namastefoods.com

PAMELA'S PRODUCTS
Pamela's Products not only has gluten-free baking mixes, but they also produce gluten-free cookies, cakes, and bars.
www.pamelasproducts.com

TINKYÁDA RICE PASTA
Tinkyáda Rice Pasta produces a wide variety of rice pastas.
www.tinkyada.com

APPENDIX B:

Vegan and Egg-Free Substitutions

▼ DAIRY SUBSTITUTES FOR GLUTEN-FREE VEGAN COOKING AND BAKING

TYPE OF DAIRY	SUBSTITUTIONS
1 cup 2% or regular milk	1 cup almond milk, full-fat coconut milk, hemp milk, soy milk (if tolerated)
1 cup 1% or fat-free milk	1 cup rice milk or ½ cup almond milk mixed with ½ cup water
1 cup buttermilk	1 cup almond milk or hemp milk mixed with 1 tablespoon lemon juice or apple cider vinegar
1 cup heavy cream	1 cup full-fat coconut milk cream (skimmed off the top of full-fat coconut milk), 1 cup reduced nut milk
1 cup yogurt	1 cup coconut milk yogurt, 1 cup almond milk yogurt, 1 cup unsweetened applesauce or plain pumpkin purée
1 cup sour cream	1 cup full-fat coconut milk cream mixed with 1 tablespoon lemon juice or apple cider vinegar, 1 cup unsweetened applesauce or plain pumpkin purée
1 tablespoon butter	1 tablespoon light-tasting olive oil, 1 tablespoon coconut oil, 1 tablespoon Spectrum Organic Shortening
1 cup cream cheese	1 cup Tofutti (soy substitute, if you tolerate soy), 1 cup Daiya "cream cheese style" spread
1 cup shredded cheese	1 cup shredded Daiya "cheese" shreds, 1 cup Galaxy Vegan Shreds, ¼ cup nutritional yeast
1 cup grated Parmesan	1 cup blanched almond flour, ¼ cup nutritional yeast, ½ cup finely chopped toasted pecans or cashews

▼ EGG SUBSTITUTES

EGG REPLACED	SUBSTITUTION
1 egg	2 tablespoons potato starch
1 egg	¼ cup mashed potatoes
1 egg	¼ cup pumpkin or squash purée + ½ teaspoon baking powder
1 egg	¼ cup puréed prunes + ½ teaspoon baking powder
1 egg	¼ cup unsweetened applesauce or mashed bananas + ½ teaspoon baking powder
1 egg	2 tablespoons water + 1 tablespoon oil + 1 teaspoon baking powder
1 egg	1 tablespoon ground flaxseeds + 3 tablespoons warm water
1 egg white	1 tablespoon plain agar + 1 tablespoon water
1 egg	¼ cup firm tofu, crumbled

Six-Week Meal Plan

WEEK 1	Spinach, Kale, and Mushroom Pizza (Chapter 13); Waldorf-Inspired Quinoa Salad (Chapter 5)	Slow Cooker Thai Curried Chicken Soup (Chapter 4)	Biscuit-Topped Chicken Pie (Chapter 8); Apple, Walnut, Cranberry, and Spinach Salad (Chapter 5)	Sesame-Glazed Planked Salmon (Chapter 9); Snow Peas with Water Chestnuts and Ginger (Chapter 11)	Spicy Steak Fajitas (Chapter 6)
WEEK 2	Beef and Broccoli Stir-Fry (Chapter 6)	Mini Turkey Meatloaves (Chapter 8); Roasted Red Potatoes with Garlic (Chapter 11)	Spicy Thai Chicken and Peanut Noodles (Chapter 12)	Confetti and Rice Pasta with Chicken (Chapter 12); Balsamic Roasted Brussels Sprouts (Chapter 11)	Fish Tacos with Tropical Fruit Salsa (Chapter 9)
WEEK 3	Pasta Primavera with Summer Vegetables (Chapter 12)	One-Pot Spaghetti and Meatballs (Chapter 14)	Honey Mustard Chicken Fingers (Chapter 14); Mexican-Seasoned Baked Avocado Fries (Chapter 11)	Chicken Piccata (Chapter 8); Lemon Rice with Toasted Pine Nuts (Chapter 11)	Sloppy Joes (Chapter 15); Sweet Rainbow Coleslaw (Chapter 5)
WEEK 4	Spaghetti with Mushroom Cream Sauce (Chapter 12); Fresh Tomato and Basil Bruschetta over Portobellos (Chapter 5)	Orange Chicken (Chapter 8); Quinoa Fried "Rice" (Chapter 11)	Spicy Vegetarian Chili (Chapter 4); Crunchy Cornbread Squares (Chapter 11)	Four-Cheese Baked Penne with Prosciutto (Chapter 12); Classic Caesar Salad with Gluten-Free Croutons (Chapter 5)	Retro Tuna Pasta Casserole (Chapter 12); Balsamic Fruit Salad (Chapter 5)
WEEK 5	Zucchini Pasta with Parmesan and Spicy Marinara Sauce (Chapter 13)	Spanish Tortilla (Chapter 10); Garlicky Parmesan Roasted Potatoes (Chapter 11)	Buffalo Chicken Nuggets (Chapter 14); Cheesiest Macaroni and Cheese (Chapter 14)	Gluten-Free Chicken and Waffles (Chapter 10); Confetti Corn with Bacon (Chapter 11)	California Burgers (Chapter 6); Asian-Spiced Kale Chips (Chapter 11)
WEEK 6	Potato Frittata with Cheese and Herbs (Chapter 13); Fried Potato Balls (Chapter 13)	Thick and Hearty Lancashire Lamb Stew (Chapter 4)	Tequila Grilled Swordfish with Pico de Gallo (Chapter 9); Blue Cheese, Grilled Pears, and Arugula Salad (Chapter 5)	Barbecue Pulled Pork and Cheesy Spaghetti (Chapter 7)	Mexican Lasagna (Chapter 14)

Standard U.S./Metric Measurement Conversions

VOLUME CONVERSIONS

U.S. Volume Measure	Metric Equivalent
⅛ teaspoon	0.5 milliliter
¼ teaspoon	1 milliliter
½ teaspoon	2 milliliters
1 teaspoon	5 milliliters
½ tablespoon	7 milliliters
1 tablespoon (3 teaspoons)	15 milliliters
2 tablespoons (1 fluid ounce)	30 milliliters
¼ cup (4 tablespoons)	60 milliliters
⅓ cup	90 milliliters
½ cup (4 fluid ounces)	125 milliliters
⅔ cup	160 milliliters
¾ cup (6 fluid ounces)	180 milliliters
1 cup (16 tablespoons)	250 milliliters
1 pint (2 cups)	500 milliliters
1 quart (4 cups)	1 liter (about)

WEIGHT CONVERSIONS

U.S. Weight Measure	Metric Equivalent
½ ounce	15 grams
1 ounce	30 grams
2 ounces	60 grams
3 ounces	85 grams
¼ pound (4 ounces)	115 grams
½ pound (8 ounces)	225 grams
¾ pound (12 ounces)	340 grams
1 pound (16 ounces)	454 grams

OVEN TEMPERATURE CONVERSIONS

Degrees Fahrenheit	Degrees Celsius
200 degrees F	95 degrees C
250 degrees F	120 degrees C
275 degrees F	135 degrees C
300 degrees F	150 degrees C
325 degrees F	160 degrees C
350 degrees F	180 degrees C
375 degrees F	190 degrees C
400 degrees F	205 degrees C
425 degrees F	220 degrees C
450 degrees F	230 degrees C

BAKING PAN SIZES

U.S.	Metric
8 × 1½ inch round baking pan	20 × 4 cm cake tin
9 × 1½ inch round baking pan	23 × 3.5 cm cake tin
11 × 7 × 1½ inch baking pan	28 × 18 × 4 cm baking tin
13 × 9 × 2 inch baking pan	30 × 20 × 5 cm baking tin
2 quart rectangular baking dish	30 × 20 × 3 cm baking tin
15 × 10 × 2 inch baking pan	30 × 25 × 2 cm baking tin (Swiss roll tin)
9 inch pie plate	22 × 4 or 23 × 4 cm pie plate
7 or 8 inch springform pan	18 or 20 cm springform or loose-bottom cake tin
9 × 5 × 3 inch loaf pan	23 × 13 × 7 cm or 2 lb narrow loaf or pâté tin
1½ quart casserole	1.5 liter casserole
2 quart casserole	2 liter casserole

Index